ENGLAND

Everyday Vegan Breakfasts
Nettle Soup
Nut Roast
Vegan Mushroom Gravy
Yorkshire Pudding and Pancakes
Green Lentil Shepherd's Pie
Store-Cupboard Soup with Dumplings
Baked Apples
Sloe Gin
Further Liquor Experiments

MIDDLE EAST

Spice Mixes
Labneh
Kuku Sabzi
Falafel
Cacik
Tahini Sauce
Tabbouleh
Ful Medames
Shakshuka
Pilaf
Hummus
Roast Rhubarb with Yoghurt
Chai
Black Sweetened Tea

CHINA

Easy and Quick Chinese Dinner
Chargrilled Greens
Tofu and Peanut Stir-fry
Egg Fried Rice
Smashed Cucumbers
Pomelo and Lychee

FRANCE

Sautéed Scallops with Lemon
Green Beans
Eggs en Cocotte
Potatoes Dauphinoise
Potatoes Boulangère (vegan)
Celeriac Mash
Poached Pears
Hot Chocolate

ITALY

Homemade Pasta
Spaghetti Aglio e Olio
Lemon Spaghetti
Tinned Tomato Sauce
Fresh Tomato Sauce with Basil
Spaghetti Vongole
Rocket and Parmesan
Wild Garlic Pesto
Roasted Zucchini and Garlic
Raspberry 'Gelato'
Campari Spritz

INDIA

Saag Paneer
Roast Aloo
Fresh Pickled Onions
Jeera Rice
Daal
Coriander Chutney
Vaghar
Egg Curry
Store-cupboard Curry
Chapati
Raita
Carrot Salad
Vegan Rice Pudding
Lassi

JAPAN

Horenso Goma-ae
Tofu and Sesame
Chirashi
Easy Pickled Carrots
Teriyaki Sauce
Dashi
Japanese Hotpot
Sunomono
Green Tea Ice Cream

'When baking,
follow directions.
When cooking,
go by your own taste.'

**LAIKO BAHRS
SAN FRANCISCO FOOD WRITER**

PARTICULAR BOOKS

UK | USA | Canada | Ireland | Australia
India | New Zealand | South Africa

Particular Books is part of the
Penguin Random House group of companies
whose addresses can be found at
global.penguinrandomhouse.com.

Penguin Random House UK

First published by Particular Books 2019
001

Text copyright © Cerys Matthews, 2019
Food photography pp. vi, 52, 79, 80, 83, 111, 119, 122, 123,
139, 149, 189, 195, 197, 198, 199, 213, 215 © Oli Green, 2019
All other food photography copyright © Sam Folan, 2019
Illustrations copyright © Elisa Cunningham, 2019

Designed by Evelin Kasikov

The moral right of the author has been asserted

The Acknowledgements on p. 260 constitute
an extension to this copyright page

Printed and bound in Italy by Printer Trento Srl

A CIP catalogue record for this book
is available from the British Library

ISBN: 978-1-846-14961-0

www.greenpenguin.co.uk

FSC MIX Paper from responsible sources FSC® C018179

Penguin Random House is committed to a sustainable future for our business, our readers and our planet. This book is made from Forest Stewardship Council® certified paper.

THANK YOU/DIOLCH Steve, Mam, Nan, Red, Harvey, Hope, Aunt Dilys, John, Jean and Rita, Gwenddydd Mai, Glenys, Saiid, Fatima, Yasmin, Evelin, Helen, Roger, Ann, Nuri, Apexa, Mrs Boora, Mudrika, Phoebe, Llio, Rhys, Terni, Papa Cunningham, Father Michael, Nupur, Claudio, Andrea Pulcinella, Fred, Sheila, Andy, John Tupelo, Anna/Pooch, Oli, Tiger, Eileen, Gary, Elina, Roi, Uli, B, Yumiko, Janice, Bob, Hillary, Joanna, Madeleine, Ana, Lulu, Aziz, Lisa, Sue, Claire, Matt, Sam, Faye, Emyr, Charlie, Mari, Matthias, Ian, Billie, Sonia, Chris, Hannah, Maria, Carla, Elisa, Lia, Jim, Chloe, Rebecca, Pen, Margaret, Tom, Angela, Lucy, Trish, Thomasina, Susannah, Caroline, Fergus, Louvain and all the feast makers who've shared their love of cooking over the years, and lastly, never leastly, the world-roving, horchata-loving, Silver Fox.

CERYS MATTHEWS

WHERE THE WILD COOKS GO

*love
cerys x*

RECIPES, MUSIC, POEMS AND COCKTAILS

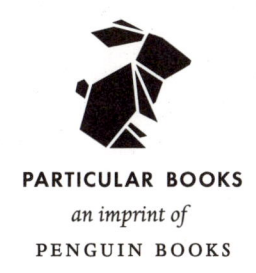

PARTICULAR BOOKS
an imprint of
PENGUIN BOOKS

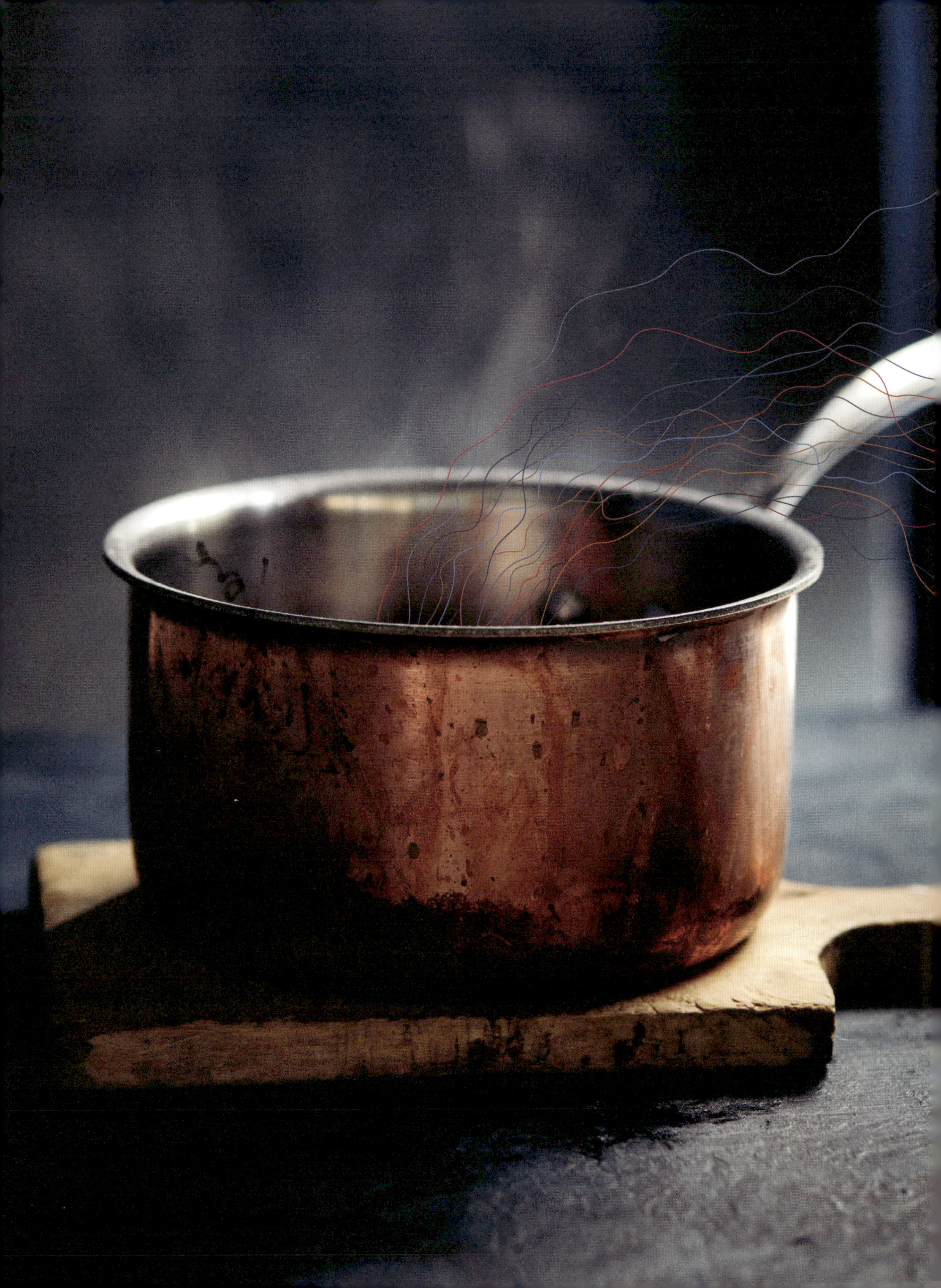

Introduction vii

Notes for cooking viii

AMERICAN SOUTH 1

MEXICO 18

JAMAICA 36

MOROCCO 52

SPAIN 70

IRELAND 88

WALES 104

SCOTLAND 124

ENGLAND 140

FRANCE 158

ITALY 174

MIDDLE EAST 190

INDIA 206

CHINA 226

JAPAN 242

Index 257

Acknowledgements 260

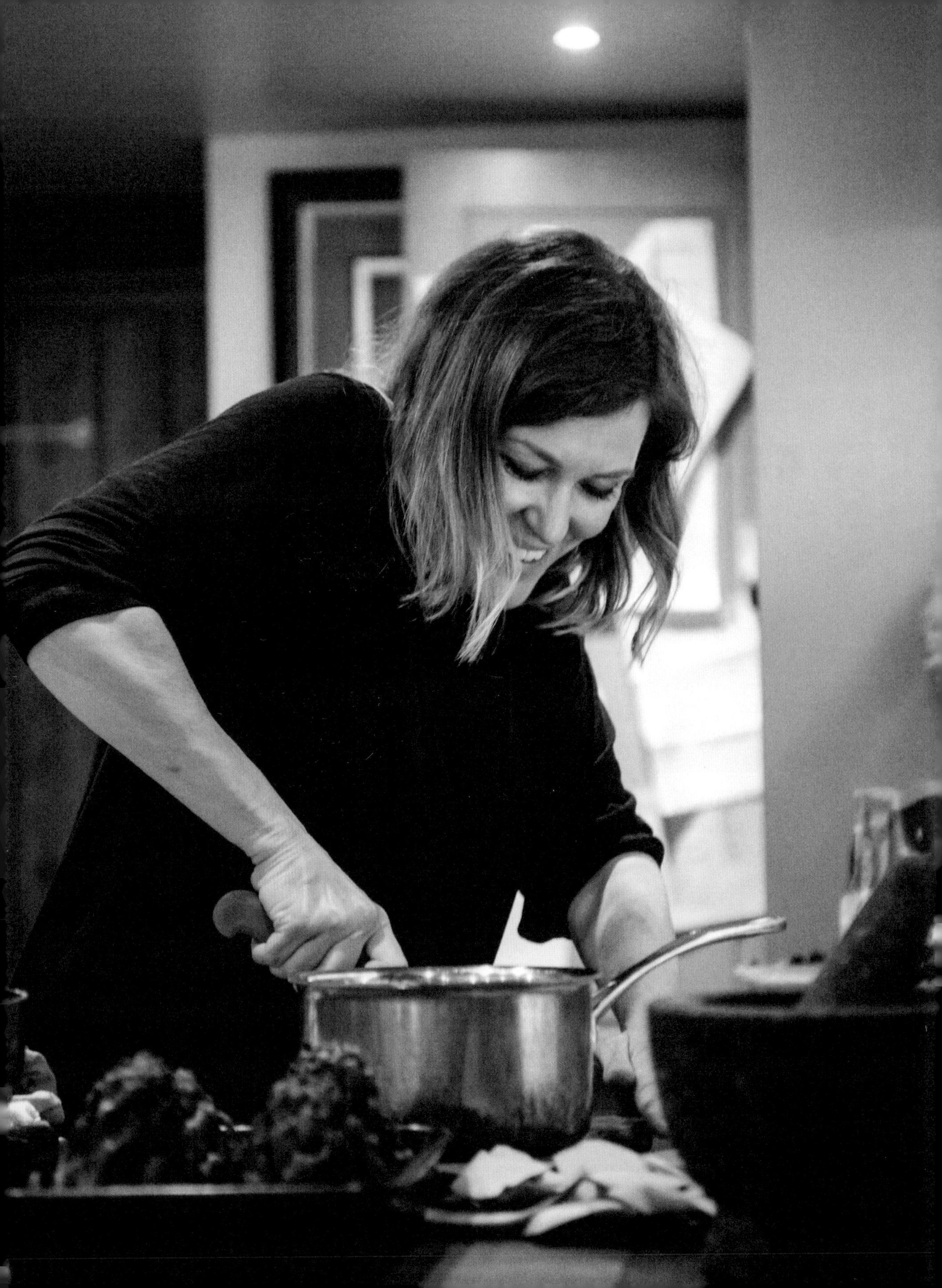

INTRODUCTION

> *'Let your food be your medicine and your medicine be your food.'*
>
> **HIPPOCRATES**

These days you can cook your way round the world without even leaving your home, and with a great playlist on the go, you've got yourself a ticket to ride. For the everyday cook, navigating by country is a great source of inspiration: shall we go Spanish? Mexican? Japanese? Scottish? Jamaican? Shall I cook inside or go outside and light a fire? Bingo. With this approach, the world, as they say, is your oyster.

I'm neither a foam-creating mad scientist chef nor a cool-headed baker. I'm a culinary explorer. And I've written this for those wild cooks like me, who love to cook but don't always have the time or logistical means to go shopping and who like instant, fuss-free results. Improvisation and a nod to the key ingredients of a particular cuisine are what I find works best. This is especially the case if you're cooking for a gang with differing requirements: mine includes vegans, vegetarians, pescatarians and meat-eaters.

This collection works for all. These are my go-to, everyday recipes. They're easy on the pocket, the planet (plant high, low meat and minimal packaging), the body (low in hidden salts, sugars, chemicals) and they taste great.

Wherever I've travelled, home or away, I've collected music and recipes. I try to go where the locals eat and drink, and taste the regional dishes and brew, often ending up singing the same songs. Great food, music and company inextricably linked. I get to share my music collection every week as DJ on BBC Radio 2 and 6, and it feels natural, now, to share the recipes.

I know many listen to the radio while cooking, myself included. There's an escape to be had, lost in music, wine in hand, pans bubbling. A moment of peace in a mad world.

I've included some curiosities, playlists and a poem from each country, to help with the vibes.

Now, press play.

NOTES FOR COOKING

Most dishes serve four people unless otherwise stated. For many chapters – for example Mexico, Spain and the Middle East – it's a case of picking out a few recipes you fancy making and serving them to share, as you would do with tapas.

SALT AND PEPPER
I use flakes of coarse sea salt, which you can grind between your palms when you need it to be finer. Pepper is always freshly ground black pepper unless otherwise stated.

STOCK
I rarely have time to make stocks, and my quick and easy replacement is Kallo organic vegetable cubes. They're low salt, contain no artificial colours or MSG, and they're coeliac- and vegan-friendly. They also let the main ingredients do the talking.

FRUIT AND VEG
I buy organic, local and seasonal if I can.

WHOLE SPICES
Instead of buying ready-mixed spices, buy whole. They store better, and toasting the whole spices makes for a taste sensation. With these in your cupboard, you can make up your own baharat, garam masala, fajita mix, za'atar and other spice mixes. Some of the recipes for these are in the chapters that lie ahead.

PESTLE AND MORTAR
Buy a large granite pestle and mortar, big enough to make guacamole, Thai curry pastes and tahini sauce, as well as grinding your spices. A blender is handy too, stick or otherwise. And a great knife.

> *'Worries go down better with soup.'*
>
> **JEWISH PROVERB**

SEEDS AND NUTS
Before using, like whole spices, try toasting them for a minute or two in a dry heavy pan; the taste makes it worth it.

LIMES AND LEMONS
To juice if they are hard, press down and roll, cut them in half, then stab and twist the insides with a fork.

BUTTER
I usually use lightly salted. If you don't eat butter, replace with your choice of fat/oil.

MILK
All the recipes work with either semi or whole milk.

OATS
I usually use whole rolled wholegrain.

RICE
To move away from refined foods and packaging, I buy huge bags of brown basmati rice. You can now pretty easily find brown sushi, paella and long-grain rice. Just adjust the timings accordingly. As a rough guide, brown rice takes 20–25 minutes to cook and 5 minutes resting, and for white rice 15 minutes to cook and 5 minutes resting. You can also try the **'knuckle'** method: add your rice to the pan, and cover with enough water so that there is a one-knuckle gap between the top of the rice and the top of the water. Bring to the boil, then turn down the heat, put the lid on and let the rice absorb the water until cooked (approx. 15–25 minutes, depending on the type of rice). Then rest for 5 minutes, as above.

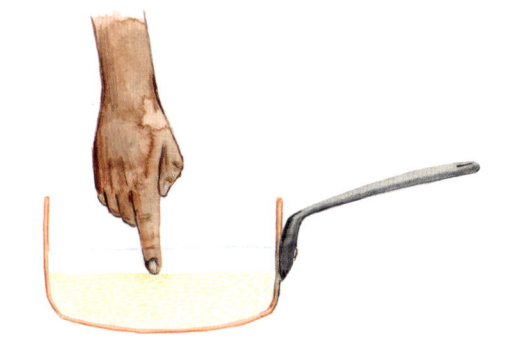

QUINOA
Throw a handful of quinoa (black, red or white) into your rice to add protein and roughage. You can buy locally grown – for example http://hodmedods.co.uk – a British supplier and grower of grains, pulses and beans; try their roasted quinoa, it's like micro popcorn (keeping our carbon footprint in mind: Peruvian quinoa is one hefty flight away.) Cooking ratio: 1 portion quinoa to 1.5 portion water. When cooking quinoa on its own, throw in a stock cube.

SUGAR
Where I use honey or soft brown sugar, feel free to replace with white sugar, agave syrup etc.

POTATOES
I wash and cut out any bruises/blemishes, but never peel. Again, your call. I do peel onions, parsnips, swede and carrots, but won't specify that in the recipes.

SOY
I use reduced salt soy. If you're using fully salted, adjust to your taste. Tamari is a gluten-free soy sauce alternative.

TOFU
Use firm tofu as you would use cooked prawns – it's ready to eat, but is improved with flavourings/sauces. Smoked firm tofu is good too. Some packs keep in the fridge for 2–4 weeks; check use by date. Silken tofu is more like jelly/blancmange and falls apart easily. Use for miso soups, or just heat up with soy and sesame oil in a pan and serve as additional protein and interest with rice or noodles. You can get this tofu in cartons that are long-lasting – so good for the store cupboard.

TOMATOES
You'll need to cook about 5–6 large tomatoes, around 600g to get an equivalent weight of a 400g can of tinned tomatoes.

BEANS AND PULSES
I buy dry as it's way cheaper, plus better for the planet (less processing and packaging) and they come with no hidden salts, sugars and chemicals which most pre-cooked options do: most varieties work out at a ratio of 1:2 dry beans to cooked bean weight. So, for a tin of beans that usually contains 230–240g drained cooked beans, you'll need to soak 115g dry beans, soak overnight (or 6–8 hours), then boil/simmer in about 400ml of water until soft. Depending on their size and age, it'll take from 30–60 minutes. 200g chickpeas weigh 500g when cooked. The only ones to watch out for are red kidney beans: with these you need to boil them for 10 minutes to kill the toxins. Then you're good to go. Simmer until soft.

NOTES FOR COOKING

BAKESTONE
A bake stone, aka 'maen' or 'planc' is handy for making more than just Welsh cakes and flat breads: try putting it on your barbecue, grease with some oil and you've got a perfect surface to cook smaller things and vegetarian fare: cherry tomatoes, garlic, prawns, eggs, green beans …

COOKING OUTSIDE ON A FIRE OR KOTLICH
This is a great alternative to a barbecue: it's basically a cauldron and tripod on a chain, and makes all sorts of stews, daals, soups and paellas.

DESSERTS
As these are everyday recipes, most of the desserts are pretty close to nature. There are exceptions. One's in the Irish chapter.

KEYS
Many of these dishes can be adjusted to suit vegetarians, vegans or meat-eaters. Check the recipe for the symbols used, i.e.: V, VG, NV – it means the recipe can be prepared to suit the dietary requirement of your choice.

- **V** Vegan
- **VG** Vegetarian
- **GF** Gluten Free
- **DF** Dairy Free
- **NV** Non Veg (i.e. meat or fish)

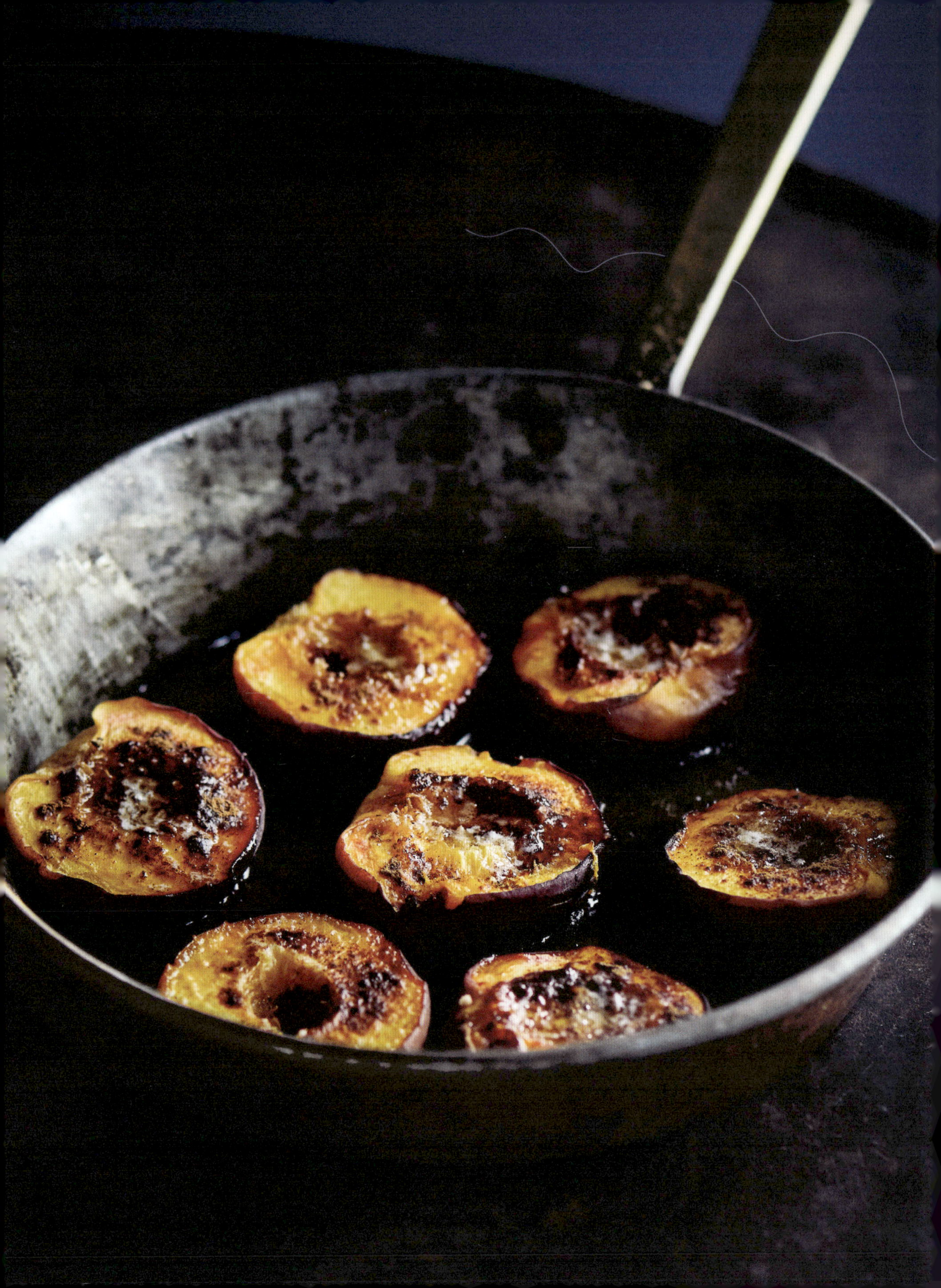

AMERICAN SOUTH

'I Saw in Louisiana a Live-Oak Growing'

I saw in Louisiana a live-oak growing,
All alone stood it and the moss hung down from the branches,
Without any companion it grew there uttering joyous leaves of dark green,
And its look, rude, unbending, lusty, made me think of myself,
But I wonder'd how it could utter joyous leaves standing alone there without its friend near,
    for I knew I could not,
And I broke off a twig with a certain number of leaves upon it, and twined around it a little moss,
And brought it away, and I have placed it in sight in my room,
It is not needed to remind me as of my own dear friends,
(For I believe lately I think of little else than of them,)
Yet it remains to me a curious token, it makes me think of manly love;
For all that, and though the live-oak glistens there in Louisiana solitary in a wide flat space,
Uttering joyous leaves all its life without a friend a lover near,
I know very well I could not.

WALT WHITMAN (1819–1892)
The father of free verse was a humanist.
I selected this poem from his collection
Leaves of Grass which celebrates democracy, love,
friendship and nature. You can't visit some areas of
the South without being absolutely taken in by the sight
of the huge dark silhouette of live oaks and the Spanish moss,
a long, bushy lichen, that grows down in dark rather eerie
bunches from the branches (think *Scooby Doo*). I love how he
takes a simple action and ends up revealing a truth about himself.

American food writer Michael Pollan said, 'Eat all the junk food you want as long as you cook it yourself.' Which I get to a certain degree, but take this recipe for a very popular southern 'homemade' dish: **BROCCOLI CASSEROLE:** put a pack of frozen broccoli florets in a Pyrex dish, pour over a can of Campbell's cream of mushroom soup, sprinkle cornflakes, add some grated 'cheese' and bake. Yes, cornflakes.

Sweet potato is evidently not sweet enough in the US. Put your cooked and **MASHED SWEET POTATO** in a dish, cover with marshmallow sweets, and bake in the oven.

Serve with pumpkin pie and sweet tea (the **'HOUSE WINE'** of the South, according to Dolly Parton's character in *Steel Magnolias*).

Thanksgiving Day

commemorates the generosity of members of the Wampanoag tribe. They taught Pilgrims at the Plymouth Colony how to grow corn, beans and squash (known as 'the three sisters') as well as to collect seafood and catch fish. This followed a terrible winter in 1620 when many of these religious refugees from England starved to death as their harvest had failed. In 1621 they invited the Native Americans to a harvest feast to say thank you.

Turkey is now associated with the Thanksgiving Day feast, but according to some sources it wasn't on the menu for the 1621 feast: lobster, cod, deer and goose were served up by the Pilgrims.

CHILLI con carne started off as a dish with no tomatoes or beans. It is sometimes credited to south-western cattle drivers who cooked it on a fire using pounded dried beef, with suet, wild onions, garlic and oregano. An alternative theory is that it began with the Mexican 'Chilli Queens of San Antonio', who sold bowls of steaming hot stew, spiced with chilli peppers from their street carts to the locals. It is now the state dish of Texas.

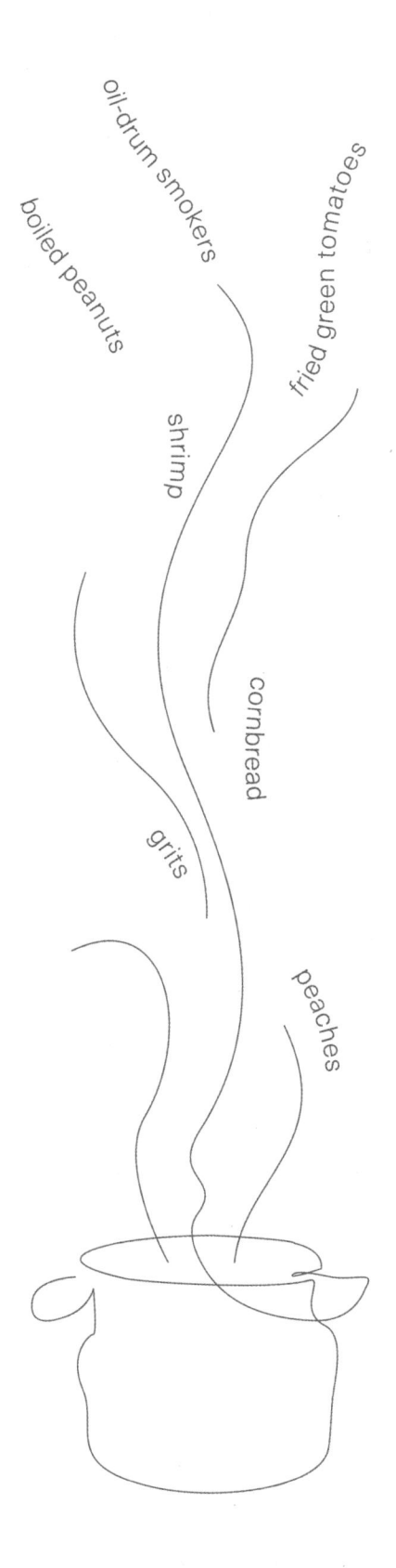

oil-drum smokers
boiled peanuts
fried green tomatoes
shrimp
cornbread
grits
peaches

The Luxembourgish name for turkey is shnuddelhong – 'snot hen'.

One icy winter day I **DEEP FRIED A TURKEY** in piping hot peanut oil on the wooden front porch. Slowly dipping it down from a tripod into a 10-gallon pot full of hot peanut oil. A 10lb bird (defrosted – important to avoid an explosion!) took forty-five minutes to cook. It was crispy on the outside, and inside was the juiciest turkey meat you can imagine. All the while drinking ice-cold Pabst Blue Ribbon beer served with salt and lime.

Tack a collard green leaf to the ceiling or over your door to ward off evil sprits, or paint your window and doorframe blue, and place a dead tree outside your house and feed empty glass bottles onto the end of the branches. The **boogey-bo man** gets stuck in the bottles or is repelled by the colour blue . . . and so doesn't bother you.

New Year's meal is rife with symbolic meaning:

Cornbread freshly made on a century-old skillet. Corn = yellow: gold.

Black Eyed Peas: luck/coins/prosperity. You can also add a real coin to the cornbread mix, like we do with the Christmas pudding; whoever finds it, teeth intact, will have future monetary luck.

Collard greens: green dollars = wealth

Pig cheek/Jowl: good luck and full bellies in the coming year.

New Year's Eve countdown: each person swallows a grape with each dong of the bell.

Go and compete in hog-squealing contest. No pigs involved in this.

People add bourbon to sweet tea, a neat way of camouflaging your vice in the **BIBLE BELT.** Ditto red wine in coffee cups, like the songwriters of Music Row, Nashville.

> *'Next to jazz music, there is nothing that lifts the spirit and strengthens the soul more than a good bowl of chilli.'*
>
> **HARRY JAMES**

Catfish sandwiches: white fish fillets covered in ground corn and deep fried, served between cheap sliced white bread, with slivers of white onion, yellow mustard and Tabasco sauce. Biscuits and gravy (savoury hot scones with gloopy sausage meat in pale gravy), Tex-Mex and barbecue (the slow-cooked meat cuisine, rather than grilling outside on charcoal). And in Louisiana, shrimping off the coast, returning to shore to quickly boil and serve, shrimping by hand-net in bayous, baiting them with fish-meal balls. Crayfish boils, spreading newspapers across the tables. Blue crab, caught overnight in metal mesh boxes. Jello shots. Deeper into the swampy groves, so very spooky, with Spanish moss hanging from every tree, fire ants under every little bump under your feet. The drive-in daiquiri stalls. And the boudin sausages, gumbo and jambalaya, where the rich tapestry of different cuisines and cultures meet on a dish, with Native American, African, Spanish and French cuisine brought by the Arcadians ejected by the British from Canada, forced south on the waters of the mighty Mississippi.

Louisianan food is good and spicy, and so is the music, with the iron triangle call of the *petite fer* in Cajun dance music, the rambunctious accordion of zydeco, jazz, boogie-woogie piano, the deep grooves of New Orleans. *Laissez les bonne temps roulez.* Cooking outside, picking parties on porches with guitars and banjos, mimosas (Champagne and orange juice – i.e. a Buck's Fizz). Or try a mint julep: sugar, muddled with mint and crushed ice, poured on bourbon whiskey, add a sprig of mint between that you've 'smacked' between your palms to release the oils – for the garnish. Perfect in a rocking chair as the sun and humidity start to drop and you look over your garden. In the heat (one August, it didn't drop below 100F) it's easy to grow okra, tomatillos and plenty of tomatoes. In season you'll see stall after stall of peaches for sale at the side of the road. Also try boiled peanuts sold at truck stops and road stalls. Salty, totally more-ish, eaten rather like edamame, as they come boiled in the shell.

Songs have a lot to answer for: 'Peach Picking Time in Georgia', 'Tupelo Honey', 'Avalon Blues', 'Alabama Bound', lyrics about crossing the Mississippi Delta, the Tallahatchie Bridge. Songs that like Sirens seemed always to be calling me to the southern states. The first thing I did when I left the band was to make endless road trips: Louisiana, Arkansas, Alabama, Tennessee, Mississippi. I ended up stopping in

South Carolina and then Tennessee for almost six years, loving the music, hating the history and inequality which is still evident in city layouts, life and health expectancy and the judicial system, and which, in the end, brought me back to Europe.

What I learnt food-wise in the US was no less bittersweet. All hail grilling out in family reunions, Friday fish fries, local blues festivals and the queues of smoking oil drums offering whole grilled corn, turkey legs and ribs. Ditto the barbecue shops and soul food restaurants with their recipes rendering cheap cuts both of vegetables and meats (turnip greens, trotters, skirt steak and chitterlings/pig's intestine) not just palatable, but delicious. But you could never escape the history behind the meals: these were the only cuts made available to the poor and enslaved.

Profiteering still impacts every aspect of food in the US. 'Government cheese' is handed out to people in social housing and probably never saw an animal in its production; junk food at every corner – Twinkies, Honey buns, Goo Goo Clusters, Moon Pies – shelf upon shelf of refined processed carbohydrates, high-fructose-corn-sugared-chemically-made-factory foods – with most brands of 'seasoning' really a helping of MSG and colouring. The impact of these 'affordable foods' on the human body is there for all to see: eye-popping, button-popping levels of morbid obesity, short life expectancies, heart and vascular disease, missing limbs through diabetes and tooth decay. Cheap food has its price. And it's people living on the lower end of the income bracket that are paying for it. The planet too: add to this equation the impact on biodiversity of growing GM products, the effects of deforestation of land for growing food crops for beef cattle or dairy cattle on a mass scale, plus there's the huge contributing factor in global warming of the methane the animals produce. It's left me passionate, like so many people around the world, about trying to get back to the basics of food, reducing the amount of sugar, meat, dairy and chemicals in our everyday diet, eating fewer takeaway meals to avoid packaging and hidden ingredients. These roads all lead back to home cooking.

> *'Foreigners cannot enjoy our food, I suppose, any more than we can enjoy theirs. It is not strange; for tastes are made, not born.'*
>
> **MARK TWAIN**

AMERICAN SOUTH

6

'I cook with wine, sometimes I even add it to the food.'

W. C. FIELDS

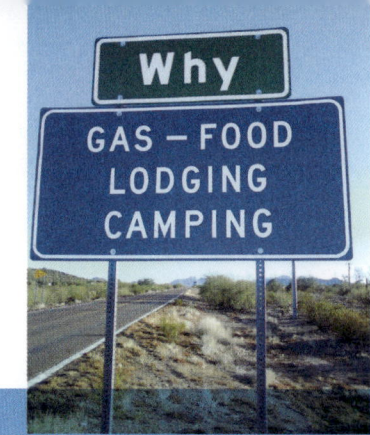

'I will not move my army without onions.'

GENERAL ULYSSES S. GRANT

'Cheese is milk's leap towards immortality.'

CLIFF FADIMAN

AMERICAN SOUTH

'Red beans and ricely yours.'

LOUIS ARMSTRONG

'Sometimes', Bird responded with a wink, 'I have a sherry before dinner …'

FROM *NICA'S DREAM: THE LIFE AND LEGEND OF THE JAZZ BARONESS*

'My doctor told me to stop having intimate dinners for four, unless there are three other people.'

ORSON WELLES

ON THE MENU

FRIED GREEN (OR RED) TOMATOES

COLESLAW

EASY POACHED EGGS

JAMBALAYA

GRITS

SHRIMP AND GRITS

CLASSIC BURGERS (VEG AND NON VEG)

CORNBREAD WITH JALAPEÑO

DESSERT

CINNAMON BAKED PEACHES

Fried Green (or red) Tomatoes

(VG)

Ingredients

2 tomatoes

30g flour

salt and pepper

1 egg, beaten with a splash of milk

30g cornmeal (any grade)

50g vegetable/peanut oil about ½cm in the pan

Method

Slice the tomatoes across the equator to form discs of about a centimetre thickness.

1. Place the flour with the salt and pepper in a small saucer, pour the beaten egg with milk in a similar dish, the ground cornmeal in a third dish.

2. Dip each disc of tomato first in the flour, then the egg and milk. Finally dip in the cornmeal and put on a plate until you've dipped all slices.

3. Heat the oil in a cast-iron pan or skillet on medium. When hot, start frying the tomatoes 3–4 minutes each side. (Some do deep fry these, but I like them fine this way.)

4. Either way, drain on a kitchen towel, season to taste, and serve hot.

Tony Joe White 'Polk Salad Annie'

The Carter Brothers 'Roast Possum'

Coleslaw

(VG) (DF)

Ingredients

½ white cabbage, finely shredded
1 large carrot, grated
2 spring onions, very finely chopped
1 tbsp celery seeds, optional

For the dressing:

4 tbsp cider vinegar
1 tsp honey
1 tsp mustard of your choice, e.g. Dijon or American mustard
4 tbsp olive oil
salt and pepper

Method

1. Mix cabbage, carrot and onions in a bowl. Sprinkle in the celery seeds if using and mix.
2. Meanwhile, shake together the dressing ingredients, along with a good pinch of salt and pepper in a jam jar. Taste and adjust the seasoning if necessary.
3. Pour over the vegetables and mix well. Do this step just before serving to avoid floppy coleslaw.

Options:

This dressing makes a great generic dressing for almost all salads. Experiment by adding a tablespoon of pickled gherkin/pickle juice to it, or a squeeze of lime or lemon.

You can also try upping the vinegar or citrus juice measurements and reducing the oil – this coleslaw is sometimes served with no oil at all.

Easy Poached Eggs

(VG) (DF)

- Boil up water in a saucepan, turn down to keep on a gentle simmer.
- Break a very fresh egg into a cup with a long handle, add 1 tablespoon of vinegar.
- Ease the egg and vinegar into the water and time 4 minutes.
- Use a slotted spoon to remove.

The Southern Tones 'It Must Be Jesus'

Noble Sissle's Swingsters with Sidney Bechet 'Southern Sunset (When The Sun Sets Down South)'

Clifton Chenier 'Ay-tete Fee'

Steve Riley and the Mamou Playboys 'La Danse De Mardi Gras'

Jambalaya

DF NV

The holy trinity of Creole and Cajun cooking is onions, bell pepper and celery. Add to these smoky sausages and rice, and you have the wonderfully named jambalaya. This version is akin to red jambalaya, the Creole type, which includes tomatoes. The Cajun type omits these and gets its colour from browning the sausages.

Ingredients

2 tbsp oil
6 smoked sausages/ hot dogs, vegetarian if you prefer. (If you don't have smoked sausage, use smoked paprika to give you the smoky jambalaya flavour.)
1 onion, chopped
2 stalks celery, chopped
½ green pepper or 1 small one, chopped
2 cloves of garlic, chopped
4 large fresh tomatoes, diced – or 1 tin tomatoes
½ tsp paprika (change for smoked paprika, if you're using unsmoked sausages)
¼ tsp thyme
½ tsp cayenne (or more if you like a kick)
2 bay leaves
salt and pepper
200g rice brown basmati (or brown long grain)
1L vegetable stock

Method

1. Heat a large wide frying or sauté pan over a medium heat. Add oil and fry the sliced sausages. Remove and leave to one side.

2. Add the onion, green pepper and celery to the pan and cook for 6–8 minutes or until the onion is translucent. Stir in the garlic and cook for a further 2 minutes. Then stir through the tomato.

3. Add spices and bay leaves, along with a really good grinding of pepper and a couple of pinches of salt. Mix well. Return the sausages to the pan and stir in the rice.

4. Pour in ¾ of the stock and bring to a simmer. Simmer gently for 10 minutes, only stirring when absolutely necessary. After 10 minutes, cover the pan, reduce the heat to low and cook for a further 15–20 minutes or until the rice is cooked through (it'll be less if using white rice). If at any point the mixture is looking really dry, add a bit more of the reserved stock.

5. Taste and adjust the seasoning as necessary. Serve with hot sauce on the side.

AMERICAN SOUTH

Mississippi John Hurt 'Avalon Blues'   JJ Cale 'Cajun Moon'   Snooks Eaglin 'Brown Skinned Woman'

Grits

(VG) (GF) (NV)

Grits are the southern equivalent to Italy's polenta, both made with ground corn. Like our porridge you can cook them up using milk or water, or a third option is to cook with stock. You can buy grits online. Look for stoneground grits, which are the best option for this recipe. If you can't get grits, try using coarse or medium stoneground polenta. With either, you're looking to whisk the cornmeal into the hot liquid until it's cooked, i.e. soft not gritty. The usual ratio of liquid to grits is about 4:1. Once cooked, it's entirely your call what flavours and ingredients you want to add. It's supremely versatile and a good change from rice or quinoa.

Ingredients

500ml milk (or water)
750ml water
200g grits
1 tsp sea salt
salt and pepper

Method

1. Bring the milk and 750ml of water to just below a simmer in a heavy-base saucepan or casserole dish. Slowly pour in the grits and the salt, stirring as you pour. Turn the heat down to the lowest setting and cook for 45–60 minutes, stirring very often until no crunchy bits of the grits remain. You are aiming for a consistency of slightly runny porridge, rather than anything thicker.

2. Once cooked, remove from the heat, season if necessary (it may need a little more salt).

3. Now decide on what you're serving it with, e.g. fried garlic mushrooms in olive oil, cheese, butter, or poached egg…

Shrimp and Grits

(GF) (NV)

Ingredients

25g butter
olive oil
12 raw peeled king prawns
parsley or chives

Method

1. Heat a large frying pan over a medium heat. Add the butter along with a dash of oil and once the butter has melted and is beginning to bubble gradually add the prawns. Cook for 2–3 minutes on each side or until just cooked through, spooning the hot butter over them as they cook.

2. Serve the grits with the prawns and butter poured over them, garnish with chopped herbs like parsley or chives.

Option to add that poached egg, too.

Further ideas:
Add any of the following to the prawns as they are cooking – chopped garlic, chilli flakes, diced tomato, spring onions, saffron, paprika, bacon pieces, chopped peppers – and then add to the grits.

Doc Watson 'Shady Grove'

Osborne Brothers 'Rocky Top'

Johnny Cash 'Tennessee'

George Jones 'Love Bug'

Bill Monroe 'Blue Moon Of Kentucky'

Burgers

Burgers in the south are served in a bap with a leaf of cold iceberg lettuce, the thinnest slice of sweet white onion and a slice of fresh ripe tomato. I love the crunch it makes when you bite into it. I serve vegetarian burgers the same way. People can build their own burgers, if you set everything out on a table. Add ketchup, homemade mayonnaise and mustard to the table offerings. If you're like me and want to eat less processed white bread, serve with wholemeal or granary baps.

Coleslaw is always served with pulled pork, and often made without mayonnaise, I imagine because of the climate. I loved its crispy freshness, which is why I have included a recipe for it.

Classic Burger

GF NV

This simple patty recipe was taught to my chef friend Anna by burger-maestro Fred Smith.

Ingredients:

750g freshly minced chuck steak (ask your butcher if they can mince for you)

salt and pepper

Method

1. Divide the mince into 4 balls. Shape into patties measuring about 12cm across and 1.5cm thick.

2. Heat a heavy-base frying pan or grill/bbq to a high heat. You want the pan/grill to be as hot as possible. Just before you cook the patties, season on each side with a good pinch of salt and pepper. Place the patties into the hot pan and lightly press down the middle of the patties to prevent them curling up.

3. Cook for 1 minute (use a timer), then turn them. Cook for a further minute then turn again and repeat this again until you have cooked them for 4 minutes in total. This will give you a perfectly medium burger. Cook for less or longer if you prefer yours more or less cooked.

4. If you'd like melted cheese on the burgers then place the cheese over the patties for their last minute of cooking. Cover with a lid of the bbq or an upturned metal bowl or pan lid to increase the melting if necessary.

Jimmie Rodgers 'Peach Picking Time In Georgia'

James C. Booker/aka Waynes 'Junco Partner (Worthless Man)'

Bean Burgers

(V) (VG) (GF)

Ingredients
(Makes 8 large burgers)

25g dried shiitake mushrooms
1 onion, finely chopped
salt and pepper
olive oil for cooking
2 cloves garlic, finely chopped
2 tsp smoked paprika (hot or sweet)
200g cooked chickpeas
200g cooked kidney beans
150g cooked puy lentils
50g plain flour, plus extra for dusting (or ground cornflour = gluten free)

Method

1. Rehydrate the dried mushrooms in a bowl, covering them with boiling water. Leave to one side.

2. Fry the onion with 1 teaspoon of salt in a tablespoon of oil over a medium heat until really soft, about 10–15 minutes. Once soft, add the garlic and smoked paprika and stir through over the heat for 3 minutes or until the garlic is soft. Remove from the heat.

3. Put the onion mixture into a food processor and add half of the chickpeas, half of the kidney beans, half of the lentils and 50g of flour. Drain the mushrooms, squeezing out any liquid, roughly chop (the liquid makes a delicious vegetarian stock if you'd like to keep it) and blend until you have a coarse paste. Taste and season. (Beans soaked then boiled from dry will need more seasoning than tinned equivalent.)

4. In a bowl, mash the remaining chickpeas, kidney beans and lentils with a fork or potato masher until they are roughly mashed up but still have quite a bit of texture. Season with salt and pepper. Tip the contents of the food processor into the bowl and mix into the mashed mixture.

5. Shape into four equal-sized patties, about 1.5cm thick. Place in the fridge for at least an hour to firm up.

   (You can store them, covered in the fridge for up to three days.)

6. Once ready to cook, dust the firmed-up patties in flour (or cornflour), shaking off any excess.

7. Heat a large heavy-based non-stick frying pan over a medium heat. Once hot, add a tablespoon of oil and cook the patties on either side until dark golden and warmed through (about 3 minutes on each side).

Options:
Melt slices of cheese on top when cooking, as before with the meat burgers. A Scandinavian cheese slice is useful for slicing cheese for this.

Further ideas:
Add a bunch of herbs (e.g. coriander, parsley or mint) (about 50–75g) and a squeeze of lemon juice to the mix when you blitz in the food processor.

Dorothy Love Coates 'Strange Man'
Scott Joplin 'A Breeze From Alabama'
Professor Longhair 'Tipitina'

Cornbread with Jalapeño

VG

This recipe is based on one written by the late great Lucille Howell, from Greer, South Carolina, my daughter's great-grandmother. It's a savoury Southern version, great with piping hot stews as an alternative to bread or rice. It's not the sweeter Northern cornbread, which is more like cake. You don't have to add the pickled jalepeños, but I enjoy the moistness and blast of flavour that they bring. Serve with chilli or stew.

Ingredients

50g butter

1 egg

100ml hot milk (whole or semi), soured with juice of 1 lemon (squeeze juice of half lemon in the milk and wait 10 mins until it curdles; or, if you have it, use 100ml buttermilk)

100g self-raising flour

200g cornmeal (medium)

handful of pickled jalapeños

Method

1. Preheat oven to 180°C.
2. Put the butter in the heavy pan or skillet and place in the oven to melt the butter and grease the pan.
3. In a bowl mix all the ingredients, adding the melted butter, and put the grease-covered skillet back in the oven again.
4. Cut up the jalapeños into small pieces, add to mix.
5. Pour mix straight into the hot skillet.
6. Bake for 20 minutes.
7. Serve immediately.

Cinnamon Baked Peaches

VG GF

Ingredients

4 ripe peaches, halved

2 tsp brown sugar or honey

2 tsp butter

2 tsp ground cinnamon

Method

1. Preheat the oven to 180°C.
2. Remove the stones from the halved peaches. Place the peach halves cut side up onto a lined baking tray. Divide the brown sugar and butter between the holes. You want about ¼ tsp of each in each hole. Sprinkle over the cinnamon.
3. Bake in the preheated oven for 30–40 minutes.

Options:
Serve with ice-cream, cream or yoghurt, crumbled digestive biscuits, chopped nuts or/and seeds, drizzle with honey.

Bobby Charles 'Small Town Talk'

Glen Campbell 'Wichita Lineman'

Clarence Carter 'Patches'
Fats Domino 'Jambalaya (On The Bayou)'

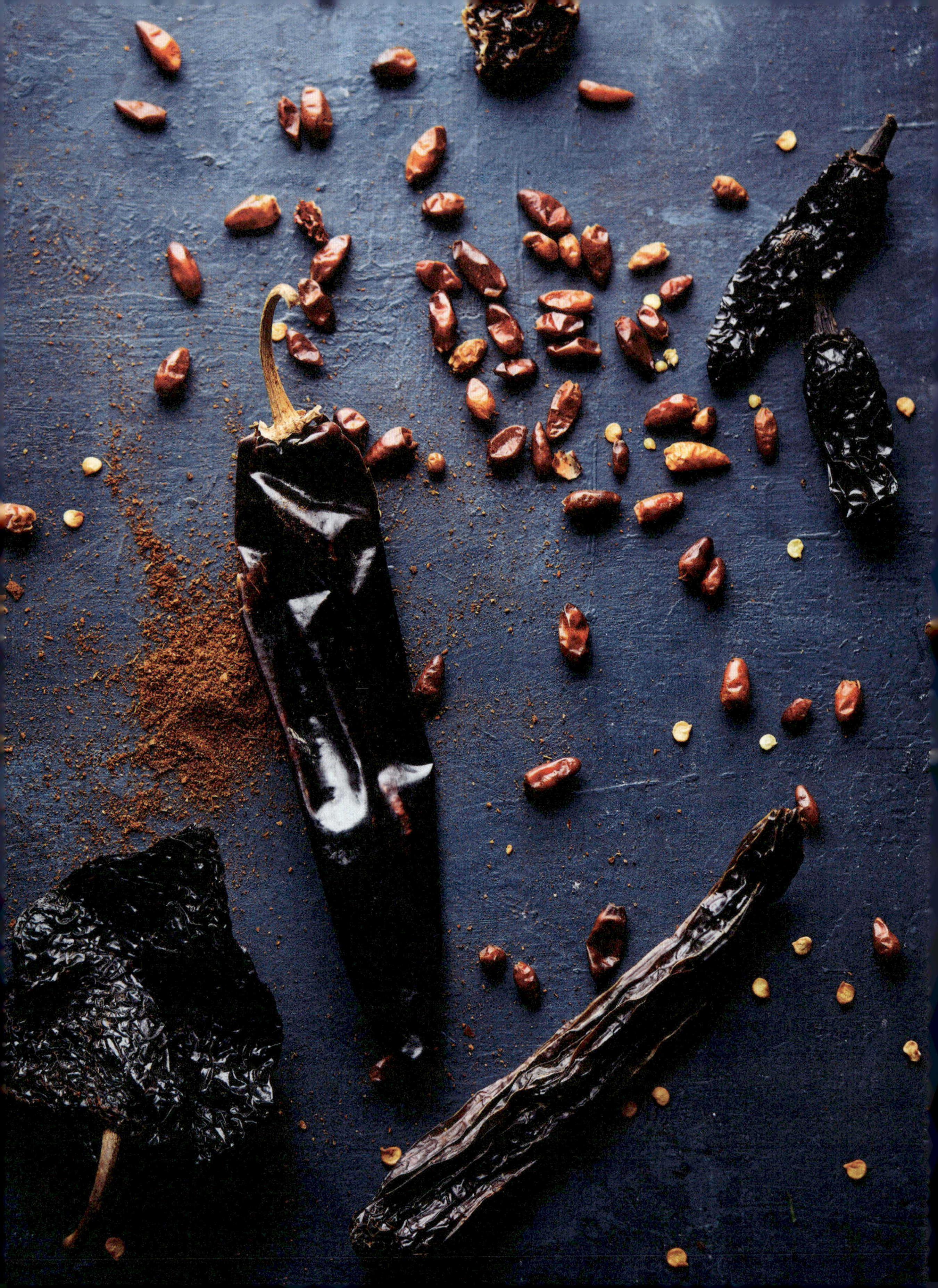

MEXICO

Sonnet 189

They die with you, Laura, now that you are dead,
Along with their longings that are now in vain,
Their eyes, on which you once bestowed
a lovely light, will never gleam again.

Let this poor lyre, still echoing with
sounds you woke, perish calling your name,
and as for these clumsy scribblings, let them be
black tears shed from this sorry pen.

Let Death itself feel pity and regret
that, bound by his own law, he could not spare you,
and Love, lament the bitter circumstance:

Where before, wanting pleasure,
he wished for eyes that they might feast on you,
now, all they'll ever do, is weep.

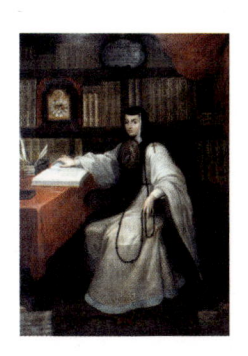

SOR JUANA INÉS DE LA CRUZ, one of the first feminist authors of the New World, had such a progressive world view and it was brave of her to publish during the seventeenth century. I could have picked any by her, but I include this. A rage against the age, it is a practical response to the loss of a loved one, by perhaps North America's first lesbian feminist writer.

FAJITAS are a Tex-Mex dish originally made with skirt beef (faja=strip). To make fajitas mix up some ground cumin, chilli powder and paprika, and use to flavour your frying onions and garlic, adding peppers and ingredients of choice.

Tequila is a particular kind of mescal that is made from one type of agave plant – the blue agave.

All limes in Mexico are called *limon*, which you'd think must mean a lemon, but in fact *limon* is the name in Spanish for the **little green fruit** we call limes.

Maize was first domesticated some 10,000 years ago in southern Mexico. The cobs on wild maize were only small: 25 millimetres or 1 inch long, with one cob per plant. Explorers took it to Europe and it proved very hardy in diverse climates. There are fifty-nine varieties of **INDIGENOUS CORN** in Mexico.

The Mayan people (whose civilizations stretched across modern-day Mexico, Belize and Guatemala) used a sophisticated, fully developed **writing system;** the earliest inscriptions date back to the third century BCE and use continued in secret well into the eighteenth century CE.

'Beso me mucho' ('Kiss me a lot') is one of the most famous *boleros* in the world. It was written by a songwriter, Consuelo Velázquez, in 1940, who wrote it when she was **A GIRL WHO HAD NEVER BEEN KISSED.**

NATIONAL FLOWER
Dahlia pinnata: these gorgeous flowers originate in the mountainous regions of Mexico and Central America.

AVOCADO aka *la manzana del invierno* (winter apple), aka alligator pear, comes from the Nahuatl word *ahuacatl* which apparently also refers to a certain part of the male anatomy, which presumably is why the Aztecs called it a fertility fruit.

Pulque is a milky, gloopy, fermented alcoholic drink made from agave sap, drunk in central Mexico for at least a thousand years. Try it in a **PULQUERIA.**

Mexican salsa verde isn't made with gherkins, capers, anchovies and herbs, but rather with tomatillos, green chillies, fresh coriander, garlic or onion and salt.

The patron saint of Mexico is the **Virgin of Guadalupe,** who appeared in an orb of light to an Aztec man called Juan Diego Cuauhtatoatzin in 1531 in what is now Mexico City. The Virgin asked him to build a shrine in her honour. The ruling bishop refused Juan, a peasant, permission. Some days later, Mary appeared to him again, asking Juan to collect flowers and carry them in his cloak made of cactus fibre to the bishop. When he opened his cloak a resplendent image of the Virgin of Guadalupe was revealed imprinted on the lining. You can even see this cloak, a 'tilmatli', in the Basilica of Our Lady of Guadalupe. Juan Diego was canonized in 2002 by Pope John Paul II, making him the first Roman Catholic indigenous American saint.

Aztec Legend: **Huitzilopochtli,** the sun god of war and human sacrifice, tore out the heart of an evil prince and threw it in a lake. The first prickly pear grew on an island in this lake, its red fruit supposedly symbolizing the dead prince's heart. The Aztec capital Tenochtitlan was then built on this very spot, where today you find the capital, Mexico City.

Piñatas were thought to have originated with the Aztecs in Mexico, when clay pots were filled with goodies as offerings to **HUITZILOPOCHTLI,** the sun god of war, on his birthday in December.

The **PRICKLY PEAR** cactus is considered sacred by the Aztecs and can be eaten, drunk, used in medicine, shampoo, and potentially as a source of . . . green energy.

Caesar salad in theory is Mexican, having been invented in a hotel in Tijuana by Italian chef Caesar Cardini, who'd moved his business there to avoid the US **PROHIBITION LAWS** of the 1920s.

The pineapple was so named by European explorers for their resemblance to the pinecone, and was first referenced in 1664. Indigenous to South America, the Aztec and Mayans cultivated it before Columbus came across it in 1493. Its Latin name is **'ananas comosus',** and comes from a South American language, Tupi, and means tufted excellent fruit. In the eighteenth century in Europe pineapples became symbols of wealth, as they were expensive to import in the age of sail, and costly to grow in our climate, needing 'pineapple stoves', or huge **'hot houses'** to thrive. In architecture, they symbolize hospitality.

'One can perfectly well philosophize while cooking supper.'

SOR JUANA INÉS DE LA CRUZ

Wanting a beer on the weekend and living in the American Bible Belt meant having to get to know US state rules. Some states ban alcohol sales on a Sunday, so with a thirst for beer on a weekend, one might have to drive over a state line from South to North Carolina, or you could head for a Mexican restaurant. I loved these oases in the Bible Belt desert, despite, much like Indian restaurants back home, the Americanized menus that made the food almost unrecognizable from the original. Take the hearty Tex-Mex cuisine, (a proper branch of cuisine in itself), giving us chimichangas (deep-fried burritos) and deep-fried whole avocado. When I did eventually get to Mexico it was a total revelation. Gone were the melted Monterey Jack-cheese-covered gloopy beans and 'easy-cook' rice; gone the soggy cheese-slathered nachos; instead came steamed tamales, fresh coriander, ceviche and fresh fruit.

Once, en route from Belize and driving into Mexico, I spotted people selling bags of yellow stuff on the side of the road and pulled over, curious. They turned out to be slices of sun-warmed pineapple, peppered with hot ground chilli and salt. The most delicious thing I'd ever tasted, and it's this that I associate the most with Mexican food: the fresh raw ingredients, the chilli, tomatoes, tomatillos, onion, coriander and tart bursts of lime. Light fare, elegantly spiced, enveloped in thin, handmade, corn tortillas. When I got back to Nashville I started growing my own tomatillos (green, savoury physalis, a Mexican native and member of the Nightshade family) and chillies. I love tomatillos and could drink a pint of salsa verde, but tomatillos are not readily available in this country year round, whilst its cousin the tomato is, so we'll be prepping salsa, aka pico de gallo, in today's menu.

As with so many cultures, food and music are inextricably linked – memories of eating chillies *toreados* while singing 'Mexico en la piel' in Nogales when we drove in from over the border – driving down highways past swaharo cacti and prickly pear, with banda or mariachi music blasting out the open car windows, passing trucks with RIP tributes, pimped up with shining rims, blue under lights and bobbing axles.

When I moved back to Europe from America, it was the Mexican culture I hankered for the most, and when Germán Lizárraga and his Banda Estrells de Sinaloa came to play the Barbican, we joined the ex-pats flying the Mexican flag in celebrating these veterans and their music to the rafters of the hall. It was a great night.

Other fabulous Mexican dishes sadly missed now I don't return every year: *mojarra frita* – deep-fried tilapia fish – so crisp, served with orange slices and raw onion slices, and *aguachile de camaron*, a super-hot dish of raw prawns marinated in lime juice and fresh blended serrano peppers (a kind of spicy ceviche), slow-cooked pork carnitas, and thick sopes and gorditas.

MEXICO

'On the day you were born, so did all flowers, And there, on the baptism font, the nightingales sang. And sunrise has begun, already bringing some daylight Get up, it's morning, look, it's already dawned!'

FROM *LAS MAÑANITAS*, SUNG ON BIRTHDAYS AND FOR SANTA MARIA DE GUADALUPE'S FEAST DATE NIGHT 11–12 DECEMBER

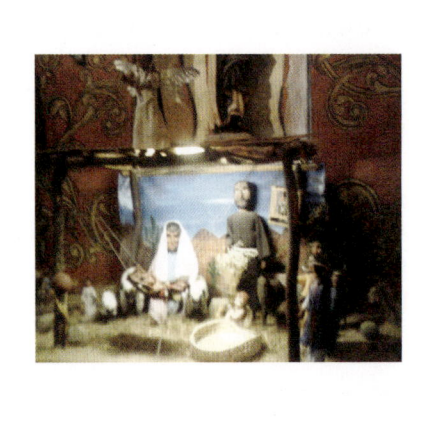

MEXICO

'They were endowed with intelligence, they succeeded in knowing all that there is in the world. When they looked ... they contemplated the arch of heaven and the round face of earth ...'

**ANON FROM THE *POPOL VUH*,
A SIXTEENTH-CENTURY BOOK, LIKE THE *MABINOGION*
(STORIES COLLECTED FROM ORAL TRADITION)**

AT THE TACO BAR

MOLE

MEXICAN MUSHROOMS

TEQUILA PRAWNS

FRIED FISH TACOS

STEWED BLACK BEANS

HOMEMADE TORTILLAS

PICO DE GALLO

GUACAMOLE

HOMEMADE HOT CHILLI SAUCE

QUESO FRESCA

CHILLIES TOREADOS

CORN ON THE COB

CEVICHE

DESSERT

PINEAPPLE WITH CHILLI

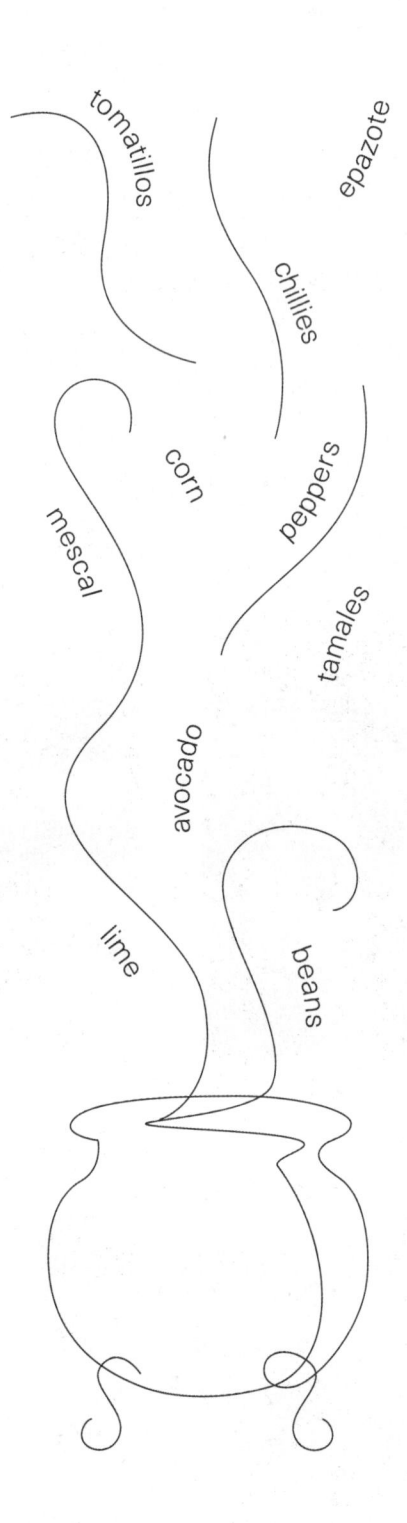

tomatillos · epazote · chillies · corn · peppers · mescal · tamales · avocado · lime · beans

Mariachi Los Vargas de Arturo Mendoza 'México Lindo'

Mariachi Vargas de Tecalitlán 'La Negra'

Mole

(V) (VG) (GF) (DF)

You can cook this Mexican national dish in so many different ways . . . here's just a start. The word 'mole' comes from the Nahuatl word for sauce.

Ingredients

2–3 tbsp oil

1 onion, finely chopped

2 cloves garlic, finely chopped

¼ tsp thyme

¼ tsp Mexican oregano (or marjoram or plain oregano failing that)

2 cloves

stick cinnamon (5cm)

5 peppercorns

½ star anise

½ tsp ground roast cumin

2 bay leaves

1 tsp smoked chipotle flakes (or chilli and smoked paprika if you don't have smoked chipotle)

1 tin tomatoes

2 tbsp ground nuts (almond, sesame or tahini, or peanut)

2 tbsp cocoa

1 tin water (use empty tomato tin to measure)

juice ½ lime

salt and pepper

optional: lime wedges, pumpkin seeds, sesame seeds, fresh coriander

Method

1. Fry the onion on medium heat for 7 minutes until soft and beginning to colour.

2. Add the garlic and whole and ground spices and cook for a further 1–2 minutes.

3. Add the tomatoes, ground nuts and cocoa powder, stir and simmer on low for around 10 minutes until it reduces down and goes a darker colour. You can keep simmering on low until you are ready to serve, adding more water if it looks too dry or is starting to catch.

4. Before serving, remove the whole spices, add lime juice, season to taste and blend, serving thick as a dip for tortilla chips (or totopos) and other sides or add a little more water at step 3, for a thinner sauce to pour on your enchiladas, tamales, meat, vegetables and rice. Serve with pumpkin seeds, sesame seeds, fresh coriander and lime wedges as garnish.

Flaco Jiménez 'Ay Te Dejo En San Antonio'

Luis Miguel 'México En La Piel'

Mexican Mushrooms

VG GF

Ingredients

1–2 tbsp oil (and/or a blob of butter)

1 small onion, chopped

pinch of sea salt

1 clove of garlic, chopped

2 dried smoky chillies, or 1 tsp chipotle flakes
1 green chilli (optional), chopped

6–8 mushrooms, sliced

juice of ½ lime

fresh coriander or mint, chopped

Method

1. Fry the onion with a pinch of salt in the oil and/or butter until soft, not browned, 3–5 minutes.
2. Add the garlic and chillies and cook for a further minute.
3. Add the mushrooms and fry until cooked, about 5 minutes.
4. Squeeze over the fresh lime juice, and serve sprinkled with fresh coriander or mint.

Tequila Prawns

GF DF NV

Ingredients

2 tbsp oil

1 small clove of garlic, chopped

250g prawns (thawed from frozen, or fresh, uncooked, no shells)

3 dried red chillies, chopped, or 1 tsp chipotle flakes

3 tbsp tequila or mescal

juice of ½ lime

salt and pepper

fresh coriander, parsley or mint, chopped

Method

1. Heat the oil in a pan on a medium heat and fry the garlic for a few seconds, without burning.
2. Add the prawns and the chillies and cook for a few minutes, until the prawns are pink.
3. Add the tequila or mescal, let the alcohol heat up, then set alight.
4. Add the lime juice, season, and serve with fresh coriander, parsley or mint.

Conjunto Medellín de Lino Chávez 'La Bamba'

Marimba de los Hermanos Paniagua 'La Sandunga'

Fried Fish Tacos

DF **NV**

Ingredients

500g firm white fish, e.g. cod, haddock, pollack, coley or tilapia (ideally from a sustainable source), skin and bones removed

50g plain flour

1 tsp paprika

salt and pepper

vegetable oil, for frying

Method

1. Cut the fish into bite-size pieces, about 2.5cm square.
2. In a wide, shallow bowl, mix together the flour, paprika and a couple of decent pinches of salt and pepper.
3. Roll each piece of fish in the flour mix until completely covered.
4. Heat a large frying pan on a medium heat. Add enough oil to come 5mm up the side of the pan. Once hot, fry the pieces of fish (in batches to prevent overcrowding the pan) for 1½–2 minutes on the first side, then 1 minute on the second, or until golden and cooked through.
5. Place on a plate lined with kitchen paper to drain.

Stewed Black Beans

VG **GF**

Ingredients

1 red or white onion, finely chopped

25g butter (or 1 tbsp oil)

salt and pepper

2 cloves of garlic, finely chopped

1 fresh jalapeño chilli, finely chopped

½ tsp ground cumin, toasted and ground

1 bay leaf

1 x 460g tin of cooked black beans, drained and rinsed (or 230g dried beans, soaked overnight)

500ml vegetable stock, (you can use the liquid from tinned beans to make up the stock)

Method

1. Fry the onion in oil or butter in a large saucepan on a medium heat with a pinch of salt until really soft (about 10–12 minutes).
2. Stir in the garlic, chilli, cumin and bay leaf and cook for 2 minutes.
3. Tip in the black beans and the stock, season, and bring to a simmer until the beans are soft and the sauce has reduced. If you are using dried soaked beans, this will take longer. Add more water if necessary.
4. Taste and adjust the seasoning.
5. Serve sprinkled with homemade cheese, queso fresco (see p. 33).

Option:
Near the end of cooking add a pinch of 'epazote' which is meant to help against intestinal gas.

Mariachi México de Pepe Villa 'Las Bicicletas'

Atrapado, Fito and Javier Olivares 'Cumbia De La Frontera'

Banda Los Lagos 'Carta Abierta'

Ignacio López Tarso 'La Persecución De Villa'

Homemade Tortillas

(V) (VG) (DF)

You can stock up with frozen corn tortillas from the Spanish market if you're ever down on Portobello Road. To make authentic corn tortillas you need *masa harina*, which I never have, so I make them using a ratio of 1:1 fine ground cornmeal with flour. (*Masa harina* is not at all the same as finely ground cornmeal. To make using *masa harina,* mix salt with this flour, then little by little add warm water until you have a dough, then make the balls and tortillas as below.)

Ingredients

100g plain flour
100g fine ground cornmeal
sea salt
1 tbsp oil
water

Method

1. Mix the three dry ingredients in a bowl.
2. Add water and oil gradually, mixing and kneading until you get a smooth dough. Set the dough aside for 10 minutes.
3. Divide the dough into small rounds about the size of golfballs.
4. Squash each ball between sheets of clingfilm, and roll them out until they're about 2–3mm thick.
5. Heat a thick iron griddle and cook the tortillas on the dry surface for 1–2 minutes each side.
6. Hold them in a tea towel and serve.

Pico de Gallo

(V) (VG) (GF) (DF)

Pico de gallo, 'rooster's beak', is apparently so called because the bits you cut are small, like chicken feed. But there's a better story: to calm fighting cocks, handlers would put the bird's head in their mouth (darkness calms the bird down in the same way as a leather hood on hawks) and sometimes the cock would bite the handler's tongue. The hot chillies in *pico de gallo* should have the same effect on your tongue. The ratio of the ingredients below is up to you, but here's an idea.

Ingredients

2 tomatoes (skinned, and seeded if you want)
¼ onion
small bunch of fresh coriander
1 or 2 jalapeños or green chillies (to taste)
sea salt and freshly ground black pepper
juice of ½ lime

Method

Finely chop the tomatoes, onion, coriander and chillies and season with salt, black pepper and lime juice.

Antonio Aguilar 'Y Andale'

Banda Estrellas de Sinaloa de Germán Lizarraga 'Bienvenida'

Guacamole

(V) (VG) (GF) (DF)

If you don't have a pestle and mortar, finely chop the ingredients and mash the avocado with a fork.

Ingredients

¼ white onion, chopped

25g fresh coriander (a small bunch), chopped

pinch of sea salt

1 green chilli, e.g. serrano (keep the seeds, they give nice flavour)

4 small avocados

pinch of Mexican oregano (use marjoram if unavailable)

juice of ½ lime

Method

1. Using a pestle and mortar, grind the onion, most of the coriander, salt and chilli.
2. Cut the avocados in half, remove the stones, then squeeze out the flesh and chop. Add the avocado flesh to the pestle and mortar.
3. Add the remaining coriander, the oregano or marjoram, and the lime juice.
4. Taste and season, adding more salt or lime juice to taste.

Homemade Hot Chilli Sauce

(V) (VG) (GF) (DF)

If you don't have a pestle and mortar, pulse in a food processor or very finely chop.

Ingredients

2 cloves of garlic

½ tsp rock salt

2 tbsp chopped chillies (a mix of chillies works really well, e.g. 2 small red and 2 small green chillies, or 1 medium green chilli, or 2 hot red dried chillies)

2 tbsp lime juice

1 tsp fresh marjoram (or Mexican oregano)

8 tbsp water

Method

1. Using a pestle and mortar, grind the garlic with the salt.
2. Add the chillies and grind them in.
3. Add the lime juice and water and a pinch of marjoram or Mexican oregano.
4. Serve immediately.

Chavela Vargas 'Macorina'

Mexrrissey 'El Primero Del Gang'

Queso Fresca (Homemade Cheese)

VG GF

My gramma used to make this and called it 'farmer's cheese' – it is called paneer in India. 500ml of milk makes a tiny amount of solid, but it is worth it for the novelty of making instant cheese.

Bring 500ml of milk (semi-skimmed or whole) to just under boiling point in a saucepan. Add 3 tablespoons of fresh lemon juice (or vinegar, if you have no citrus). Leave it to separate.

Using a jiffy cloth, a muslin, or a clean old T-shirt, filter out the solids, retaining the whey (use it in smoothies or for making soda bread; it can be frozen). Twist the cloth to squeeze out the liquid.

Season the cheese with a little salt and crumble it on to your beans, tacos or toast.

Corn on the Cob

VG GF

Cook corn cobs in a saucepan of boiling water for 5 minutes, then drain. Either cover them with oil or butter and flash-grill them on hot charcoal or a hot griddle, or just drizzle them with melted butter and sprinkle them with paprika, with or without a pinch of cayenne, a squeeze of lime, and a pinch of sea salt.

Chillies Toreados

V VG GF DF

Ingredients

4 jalapeño chillies

1 tbsp oil

sea salt

Method

1. Get a pan or griddle smoking hot.
2. Grease the chillies with the oil and grill them for 3–4 minutes, turning them around so that each side scorches.
3. Season and serve.

Mariachi Nuevo Tecalitlán 'Cielito Lindo'

Mariachi Nuevo Tecalitlán 'Guadalajara'

Ceviche

(GF) (DF) (NV)

All you need for this is fresh fish and fresh lime or lemon juice – you can add pretty much anything to it in whatever ratio you like: tomatoes, hot sauce, red peppers, parsley, mint, a drizzle of oil before serving. Here's a start.

Ingredients

2 fillets of white fish, e.g. sea bass (about 200g)
¼ tsp sea salt
juice of 2 limes
¼ sweet onion or 1 spring onion
1 hot green chilli or ¼ small sweet green pepper, finely chopped
small bunch of fresh coriander, finely chopped
1 small avocado, diced
freshly ground black pepper

Method

1. Remove any skin from the fish fillets and cut them into small pieces about 1cm x 2cm (the easiest way to do this is to cut the fillets into three strips lengthways, then across).

2. Put the fish pieces into a bowl with the salt and lime juice and leave to marinate in the fridge for 10 minutes.

3. Remove from the fridge and add all the other ingredients.

Option:
Serve with or without the marinating juice. Note, in Peru the tradition is to drink this juice, the 'tiger's milk', with a shot of Pisco, Peruvian/Chilean brandy.

Pineapple with Chilli

(VG) (GF)

Warm pineapple, sprinkled with sea salt and cayenne pepper. You can simply serve it at room temperature, or you can sauté slices in hot butter, then sprinkle with a pinch of salt and cayenne.

For that extra something, serve it with ice cream drizzled with mescal, a tip picked up at the home of Thomasina Miers (chef and founder of the Wahaca restaurant chain).

Guitarte 'La Pajarera'
Louis Armstrong 'La Cucaracha'

Mariachi Aguila Real 'El Jarabe Tapatio'

Carla Morrison-Eres Tu

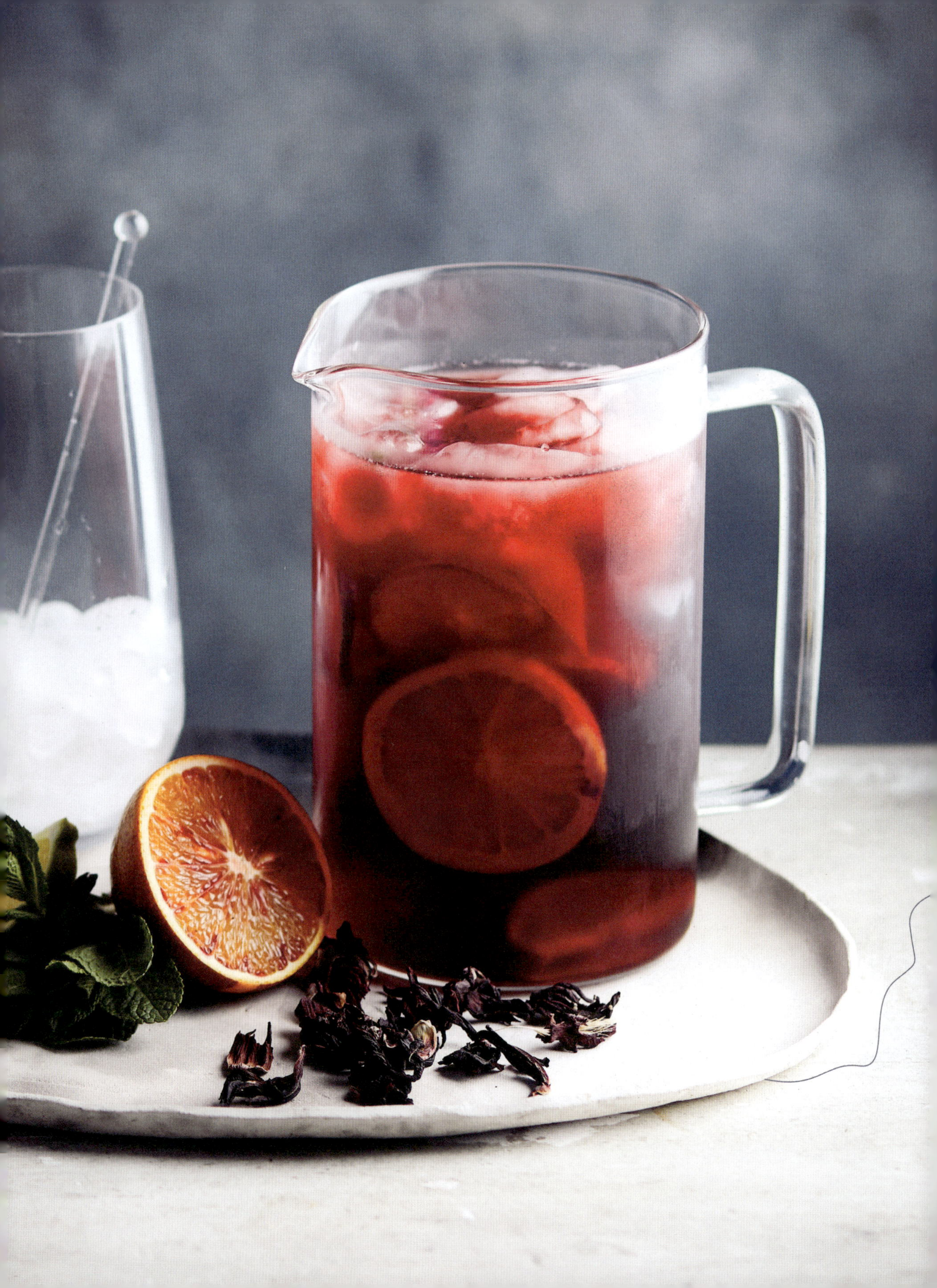

JAMAICA

Here's an excerpt of a poem by Kingston-born Kei Miller, from his 2014 Forward Prize-winning collection, *The Cartographer Tries to Map a Way to Zion*. Kei writes in one poem about borders wriggling over the centuries, an image that's stayed with me:

x. in which the cartographer asks for directions

Sometimes the cartographer gets frustrated when he asks an I-formant how to get to such and such a place, and the I-Formant might say something like –

> Awrite, you know the big white house at the bottom of
> Clover Hill with all the windows dem board up, and
> with a high shingle roof that look almost like a church?

Yes, the cartographer says.

> And in front the house you always see a ole woman,
> only three teeth in her mouth, and she out there selling
> pepper shrimp in a school chair with a umbrella tie to it.
> And beside her she always have two mongrel dog and
> one of them is white and the nedda one is brown?

Yes, I know exactly where you mean, the cartographer says.

> And in the year there is a big guinnep tree that hang
> right out to the road, so school pickney always stop
> there to buy shrimp and eat free guinnep?

Yes, yes, the cartographer insists. I know it.

> Good, says the I-formant. Cause you mustn' go there.

Famous Son:

PAUL BOGLE (1822–1865), was recognized as a national hero in Jamaica in 1969. His name appears in songs by Lee Scratch Perry, Bob Marley and Burning Speer. Bogle was a rare African Jamaican landowner, prosperous enough to be able to pay the fee to vote. Jamaican slavery officially ended in 1833, but former slaves were still facing discrimination. In 1865, Bogle and his brother Moses led nearly 300 people on a march from Stony Gut to Morant Bay Courthouse in Spanish Town in protest at continued acts of oppression. The colonial militia opened fire on them, killing seven. In retaliation, sixteen officials were killed and Bogle and his brother Moses were hung at Morant Bay for taking part in the uprising.

The national airport is named after **Norman Washington Manley,** a politician who helped lead Jamaica to independence in 1962. His grandfather was a migrant worker from Yorkshire.

NANNY OF THE MAROONS, seen here on the $500 note, was a renowned resistance and freedom fighter, leader of escaped slaves in Jamaica in the early eighteenth century, and founder of Nanny Town.

Coffee from Blue Mountain is among the world's most famous and expensive.

Johnny cakes are deep-fried balls made from flour (or cornmeal and sugar). Dumplings are made of flour and can be fried or boiled.

Noni (pronounced noonie) is another name for the duppy **soursop,** thought to have medicinal properties.

DUPPY is a word meaning 'ghost' or 'bad spirits'. You can hear about it in Bob Marley's song 'Duppy Conqueror'.

COCONUT is the one tree that has everything to sustain life; known in Sanskrit as 'kalpavriksha', it has one of the biggest seeds in the world and can float across oceans.

English is the official language but most speak Jamaicans speak patois, a mixture of English and African Creole.

Sorrel is a dark berry-coloured spicy drink made from dried flower parts and drunk at Christmas.

BREADFRUIT is related to the **JACKFRUIT** and arrived in Jamaica from the Pacific. Starchy, like a potato, it is one of the highest-yielding food plants known.

Besides the USA, Jamaica holds the most **Olympic world records.**

A **railway** was built in Jamaica in 1845.

The name Jamaica is thought to come from an **ARAWAK** Indian word – *Xaymaca* – meaning land of wood and water.

Jamaica has more **churches** per square mile than any other Christian country in the world.

Jamaica's national bird is the doctor bird, aka the **SWALLOW TAIL HUMMINGBIRD** or *Trochilus Polytmus*. It only lives in Jamaica. The Arawaks believed it had magical powers.

National dish:
ACKEE AND SALTFISH.
Ackee are part of the soapberry family, as are lychee and longan. The soapberry is a native of West Africa and was imported to Jamaica some time before 1778.

> *'Mi nuh drink coffee tea: mango time,*
> *Care how nice it may be – mango time*
> *In the heat of the mango crop*
> *When di fruit dem a ripe an' drop*
> *Wash yu pot, tun dem dun' – mango time.'*
>
> **JAMAICAN FOLK SONG**

Cho-cho, breadfruit, green banana, coconuts, plantain, mango, duppy soursop, rum, red stripe and humidity. Sound systems, vinyl Sundays, jerk stalls, wood smoke (which doubles as a good mosquito repellent), markets with stalls heaped with callaloo, clothes and trainers emblazoned with the Jamaican flag, knitted hats in Rasta colours for dreads, pineapples, okra, seasonings and Scotch bonnets. Johnny cakes, ital soup, fresh in season gunga peas, (they are in season around December time, like sorrel, that dark, berry, spicy festive drink), spinners in stews, bamboo rafts up the Rio Grande, lunch cooked on wood and stone, cray fish coconut curry and dumplings, Manish water and a million other aphrodisiacs, Guinness in bottles (the Caribbean version has more alcohol), kayaking, white sands, turquoise seas and rainbows over Alligator Head. So many varieties of yam (they look woody and muddy, but cut easily, and cook up like potato), ginger, fresh from the ground, and a passion for food that embraces you as much as the sounds of the islands.

We stayed in a tree reservation once. At night the frogs sounded like birds; in the day, the birds looked like flowers, the trees lush, dizzyingly high, a nice change to look up skywards instead of at a screen; cheese plants recognizable from home in the seventies (dusty and dry in corners of offices or empty shop windows) here climb up to heaven on the trunks of their giant host trees, aerial roots hanging down as in *Tarzan* films.

I'd never seen ackee trees in fruit before. The fruit hung like rose-coloured sweet peppers, and shouldn't be eaten until they split, when they reveal beetle-black seeds and yellow castings, which form part of the national dish. Fresh ackee tastes a little like new potatoes, creamy and delicate, but with a more complex aftertaste.

From jerk chicken to rice and peas and patties; from mento, ska, rock steady to reggae and sprinting, Jamaica packs a big cultural punch for a small island. My neck of the woods is Ladbroke Grove: famous for its Notting Hill Carnival. Reggae music, stalls and sound systems, oil-drum smokers and jelly coconuts are a big part of Portobello Road market; dominoes is played in bar corners on a Sunday and words from Jamaican patois and other African-Caribbean communities are used across London every minute of the day.

Jamaica itself is a rich mix of cultures, and its history can be traced in the cuisine. From the Chinese you'll see pak choy, and soy used as an umami ingredient, or as a browning alternative in jerk. From the Indian diaspora (indentured labourers arrived between 1845 and 1917 following the end of slavery) comes curried goat and shrimp, and, from the English, Easter buns and Christmas spice cake.

Let's give a nod to a huge Jamaican export: rum, first distilled in the Caribbean in the seventeenth century when plantation workers (mostly slaves) discovered that molasses, a by-product of the sugar-refining industry, could be used to make liquor. Jamaica was one of the first countries in the world to commercially produce it.

Smoking fires remind me both of home and Jamaica, and if you do come across fresh breadfruit, try cooking it for ten minutes direct on a charcoal fire or roast in an oven for twenty minutes. Once cooked, cut off the outside shell, take out the inside nut and cut off pieces shaped like crescent moons, serve as you would boiled potatoes, adding butter if you want and salt and pepper.

In Jamaica unripe green bananas are used as a savoury vegetable. Cut off the green skin, trying not to break the banana inside, and put into a saucepan and boil up for about ten minutes with peeled and chopped cho-cho (from the squash family) and yam (also peeled and chopped). Test with a fork to see if they are soft and cooked through. Serve with butter, salt and pepper, just like potatoes. Green plantains are easy too: remove the skin and fry in vegetable oil for 1–2 minutes each side, take out of the pan, squash between tea towels or paper towel, then put back in the pan, and fry a second time. With ripe yellow/black plantain, fry once in oil for 1–2 minutes each side, drain and serve immediately with salt.

JAMAICA

Port Royal, now known as the city that sank, was once known as the
'WICKEDEST PLACE ON EARTH',
due to its pirates, ladies of the night and other characters …

Port Royal's sandy ground was liquefied by an earthquake in 1692: a gravestone tells the miraculous story of a man who was buried twice:

'Here lies the body of Lewis Galdy who departed this life at Port Royal on December 22, 1739 aged 80. He was born at Montpelier in France but left that country for his religion and came to settle in this island where he was swallowed up in the Great Earthquake in the year 1692 and by the providence of God was by another shock thrown into the sea and miraculously saved by swimming until a boat took him up. He lived many years after in great reputation. Beloved by all and much lamented at his Death'

These mighty trees in regal robes
Now call the land to worship,
And the bees, hungry for hidden honey,
Swarm among its blossoms and buzz and buzz.

An excerpt from a poem, 'Home Thoughts' by pioneering Jamaican feminist, poet, playwright, activist and first black BBC journalist **UNA MARSON**.

'Jamaica has the best coffee, the best sugar, the best ginger and some of the best cocoa in the world.'

CHRIS BLACKWELL

'If you want real fresh Jamaican produce, you need to head to Coronation Market in Kingston. It's the real Jamaica – you can try all the authentic fruits, meat and fish you can think of.'

USAIN BOLT

'Better belly bust than waste good food.'

'Those who can't dance say the music is no good.'

ON THE MENU

CHICKPEA AND POTATO CURRY

RICE AND PEAS

CALLALOO

ITAL SOUP

CURRIED TOFU OR PRAWNS

HOMEMADE JERK SEASONING

SALT FISH ACKEE

DESSERT

MANGO AND MINT SORBET

COCKTAILS

DARK AND STORMY
TING-A-LING
RUM PUNCH
SORREL

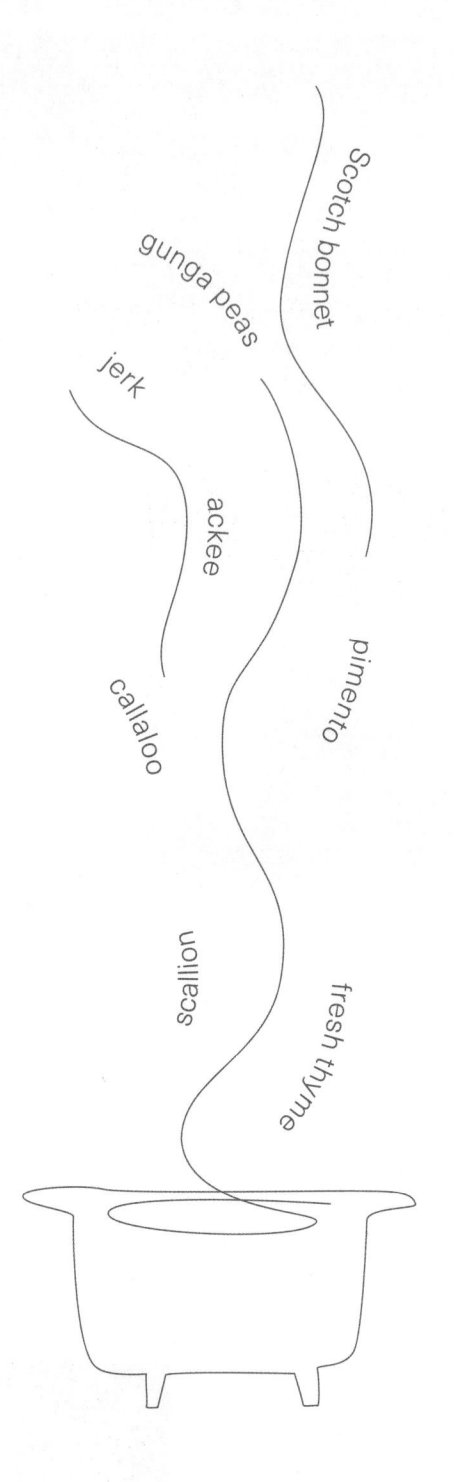

Scotch bonnet
gunga peas
jerk
ackee
pimento
callaloo
scallion
fresh thyme

Joe Gibbs and the Professionals 'Chapter Two'

Desmond Dekker '(Poor Mi) Israelites'

Rico 'Take Five'

John Holt 'Ali Baba'

Jimmy Cliff 'The Harder They Come'

JAMAICA

Chickpea and Potato Curry

V VG GF DF

Curry powder packaged up and sold in Jamaica includes: cumin, coriander, fenugreek, ginger, cayenne, turmeric, pepper and chilli pepper.
I mix my own, but if you want to use ready-made, remove the spices* I include below and use 2–3 tablespoons of Jamaican curry powder instead.

Ingredients

1 onion, finely chopped
salt and pepper
3 cloves of garlic, finely chopped
¼ green pepper, diced
1 Scotch bonnet chilli, halved
1 spring onion, finely chopped
sprig of fresh thyme
1 tsp grated ginger
*½ tsp ground turmeric
*½ tsp ground cumin
*½ tsp ground coriander
*10 allspice/pimento berries
*¼ tsp cayenne pepper
*¼ tsp ground fenugreek
1 tomato, diced (and skinned if you want)
400g potatoes, cubed
1 x 400g tin of chickpeas (or approx. 100g dried, soaked and cooked for 45 minutes to 2 hours, depending on the chickpeas) – keep the liquid
200ml vegetable stock (including the chickpea cooking liquid)
1 x 400ml tin of coconut milk (or you can use coconut powder mixed in water)
sprig of fresh parsley, finely chopped

Method

1. In a large wide pan, fry the onion with a pinch of salt until soft – about 5–7 minutes.

2. Add the garlic and let it soften for a minute, then add the green pepper, Scotch bonnet, spring onion, thyme and spices/curry powder, and fry for a minute to release the flavours.

3. Add the tomato, potatoes, chickpeas and stock, then put a lid on the pan and simmer on a low heat for 35–40 minutes. Add the coconut milk for the last ten minutes.

4. Take out a few of the potato pieces and mash them with a fork, then return them to the pan to thicken the sauce. Add the chopped parsley.

5. Taste, season and serve.

Rudy Mills 'John Jones'

Augustus Pablo 'Addis-A-Baba'

Alton Ellis 'My Willow Tree'

Rice and Peas

(V) (VG) (GF) (DF)

Ingredients

100g fresh gunga or garden peas, or 100g cooked gunga peas, drained (alternatively use cooked red kidney, pinto beans, or black-eyed peas)

1 clove of garlic, sliced

sea salt, a pinch, or to taste

250g brown rice

600ml water (you can use the bean-cooking water as part of this)

100ml coconut milk (or coconut powder with water)

large sprig of fresh thyme

1 small Scotch bonnet chilli (or to taste – they pack a big punch)

1 spring onion, sliced

10 allspice/pimento berries

Method

1. Boil the fresh gunga peas or garden peas in a pan of water with the sliced garlic and a touch of salt until soft – about 10 minutes – then drain, reserving the water. If you are using pre-cooked peas, you can go straight to step 2.

2. Put all the ingredients into a saucepan. Put the lid on, bring to the boil, then turn down the heat and cook until the liquid has been absorbed and the rice is cooked – about 15–30 minutes, depending on the rice you've used. Brown basmati takes 30 minutes. Turn off the heat and keep the lid on the pan until you are ready to serve.

Callaloo

(VG) (GF)

Ingredients

1 tbsp oil or butter

½ onion, finely chopped

¼ tsp jerk seasoning (see p. 49)

2 small tomatoes, chopped

250g callaloo, washed and with ends trimmed, then chopped (or use tender greens like kale/chard/spinach)

50ml water

salt and pepper

Method

1. Heat the oil in a pan on a medium heat, add the onion and jerk seasoning, and cook for 5 minutes, until the onion has softened.

2. Add the tomatoes and fry for 1 minute.

3. Add the callaloo, stir, add the water, then put a lid on the pan and cook until the leaves are tender – about 3–5 minutes. Season to taste.

The Wailers 'Soul Rebel'

Dr Alimantado 'Born For A Purpose/Reason For Living'

Ital Soup

V | VG | GF | DF

My other half, Steve, met the Georgie mentioned in Bob Marley's song 'No Woman, No Cry', and they had food together. Like a master of ceremonies, Georgie kept a huge cauldron hot on a fire in Trenchtown, Kingston. He always had a stew or porridge on the go, always overflowing, never to run out. He'd give you a bowl and then, if you asked how much you owed, he'd reply, 'Whatever you can afford.'

Once you know how to cook a vegetable and pulse soup, you are forever a king. Rastafarians, believing that eating meat is a form of cannibalism, cook it using a mix of seasonal vegetables and peas.

Ingredients

Approx. 1kg vegetables of your choice (cho-cho, yams, green bananas, callaloo, pumpkin, carrots, cabbage, fresh beans and peas (or pre-soaked and cooked dried beans/peas)

1 x 400ml tin of coconut milk (or make using fresh or powdered)

salt and pepper

water

Seasonings: use the classic Jamaican line-up of:

10 allspice/pimento berries

2 cloves of garlic, finely chopped

1 tsp grated ginger

sprig of fresh thyme

1 scallion (spring onion), finely chopped

1 onion, chopped

1 small green pepper, chopped

1 Scotch bonnet chilli (or to taste), chopped

2 tbsp coconut or vegetable oil

Method

1. In a large pan on a medium heat, fry the seasonings in the oil for a few minutes to release the flavours.
2. Add your choice of prepared vegetables and cooked dried beans/peas, with the coconut milk and enough water to cover them.
3. Bring to the boil, then reduce the heat and simmer until the vegetables and beans/peas are soft.
4. Season and serve.

Courtney John 'Strangers'

Desmond Dekker 'You Can Get It If You Really Want'

Curried Tofu or Prawns

GF DF NV

Ingredients

400g tofu (firm, drained), or shelled prawns (cooked or uncooked)

1 small onion, finely chopped

1 spring onion, sliced

1 small Scotch bonnet chilli (or to taste), sliced

large sprig of fresh thyme

1 clove of garlic, chopped

1 tsp grated ginger

2 tsp Jamaican curry powder (or a mix of ¾ tsp toasted cumin, ¾ tsp toasted coriander, ¼ tsp toasted fenugreek, if you have some, ¼ tsp cayenne pepper (or to taste), ¼ tsp ground turmeric, ¼ tsp freshly ground black pepper)

2 tbsp coconut or vegetable oil

100ml coconut milk (or 25g coconut powder mixed with 100ml water)

¼ tsp jerk seasoning (see below)

salt and pepper

Method

1. Mix the tofu or prawns, onion, spring onion, Scotch bonnet, thyme, garlic, ginger and curry powder in a bowl (keeping ½ teaspoon of curry powder for later) and leave to marinate for 30 minutes.

2. Heat the oil in a wide pan on a medium heat, add the remaining curry powder to release the flavours, then add the marinated ingredients and gently fry for 7–10 minutes.

3. Add the coconut milk and jerk seasoning, and simmer for 10 minutes. Season and serve with rice and peas.

Dry jerk seasoning

2 tsp thyme, ½ tsp ground cumin, ½ tsp cayenne pepper, 1 tsp paprika, 1 tsp allspice/pimento berries, ¼ tsp ground cinnamon, ¼ tsp grated nutmeg, 1 tsp peppercorns, 1 tsp sea salt, 1 tsp sugar, ½ tsp dried chilli flakes. Use as a rub or to flavour dishes.

Homemade wet jerk marinade

1 tsp grated ginger, 1 tsp chopped garlic, 2 chopped spring onions, 1 chopped Scotch bonnet, 1 tsp fresh thyme leaves, 1 tsp ground toasted allspice/pimento berries, 100ml white wine vinegar, ½ tsp ground cinnamon, ¼ tsp grated nutmeg, 3 tablespoons honey, 2 tbsp olive or vegetable oil. Grind all these ingredients in a pestle and mortar or a blender. Use as an overnight marinade: with chicken or red snapper, skin scored, or with prawns, ideally then cook over a wood fire, or roast on a high heat in the oven. Serve fish with lime or lemon wedges, breadfruit or boiled potatoes, and hot sauce.

Salt Fish Ackee

GF DF NV

Ingredients

250g salt fish

350g fresh ackee fruit (or 540g of tinned ackee, drained)

1 tbsp allspice/pimento berries

1 tbsp coconut or vegetable oil

½ onion, finely chopped

sprig of fresh thyme

1 spring onion, chopped

1 Scotch bonnet chilli, sliced

½ green pepper, chopped

1 clove of garlic, finely chopped

2 small tomatoes, chopped

freshly ground black pepper

pinch of jerk seasoning (optional)

Method

1. Put the pieces of salt fish into a bowl of cold water and rub a little to start moving the salt. Change the water and leave to soak for an hour.

2. Shell the ackee fruit, discarding the outside shell, the black nut and the orange/pink stringy core.

3. Put the ackee into a pan (about 20 pieces) with the allspice/pimento berries, bring to the boil, then reduce the heat and simmer for about 5–10 minutes, until soft but not mushy. Drain and leave to cool. If using tinned ackee, there's no need to cook it, just drain.

4. Drain the salt fish and put into a pan. Cover with fresh water, then bring to the boil and cook for 10 minutes. Remove the fish from the pan and, when cool enough, remove the bones and skin, and break up the flesh into pieces. Set aside.

5. Heat the oil over a medium heat and add the onion and the sprig of thyme. Cook for about 3 minutes, then gradually add the rest of the ingredients – the spring onion, Scotch bonnet, garlic, green pepper and tomatoes – and soften for 5 minutes.

6. Add the salt fish pieces (you can include the backbone if you like, for added taste) and stir to coat with the flavours.

7. Finally add the ackee (including the whole allspice/pimento berries) and taste – it should be salty enough, but add a pinch of black pepper and a pinch of jerk seasoning, if you like.

Note:
Never eat unripe ackee, as it is poisonous. It's fine once the fruit has opened naturally.

Mango and Mint Sorbet

V VG GF DF

Just keep some coconut powder and frozen mango in your freezer and you'll have an instant delicious vegan dessert (if you don't have any fresh mint, it still works).

500g frozen mango pieces
handful of fresh mint leaves
150ml fruit juice, e.g. pineapple (water works too, if you have no juice)
50ml coconut powder with water (or coconut milk, if you prefer)

Blend the ingredients together and serve straight away.

Cocktails

V VG GF DF

Dark and stormy
Mix a shot of dark rum ('dark') with ginger beer ('stormy'). Serve on ice, with a slice of lime.

Ting-a-ling
A shot of rum mixed with Ting (grapefruit soda, sold in Jamaica). Serve with ice.

Rum punch
My neighbours Billie and Gary make rum punch for parties. Dangerous stuff as it tastes so innocent. Here's the classic ratio in a rhyme:

One of sour, two of sweet, three of strong and four of weak.

Sour: lime juice
Sweet: sugar syrup /honey
Strong: rum
Weak: water, or fruit juice, or, apparently, Red Stripe

Sorrel
A Christmas drink. This is not the green sorrel as listed in the 'hedgerow salad', but rather the bright red drink pictured in the opening pages of this chapter, made from the sepals of the roselle plant, a species of hibiscus.

Steep 50–75g dried sorrel/hibiscus in 1.5 litres boiled water with slices of fresh ginger (about 80g, a large lump), and 8–10 pimento/allspice seeds (option: you can also use some cinnamon and cloves). The following day, strain off the solids, add a squeeze of lemon or lime, and stir in 150g of sugar until it dissolves. Add more if you like sweet things. Serve with rum (optional), ice cubes and a slice of lime or lemon.

Sorrel will keep for a week in the fridge. You can also make a herbal tea using some of the dried sorrel.

The Upsetters 'Return of Django'

P. P. Arnold 'Angel of the Morning'

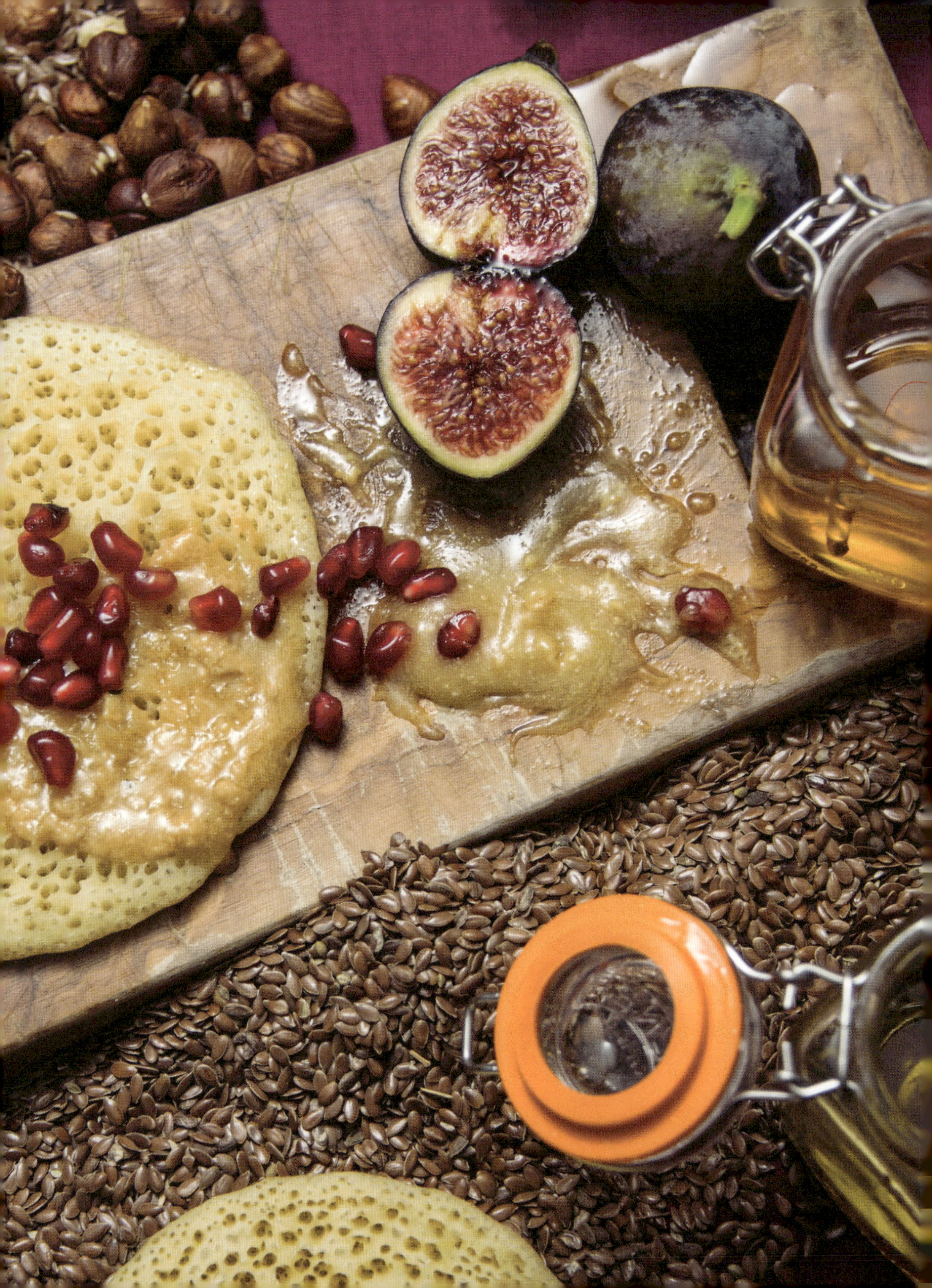

MOROCCO

'Qbet raja' ('Hold the grinder')

The grinder is in a ruthless hand
Oh God may you grind him over and over
He hit me and I became light in his hand
Love is never given by force

Anon

I've picked a poem about the desire for revenge, and rebellion against oppression, since the question of equality is still so relevant everywhere today, and the grinding brings to mind the stones used to produce argan oil. The author is unknown, but it was written around 1801 in Moroccan Arabic and published by Al-Fassi in 1957. It's translated by Fatima Sadiqi, the author of *Women, Gender, and Language in Morocco*.

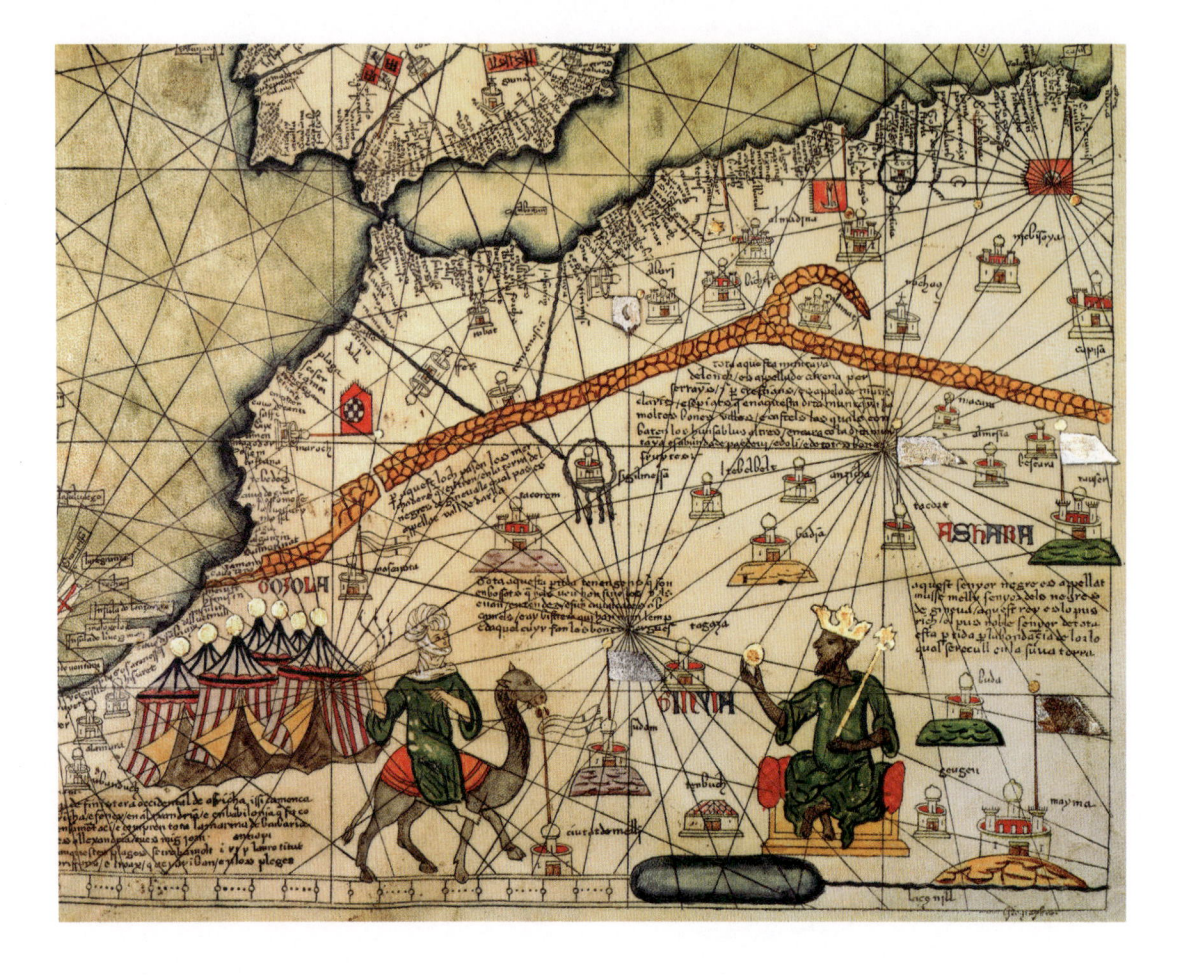

Ibn Battuta (1304–1377) spent nearly thirty years travelling an astonishing 75,000 miles across Africa, the Middle East, India, Vietnam and Spain, making him one of the greatest explorers of all time.

Battuta was of **BERBER** descent, born to a family of scholars in Tangiers. Aged twenty-one, he set off alone on a pilgrimage that normally took sixteen months. He ended up being away from Morocco for twenty-four years. The countries he visited include Somalia, Mogadishu ('an exceedingly large city'), Tanzania, Egypt, Malaysia, Palestine, Spain, Mali and Siberia. He also visited Constantinople, Afghanistan, India, the Maldive Islands, Sri Lanka, Bangladesh and China. Shortly before he died, he dictated *The Travels* 'Rihla'.

'Travelling… it gives you home in a thousand strange places, then leaves you a stranger in your own land.'

IBN BATTUTA

In Arabic, Morocco is 'Al Magrib' – the place where the sun sets – the west.

'The determined ostrich hunter will surely meet one.'

'Evening promises are like butter; morning comes and it's all melted.'

Josephine Baker had a home in Marrakech in the 1940s. Stay in her old riad and see her eccentric dresses and bright purple saxophone.

cinnamon
turmeric
tagines
couscous
cumin
flat bread
ginger
argan oil

COUSCOUS was originally made by hand in the Moroccan mountains, using sieves, and is a staple of the Berber culture of North Africa – ideal for nomads as it is so easy to transport and cook. Is it a grain or is it pasta? A bit of both: it is hard cracked wheat, produced by a first crushing in a mill, then moistened and rolled in flour. Some say it predates pasta, and has more vitamins.

The **Evil Eye** was first seen 5,000 years ago on Mesopotamian idols; now you often see these white, turquoise and black glass discs in many countries, including Morocco. It is worn as a good luck charm.

The **Hand of Fatima,** or Hamsa (five, or five fingers of hand) is named after the daughter of Muhammad, Fatima. Again, it's a protective sign, promising success, harmony, luck and protection.

*Never say 'I regret …',
always say 'I learned …'*

Some of the best seafood dishes to be eaten in London are served by a Moroccan gentleman on his street stall in Golborne Road. He serves up the freshest whole white fish grilled on charcoal, served with bunches of herbs and tomatoes. You eat on tables on the pavement in front of the patterned bowls, straw baskets, oils, rice, onions and bags of a full-to-bursting shop. Notting Dale, where I live, is home to many Moroccan families, many on the same school run as me. A plan was hatched when my friend Saiid bought me huge bags of fresh spices from his home town of Tangiers. It was time.

Arriving in Marrakech at the hot end of August, we got in a car and started the three-hour ride west, past construction sites at the edge of town, a cement factory, herds of goats and their boy shepherds, through crimson lands and on towards the coastal town of Essaouira – a walled city, and briefly home to Jimi Hendrix. The sun, looking very much like a huge, pink moon, bobbled on the horizon and left the building. The darkness deepened, we looked up, it sparkled: the sky was full of stars.

The sound of the name Essaouira gives us a clue to its other moniker: Africa's 'Windy City'. It's known for its strong coastal winds: great for windsurfers and kiters, and for those wanting some natural exfoliation. I retreated; reading was best done back inside the walled ramparts on a roof terrace with some local organic rosé. Moroccan wine is delicious, so too the food. Everywhere are mountains of fresh local produce: dates, peas, prickly pears, bananas. Throughout the day the loudspeakers rev up for the call to prayer; they sound like small motorbikes, or a cow lowing in labour. One mosque would start, then others join in in a strange polyphony. It accompanied my harmony of salads: green lentils, beetroot, tomatoes, onions, carrots, parsley, courgettes, aubergine and sweet potatoes.

One of the curious sights of Morocco is that of goats grazing in the tops of trees. These are argan trees, which only grow in a small area of the country. They're prized for the oil from the nuts they produce, and the oil is used everywhere: for hair, skin, in cooking, and, my favourite, to make *amlou,* aka Moroccan Nutella, by mixing the oil with honey and ground nuts. We visited an argan oil cooperative, where women laboriously extracted the oil by hand using tiny stone mills.

Morocco felt biblical at times: donkeys are still used to go to and from the market. Their legs look so small – dainty even – but then look at the size of their belly, then the belly of the man on top and his bulging saddlebags and netted goods. Yet there they go, trotting up the steep hill. All that weight on those four spindly legs. Friday is market day, for men only; time to exchange news, visit the barber, and, in the past, for young boys to be circumcised; to bring animals for slaughter and buy vegetables. Animals arrive, are slaughtered, butchered, then cooked in a row of stalls. Wood smoke keeps the flies away. Camel legs dangle next to lumps of white fat from their humps. We walked through to the end tent: sweet mint tea and honey nuts for a break. It was midday at this point, heavy-hot; inland, I stopped at a stall heaped with seeds and roots: more cumin, turmeric, ginger, paprika, peppercorns. Heaven scent.

After the Berber market, we stopped for lunch and sat under pomegranate trees, a rug under us as food was served: tomato and onion salad; sardine balls with courgette, carrots, parsnip, peppers, flat bread. A rest post-meal, then it was back to the coast, through the gates of the town, past the carts heaped with skinned prickly pears, which are sweet as can be, aromatic like mango, with hard nuts to spit out, and those small yellow bananas, the best I've ever tasted.

There's such an interesting mix of cultures, no surprise in a country with such a rich trading past and proud history of independence. Half the population speaks Berber, or Berber dialects – languages native to North Africa. The Arabs came here in the seventh century and converted the population to Islam; Moroccan Arabic and French are spoken widely, and practically everyone in Morocco is at least bilingual.

To the cooking: you might have a tagine in your home, but if you live in a micro house like me, you won't. No problem, they aren't strictly necessary. What's not negotiable, however, are three particular spices: cumin, ginger and turmeric. And as ever, buy cumin whole, toast it for a few minutes on a thick iron pan just before you start cooking, then grind. The puffs of smoke and the smell released are what make this pastime worth it. Also worth sourcing are some preserved lemons and harissa.

MOROCCO

58

'Travelling – it leaves
you speechless, then
turns you into a storyteller.'

IBN BATTUTA

MOROCCO

'When the stomach gets full,
it tells the head to sing.'

'A camel never sees his own
hump, but that of his brother
is always in his eye …'

ON THE MENU

FRESH TOMATO SAUCE

MOROCCAN RICE

CHICKPEA AND VEGETABLE TAGINE

SALADS

CARROT

SWEET POTATO

BEETROOT

TOMATO AND ONION

COURGETTES ROASTED IN CUMIN

GREEN LENTILS WITH PRESERVED LEMON

DESSERT

AMLOU

THOUSAND-HOLE PANCAKES WITH AMLOU *(BAGHRIR)*

DRINK

FRESH MINT TEA

Bing Crosby and Bob Hope 'The Road To Morocco'

Fresh Tomato Sauce

(V) (VG) (GF) (DF)

Goes well with fish tagine or vegetables.

Ingredients

4 tomatoes (chopped finely, skinned and seeded if you want)
2 tbsp olive oil
½ tsp ground ginger
¾ tsp ground cumin
½ tsp ground turmeric
a squirt of tomato purée
salt and pepper

Method

1. In a wide pan, fry the tomatoes in the oil on a medium heat for 5 minutes, until softened.
2. Add the spices and continue to cook, adding about 50–100ml of water if it starts getting too dry and is sticking. Stir in the tomato purée and cook for 5–10 minutes.
3. Taste and season.

This sauce is now ready to be used in a tagine dish. Add chopped vegetables, a packet of tofu or prawns, or a mix of these in any combination, to the sauce, then put a lid on the pan and simmer on a low heat until cooked. Add more water if it looks too dry. Serve with finely chopped parsley and an optional drizzle of olive oil.

Moroccan Rice

(V) (VG) (GF) (DF)

Ingredients

1 courgette, grated
2 tbsp olive oil
4 heaped tbsp fresh tomato sauce (see above)
1 tsp cumin seeds, toasted and ground
1 tsp ground ginger
1 heaped tbsp chopped preserved lemon
300g brown basmati rice, almost-cooked (i.e. it still has a little bite)
150ml water
salt and pepper

Method

1. In a wide pan on a medium heat, fry the grated courgette in the oil. Add the tomato sauce and stir.
2. Stir in the cumin, ginger and preserved lemon, then add the rice and 150ml of water. Season with salt and pepper, then put a lid on the pan.
3. Cook until the rice is cooked through and the water is all absorbed, about 5–10 minutes. (Add more water if the rice needs more cooking time.)

Najat Aâtabou 'Et Oui Mon Ami, Parle Je T'écoute'

Ahmed Drief 'Sahara Desert'

Chickpea and Vegetable Tagine

(V) (VG) (GF) (DF)

Ingredients

1 small onion, finely chopped
2 tbsp oil
salt and pepper
2 cloves of garlic, finely chopped
pinch of saffron
½ tsp ground turmeric
½ tsp ground ginger
¾ tsp cumin seeds, toasted and ground
1 parsnip, cut into large pieces (approx. 7cm x 2cm)
2 carrots, cut into large pieces (approx. 7cm x 2cm)
1 heaped tbsp chopped preserved lemon
100g dried chickpeas (soaked, then cooked), or 150g tinned chickpeas, drained
200ml liquid from the chickpeas plus added water/veg stock
1 x 400g tin of tomatoes or 5–6 fresh tomatoes (seeded and peeled if you want)
fresh parsley or coriander

Method

1. In a wide pan, on a medium heat, fry the onion in the oil with a pinch of salt for 5–10 minutes, until soft and beginning to go golden.
2. Add the garlic and fry for a minute until soft.
3. Add the spices and fry to release their flavours.
4. Add the chopped vegetables and the preserved lemon, stir to coat with the spices, then add the chickpeas, the 200ml of chickpea liquid and the tomatoes.
5. Put a lid on the pan and cook for 45 minutes, then taste and season.
6. Serve with fresh parsley or coriander. Good with the rice dish on p. 61, or couscous or Moroccan flatbread.

This more robust tomato sauce is also great if you're cooking a meat tagine: first, brown your pieces of meat, set aside, then add them at step 4 instead of the vegetables and chickpeas. Cook for longer, adding water if it's getting dry, until the meat is cooked through and tender.

Cooking couscous:
The ratio is 1:1 water and couscous. Don't overcook. Bring to the boil, then once it boils, turn off the heat, keeping the lid on. It is ready in 5–10 minutes. Taste to test, and plump up with a fork before serving.

Options:
Like quinoa, you can add half a stock cube to the cooking water and add a blob of butter or olive oil before serving.

Hamid El Kasri 'Hamouda'

Moroccan Salads

Carrot Salad

V VG GF DF

Ingredients

2–3 carrots (250g), cut into thick julienne strips
1 clove of garlic, thinly sliced
½ tsp cumin seeds, toasted and ground
¼ tsp paprika (optional)
⅛ tsp ground turmeric
small bunch of fresh parsley, finely chopped
1 tsp olive oil
1 tsp white wine vinegar or cider vinegar
salt and pepper

Method

1. Blanch the carrots with the slices of garlic in a pan of boiling water for 2 minutes.
2. Rinse them under cold water to cool and stop them cooking, then shake off the water and remove the garlic.
3. Dress the carrots with the spices, herbs, oil and vinegar, mixing and seasoning to taste.

Alabina 'Lamouni (Ligharou Meni)'

Sweet Potato Salad

V VG GF DF

As above, but use cooked and cooled pieces of sweet potato (boil them in water for 10–15 minutes until soft, then drain and leave to cool). Dress with cumin, turmeric, olive oil, salt and pepper. Also try adding toasted cumin seeds and squeeze orange juice over it.

Beetroot Salad

V VG GF DF

Ingredients

250g cooked beetroot, cooled, peeled and diced
small bunch of fresh mint, leaves finely chopped
2 slices of orange, pith removed, cut into small pieces, or a handful of pomegranate seeds
1 tsp white wine vinegar or cider vinegar
1 tsp olive oil
pinch of toasted and ground cumin seeds
salt and pepper

Mix all the ingredients together in a bowl and season to taste.

Tomato and Onion Salad

V VG GF DF

This salad seemed to be served with every meal we ate.

Ingredients

2 tomatoes, skinned if you have time, and diced
1 red onion, diced
½ tsp cumin seeds, toasted and ground
1 tsp finely chopped fresh parsley
1 tsp lemon juice
1 tbsp olive oil
salt and pepper
1 tsp honey (optional)

Method

Mix the ingredients together, adding honey to taste.

Khalid Izri 'Casablanca Medina'

Mahmoud Guinia 'Allah Allah Ya Donia'

Courgettes Roasted in Cumin

V VG GF DF

Ingredients

2 courgettes (300g), diced into small pieces, then dried with a tea towel
1 tbsp olive oil
1½ tsp cumin seeds, toasted and ground
salt and pepper

Method

1. Preheat the oven to 180°C/gas 4.
2. Massage the courgette pieces with the oil and cumin.
3. Place in a shallow roasting tin and roast for 15 minutes.
4. Remove from the oven and shake the courgettes around, then roast for a further 10–15 minutes until golden.
5. Season and serve.

Green Lentils with Preserved Lemon

V VG GF DF

Ingredients

200g green lentils
¼ onion or 1 spring onion
2 tsp chopped preserved lemon
small bunch of fresh parsley, finely chopped
1 tbsp olive oil
salt and pepper

Method

1. Put the lentils into a pan with 600ml of water and bring to the boil, then turn down the heat to low and simmer for 35–45 minutes, or until the lentils are soft. If there's any excess water left, drain it off, then leave the lentils to cool.
2. Put the onion, preserved lemon and parsley into a serving bowl.
3. When the lentils are cool, add them to the bowl and stir, then add the olive oil and season.

Mazagan 'Ya Labess'

Ammouri M'Barek 'Tamazirt Inou'

Amlou

VG GF DF

A mix of roasted ground nuts, honey and argan oil, in a ratio of 2:1:1. It's very easy to scale this recipe up.

Ingredients

4 tbsp ground almonds
2 tbsp honey
2 tbsp argan oil*

Using the back of a teaspoon, mix everything together in a dish until blended.

Options:

- Replace ground almonds with peanut butter, ground linseed (flax) or tahini.
- Add more honey to taste.

* If you don't have any argan oil handy, replace it with groundnut oil. You could also try sesame, walnut or hazelnut oil for a stronger flavour.

Ras el Hanout
Translates as 'head of the shop' – the best selection in the store. A spice mix used as a rub or flavouring. Experiment with grinding up dried ginger, chilli, turmeric, cardamom, mace, star anise, bay leaf, cassia/cinnamon, white and black peppercorns and coriander seeds. You can also try adding cumin, caraway seeds, cloves, nutmeg, allspice and paprika.

Harissa
A paste made of red pepper, chilli peppers and garlic, roasted and reduced with olive oil. Try adding to salad dressings or the tomato sauces.

Mint Tea
Put a bunch of fresh mint into your teapot and pour boiling water over it. Serve immediately.

Thousand-hole Pancakes with Amlou *(Baghrir)*

VG DF

Baghrir are traditionally served with melted butter, orange blossom water and honey for breakfast and during Ramadan. They're a bit like skinny crumpets. Serve them with amlou (see p. 67), fresh orange slices and dates.

Ingredients

125g fine semolina
2 tbsp flour
1 tbsp honey or sugar (optional)
1 tsp active dried yeast
¼ tsp salt
250ml warm water
1 tsp baking powder (not heaped)*

Method

1. Blend together all the ingredients except for the baking powder for 5 minutes, then add the baking powder and blend again for 3 minutes. Allow to rest for 30 minutes (or longer if you've time – it keeps overnight).

2. Heat a bakestone or pan, lightly greased with oil or butter.

3. Pour in enough of the batter to make a round, like a drop scone. Within seconds you'll see holes bubbling up – allow the *baghrir* to continue to cook on top, don't flip it, just turn down the heat if the bottom begins to colour.

4. Once the *baghrir* has no wetness left on top, it's done. Remove it from the pan and lay it on a tea towel, then repeat with the rest of the batter.

* If you don't like the taste of bicarbonate of soda, make the *baghrir* without it. Leave longer for the yeast to work – you'll see the batter bubbling. You'll just get less epic hole action.

Various artists 'Salanabina' Saïd Chraïbi 'Longa Nakryse'

Master Musicians of Jajouka 'Leaving Makes You Sad/Your Eyes Make Me Want To Drink Tea'

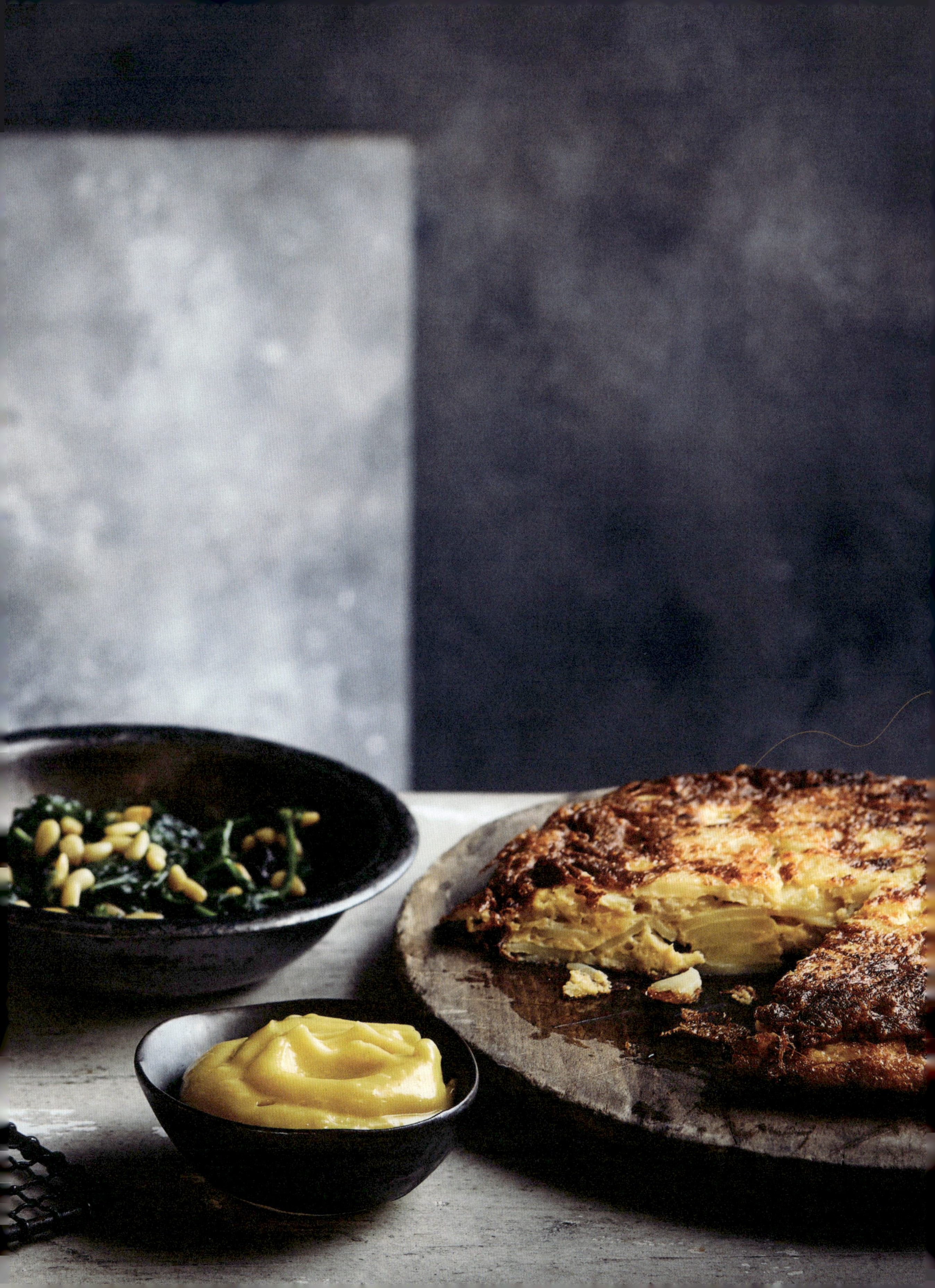

SPAIN

Agosto–

   Contraponientes de melocotón y azúcar,
    Y el sol dentro del la tarde
    Como el hueso en una fruta.

     La panocha guarda intacta
     Su risa amarilla y dura.

      Agosto.
       Los niños comen
        Pan moreno y rica luna.

August–

   Comparisons of peach and sugar,
    And the sun in the afternoon
    like the stone in a fruit.

     The corn keeps its smile steadfast,
     Yellow and firm.

      August.
       The children eat
        brown bread and rich moon.

FEDERICO GARCÍA LORCA
Lorca was born on 5 June 1898 in a town a few miles from Granada, Andalucia. He was an influential poet and dramatist and was part of group of artists known as Generation del 27 (with Salvador Dalí and Luis Buñuel). Lorca established the 'Cante Jondo festival' ('Deep Song') in 1922. Lorca visited New York and Cuba and toured Spain with his theatre group.

A prominent socialist and homosexual, he was arrested on 16 August 1936 at the beginning of the Spanish Civil War and is believed to have been murdered by Fascist forces, aged just thirty-eight. His body has never been found.

I love this poem, 'Agosto'. It is concentrated energy, where humdrum and romance, for a moment, intertwine.

Patron Saint

James, son of Zebedee, a fisherman on the sea of Galilee, one of the first disciples to join Jesus. James was also the brother of John.

Miracle 1:

The Virgin Mary appeared to him in AD 40 on a pillar (now found in Zaragoza) when preaching the gospel in Spain. He was killed with a sword by Herod in 44 CE, back in Jerusalem, and martyred. According to legend, his body is held in **SANTIAGO DE COMPOSTELA.** So how did it get here?

Miracle 2:

Angels took his body in a rudderless empty boat to Spain, a rock closed around it and these relics were found by a **HERMIT FOLLOWING A STAR,** in 813. Thereafter he was buried in Galicia (though his head apparently ended up in Jerusalem), hence Compostela (*stela*: star).

St James's emblem is the cockle shell (the French for scallops is **'COQUILLES ST JACQUES',** and in Dutch it's 'Jacobs schelp' – perhaps because St James apparently pulled a knight out of the sea covered in scallop shells …

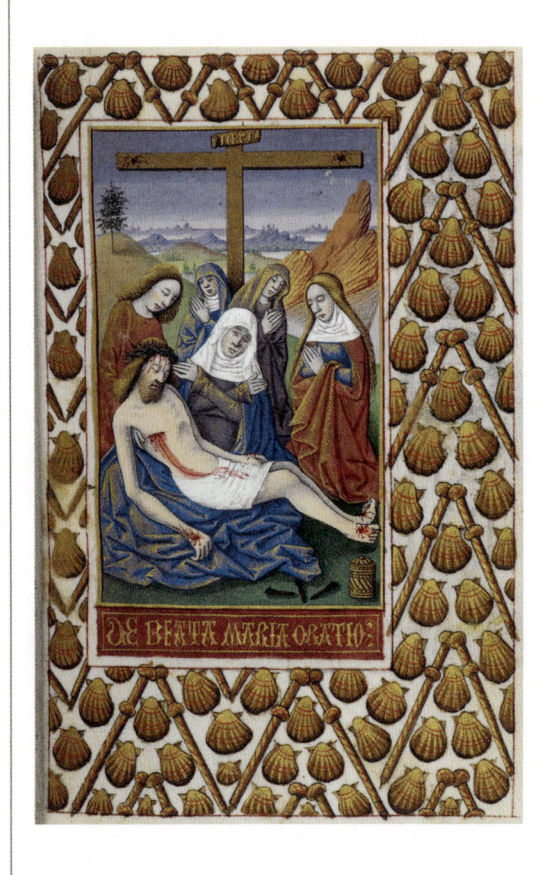

The Phoenicians and the Greeks introduced the olive to Spain and cultivation was expanded by the Romans.

'If you come from Spain, you have to play **FOOTBALL.'**

ENRIQUE IGLESIAS

The name 'Spain' may come from the Phoenician 'I-Sphanis' ('island of rabbits'), which I rather like.

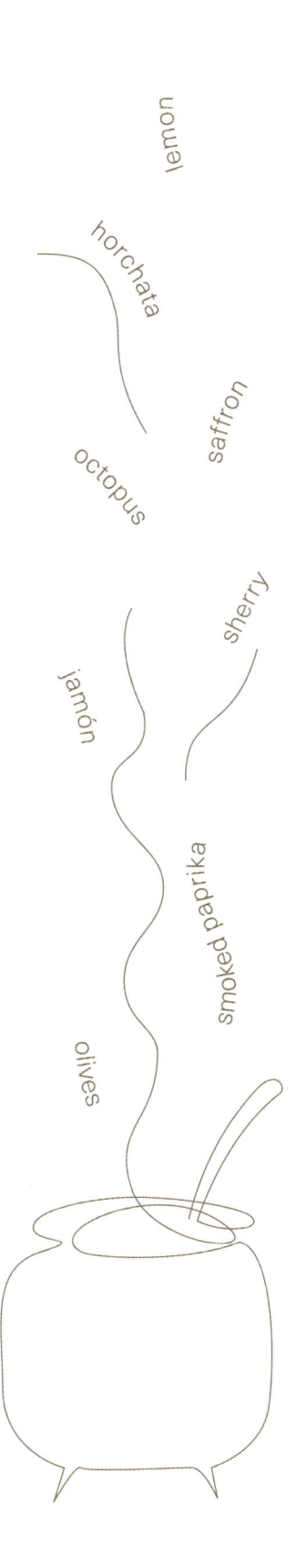

lemon
horchata
saffron
octopus
sherry
jamón
smoked paprika
olives

'Hunger is the best sauce
in the world.'

MIGUEL DE CERVANTES SAAVEDRA,
DON QUIXOTE

'De músico, poeta y loco,
todos tenemos un poco'
(We are all a little musical,
poetic and mad).

Why **Tapas**?
Morsels of food were served on top of the glass. To keep sand off? Flies out? To encourage more drinking, less drunkenness, or to show patrons what dishes are available? Our guess is as good as anyone's.

My experiences of Spanish refreshment were a lot headier than the frugal diet of Don Quixote, whose sustenance came from his high aspirations for man rather than earthier offerings. Back down to earth with a bang, then, because my memories of Spain begin aged six, tipsy on too much sangria-soaked fruit. No wonder I fell in love with the place. My dad too is an Iberiophile, with a cache of dodgy old bullfighting videos, films and photos of fishing villages like Torremolinos and Estepona and a huge collection of Spanish music.

No wonder then that the first place I wanted to visit alone was this land of many tribes. I arrived in Spain aged eighteen with an over-stuffed rucksack and guitar, with ambitions to learn how to play flamenco. I landed up in Andalucía, the heartland of this ancient tradition, and as a young, white Welsh girl, found the door to this craft had to open. With the bountiful energy of a teenager, I moved on, getting the odd job before ending up helping out a family in Santa Perpètua de Mogoda, a village just outside Barcelona. 'Adiós papá consíguenos un poco de dinero mas' ('Bye Dad, get me some more money') by Los Ronaldos was on heavy rotation on the radio. I learnt Castillano and how to cook spinach, learnt Catalan, how to make *calcots* (barbecued spring onions in a peanut sauce) and to cook paella over a fire. (If it's not cooked on a fire, it's not officially paella, so it goes ...)

My cooking was laughed at, but I soon learnt. I was sent to the market to buy green veg (mostly chard), bread and groceries each day. I hadn't ever before shopped daily for meals and haven't really done it since. But while it lasted it was great. I learnt to learn from the locals. They were drinking *carajillo*, a shot of liquor in an espresso; brandy, whisky or a shot of aniseed liquor, a *'carajillo de anis'*. It's ace, but on a hot summer's day there is nothing that will take me back more immediately than a chilled glass of Vermouth martini, with an anchovy-filled olive and ice, the sun's rays lighting up the green-gold liquid.

It goes without saying that Spain is a collection of regions with their own distinctive folk songs, dances, languages and dialects, cuisines and specialities. The mother I was working for was from Valencia, home of paella (and rice dishes in general), and this was what I was taught to cook.

'Take my advice and live for a long, long time. Because the maddest thing a man can do in this life is to let himself die.'

MIGUEL DE CERVANTES SAAVEDRA,
DON QUIXOTE

'Vivieron felices
y comieron perdices
(y a mí no me dieron).'

'They lived happily
and ate partridge
(and didn't give me any).'

MIGUEL DE CERVANTES SAAVEDRA

SPAIN

'El mundo es un pañuelo.'

'The world is a handkerchief:
it's a small world.'

'Camarón que se duerme se lo
lleva la corriente.'

'The prawn that sleeps is taken
by the current: snooze you lose.'

ON THE MENU

ROAST ARTICHOKES

HOMEMADE MAYONNAISE

GREEN LENTILS WITH WHOLE HEAD OF GARLIC

PRAWNS A LA PLANCHA

SPINACH WITH PINE NUTS

SEAFOOD PAELLA

PAELLA WITH BROWN RICE

SPANISH TORTILLA

CHORIZO IN RED WINE

PIMIENTOS DE PADRÓN

TOMATO AND ONION SALAD

PAN Y TOMATE

DESSERT

HALF A MELON FILLED WITH SHERRY

Artichokes

When I came home from Spain, I planted some artichoke seeds and they grew into huge bushes. Artichokes are part of the thistle family; if they like the soil and the view they'll give you bags of the stuff. Then you can pick them young, before the choke is fully formed. The ones in shops are usually the larger, older ones, but are also great too.

heart · choke

Roast Artichokes

V VG GF DF

Ingredients

4 globe artichokes

olive oil

salt and pepper

Caterina Valente 'Malagueña'

Currichi 'Tirititran'

Method

1. Preheat the oven to 200°C/gas 6.
2. Cut the stems off the artichokes so they can stand upright, then smash them upside down on the worktop to get rid of insects and to open up the leaves. Line them up in a shallow baking tray.
3. Drizzle with olive oil, sprinkle with salt and pepper and roast in the oven for 40 minutes, until cooked, when the bottom leaves come away easily. Keep checking: it takes ages – they can come out looking almost burnt, but they are delicious.

I like them just as they are, perhaps with lemon juice. A healthy TV snack – pull away a leaf at a time, eat the flesh from the lower part of it using your teeth, throw the spent leaf in a bowl. When you get to the middle, the leaves get tiny and thin and you'll come across the hairy thistly bit, the choke, remove with a side of a teaspoon. But eat the bit they come from, that's the heart and it's the bomb.

Many people like to dip the leaves in mayonnaise, so here goes:

Homemade Mayonnaise

VG GF DF

Ingredients

2 egg yolks from very fresh eggs, at room temperature
1 tbsp lemon juice
salt and pepper
50ml light olive oil
150ml vegetable or sunflower oil

Method

Mayonnaise is easiest done in a food processor or with an electric whisk, but you can also make it by hand. The yolks need to be at room temperature.

If using a food processor:

1. Put the egg yolks and lemon juice into the bowl of a food processor, along with a pinch of salt and pepper. Blend until creamy and slightly thickened.
2. With the motor running, slowly pour in the oil, scraping down the sides now and again if necessary, and continue until the mixture is thickened and creamy.
3. Taste and season as necessary.

If making by hand or using an electric whisk:

1. Whisk together the yolks, lemon juice and seasoning.
2. While continuing to whisk, pour in the oil in a steady stream.

Option:
For a garlic mayonnaise, add a peeled, chopped garlic clove with the yolks when you start making the mayonnaise.

SPAIN

Pata Negra 'Calle Betis'

Estrella Morente 'En Lo Alto Del Cerro' (tangos)

Green Lentils with Whole Head of Garlic

V VG GF DF

Once you've cooked this thick hearty stew, it becomes a staple. If you eat meat, add a ham hock, or a large chorizo sausage, cut in chunks. Add it at step 2, instead of the smoked paprika.

Ingredients

1 large onion, diced

2 tbsp olive oil

salt and pepper

1 tsp smoked paprika

1 whole head of garlic

250g green lentils

2 bay leaves

2 tsp tomato purée

1.5 litres vegetable stock

Method

1. Heat a large saucepan on a medium heat and fry the onion in the oil with a pinch of salt for 7–9 minutes, until soft and colouring on the edges.

2. Stir in the smoked paprika and cook for a further minute. Add the whole head of garlic, the lentils, bay leaves, tomato purée and stock (or water and stock cube).

3. Bring to the boil, then reduce to a simmer and leave to cook for 40 minutes, or until the lentils and garlic are soft and the whole mixture is oozing the most delicious smells.

4. Season to taste, with loads of ground black pepper.

5. Serve with bread or rice, yoghurt, a squirt of olive oil, lemon juice, parsley or just as it is, piping hot in a bowl.

Option:
Remove the garlic from the pan and squeeze the flesh on to a chopping board, then roughly chop and stir back into the soup, or spread on some toast. Roasting whole heads of garlic in the oven gives you the same result.

Claudya con Ramon y Sus Showmen 'Un Millón De Lagrimas'

Elia y Elizabeth 'Ponte Bajo El Sol'

Prawns a la Plancha

GF DF NV

I bought a paella dish, a stove-top coffee maker and a *plancha* when I moved back to the UK and have used them all ever since. A *plancha* is a cheap, thin corrugated tin plate for cooking on gas rings. The cooking method can kick off a lot of smoke.

Ingredients

300g raw shell-on king prawns

2–3 tbsp olive oil

2 cloves of garlic, finely chopped

salt and pepper

a handful of fresh parsley, finely chopped.

1 lemon, half cut into wedges, half for cooking

Method

1. Heat a *plancha* (or a frying pan) over a high heat.
2. Coat the prawns with olive oil and place them on the *plancha* or pan, turning them after a minute to cook the other side.
3. Add the garlic for the last 2 minutes of cooking – the prawns are ready when pink and slightly charred.
4. Add salt and finely chopped parsley, squeeze over some lemon juice, and serve hot with lemon wedges.

Espinacas a la Catalana/ Spinach with Pine Nuts

V VG GF DF

Ingredients

400g baby spinach (or chard), washed

4 tbsp pine nuts

2 tbsp olive oil

3 tbsp raisins

salt and pepper

Method

1. Blanch the spinach for 2 minutes in 150ml of salted boiling water, then drain in a colander, squeeze out the excess water, and set aside.
2. Toast the pine nuts in a frying pan on a medium heat for 1–2 minutes until golden, then set aside.
3. Add the olive oil to the pan. When it's hot, add the spinach, pine nuts and raisins, and cook for a further 3–4 minutes until heated through.
4. Taste and season as necessary, then serve.

For meat eaters, cook this dish with small pieces of bacon or pancetta (about 75g). Cook in the pan at step 3, before you add the spinach, pine nuts and raisins, and reduce the amount of oil and salt accordingly.

Los Ronaldos 'Adios Papa'

Seafood Paella

GF DF NV

Traditional paella is made with rabbit. If peas were used they would be fava beans, so fresh broad beans work well when in season (just add them when you add the clams).

Ingredients

good pinch of saffron, about 0.4g
700ml warm water
2–3 tbsp olive oil
8 raw shell-on king prawns (if you can only get the larger tiger prawns, just use 4)
100g raw squid rings
2–3 cloves of garlic, finely chopped
250g paella rice, e.g. Bomba or Calasparra
sprig of fresh rosemary
150g raw shell-on mussels, cleaned and debearded
150g raw shell-on clams, cleaned
lemons, cut into wedges
fresh parsley, finely chopped

Method

1. Heat a 28–30cm paella pan, or a large, wide, thin-based frying or sauté pan, over a medium heat. (If your pan has too thick a base, you won't end up with a crunchy layer on the bottom and may have too much liquid in the pan after the rice is cooked. Use a slightly higher hob temperature if you are worried about the thickness of your pan.) Add the saffron and stir around to toast it until fragrant but not burnt.

2. Add the toasted saffron to the warm water.

3. Add a glug of olive oil to the pan, and fry the prawns and squid until the prawns start to release their juices and have turned pink. Add the garlic, and continue to fry for a further 2 minutes until it is turning golden and fragrant.

4. Add the rice, stir briefly to combine and coat in the flavoursome oil, then pour in 550ml of the saffron water and bring to the boil, without turning the heat up any higher than medium. You need to make sure that the entire base of the pan has heat under it, so if necessary, cook over two of the burners/rings on your stove. Once boiling, reduce the temperature, add the sprig of rosemary and simmer for 10 minutes. Do not stir.

5. After 10 minutes, dot the mussels and clams around the top of the rice and continue to cook for a further 10 minutes, or until the shells of the clams and mussels have opened and the rice is quite dry and separated, and not at all watery. If at any time during the cooking the rice looks too dry, too early, add more water. Remove from the heat and cover with foil, a clean tea towel or, traditionally, newspaper. Leave for 5 minutes to rest, then serve with lots of lemon wedges and a sprinkling of parsley.

When I don't have fresh shellfish, a lower-league version works just as well – using frozen prawns and peas.

Further Spanish experiments:
Try a one-pot wonder like mussels and rice. Put the mussels, some water, rice, garlic and bunches of chopped parsley all in one pot. With lid on, heat on low and cook until the mussels are opened and rice is cooked.

Camarón de la Isla 'La Tarara'

Los Salvajes 'Soy Así'

Paella with Brown Rice

GF DF NV

Ingredients

pinch of saffron

1.5 litres hot water (optional: add a stock cube)

2 tbsp olive oil, plus a little extra to drizzle

300g frozen prawns, thawed

2 cloves of garlic

400g brown Bomba rice

¼ tsp sea salt

1 sprig of fresh rosemary

100g frozen peas

1 red pepper, sliced into rings

freshly ground black pepper

lemon wedges

fresh parsley, chopped

Method

1. Toast the saffron in a hot frying pan, then steep it in the hot water.
2. Add the oil to the pan and fry the prawns and garlic on a medium heat for 1–2 minutes.
3. Add the rice, stir it round in the oil mix, then add 1 litre of the saffron water/stock, the salt and the sprig of rosemary. Bring to the boil, then lower the heat and cook so the rice begins to soften, adding more water if it gets too dry.
4. After 35 minutes add the frozen peas, stir them gently into the rice, and place the red pepper rings on top. Drizzle with olive oil.
5. Cook for a further 5–10 minutes, until the rice is cooked through. (Use a lid if the rice on top needs help cooking.)
6. Season, serve with lemon wedges and chopped fresh parsley.

Les Paul 'Lady Of Spain'

Paco de Lucía 'La Flor De La Canela' (instrumental)

Spanish Tortilla

(VG) (GF) (DF)

Ingredients

750g waxy potatoes such as Charlottes

300ml olive oil

6 eggs, beaten

1 tsp salt

Method

1. Slice the potatoes thinly into rounds no thicker than 0.5cm. Use a mandolin, if you have one.

2. Heat the olive oil in a large frying pan over a medium heat. Stir in the potatoes, season with 1 teaspoon of salt, and cook until they are completely tender (about 10–15 minutes).

3. Season the beaten eggs really well. Using a slotted spoon, take the potatoes out of the pan and put them into a large bowl with the eggs. Stir gently so they are completely coated. Reserve the oil in the pan (you can re-use the oil for cooking more potatoes for tortilla, or for roasting or frying other vegetables in the future).

4. Heat 1 tablespoon of the oil from the potatoes in a non-stick medium frying pan (smaller than the one you used for the potatoes – 21–24cm is the perfect size) over a medium heat.

5. Tip in the egg and potato mixture and cook for about 10 minutes, or until the tortilla is firm all the way to the top of the edges, but still runny in the very middle.

6. Cover the pan with a large plate, holding it firmly in place with your hand, and flip it round so that the cooked side of the tortilla is now facing upwards on the plate. Slide the tortilla back into the pan, cooked side up, and continue to cook for a further 5–7 minutes or until almost completely set.

7. Remove the pan from the heat. Leave the tortilla in the pan for 2–3 minutes, then slide it on to a plate.

8. Serve hot or cold, even in a sandwich as a tortilla bocadillo.

Some people add a little chopped onion to the potatoes, and you can also add a pinch of saffron to the beaten egg. For a lower fat option, pre-cook the potatoes by boiling instead of frying.

Chorizo in Red Wine

(GF) (DF) (NV)

Ingredients

½ tbsp olive oil

300g chorizo, sliced 1cm thick

125ml red wine

Method

1. Heat the oil in a heavy frying pan on a medium heat.

2. Add the chorizo and cook for about 4–5 minutes, until a crust develops on each side.

3. Pour in the wine and bring it to a simmer, using a spoon to scrape up any bits of chorizo stuck to the bottom of the pan. Cook for 3–4 minutes, to let the wine reduce.

Emerson Ensamble 'El Gato Montés'

Juan Maya Marote 'Solo Guitarra'

Pimientos de Padrón

V VG GF DF

Ingredients

200g Padrón peppers

2 tbsp olive oil

sea salt

1 lemon, cut into wedges

Method

1. Heat a griddle pan over a high heat.
2. Coat the peppers with the olive oil. Place them on the hot griddle and cook, turning them so they blister all over. Ready in 2–3 minutes.
3. Add salt and serve hot with lemon wedges.

Eduardo Niebla 'My Gypsy Waltz'

La Niña de la Puebla, 'Tinieblas'

Tomato and Onion Salad

V VG GF DF

So simple. So good.

Ingredients

ripe tomatoes, at room temperature, thinly sliced
sweet white onion, thinly sliced
olive oil
1 tsp wine vinegar
fresh parsley, finely chopped
salt and pepper

Method

1. Serve the sliced tomatoes with the onions on top, drizzle with oil and a tiny bit of vinegar, sprinkle with parsley and season.
2. Mop up the juices with fresh bread; just the bomb.

Pan y Tomate/Bread with Tomato

V VG DF

This is a famous Catalan snack. It sounds like nothing, but it's more. Also a great option if you're cutting down/out the dairy.

Ingredients

1 large ripe tomato
fresh bread (toasted or not; traditionally it can be either), a thick slice per person
olive oil
sea salt and pepper
garlic (optional)

Method

1. Halve the tomato around the equator, then drag it along your slice of bread or toast, squeezing a little so it leaves a whole load of seeds, flesh and juice on the surface.
2. Drizzle with olive oil, and sprinkle with sea salt and pepper. That's it.

Option:
Toast the bread and pass a cut piece of garlic along the surface before you do the tomato bit.

Half a Melon with Sherry

(V) (VG) (GF) (DF)

Cut a ripe, small, orange-fleshed cantaloupe in half and remove the seeds. Fill the hole with Jerez sherry, or sherry of your choice, and serve.

Juan Velasquez and His Authentic Bull Ring Band 'Toreador Song'

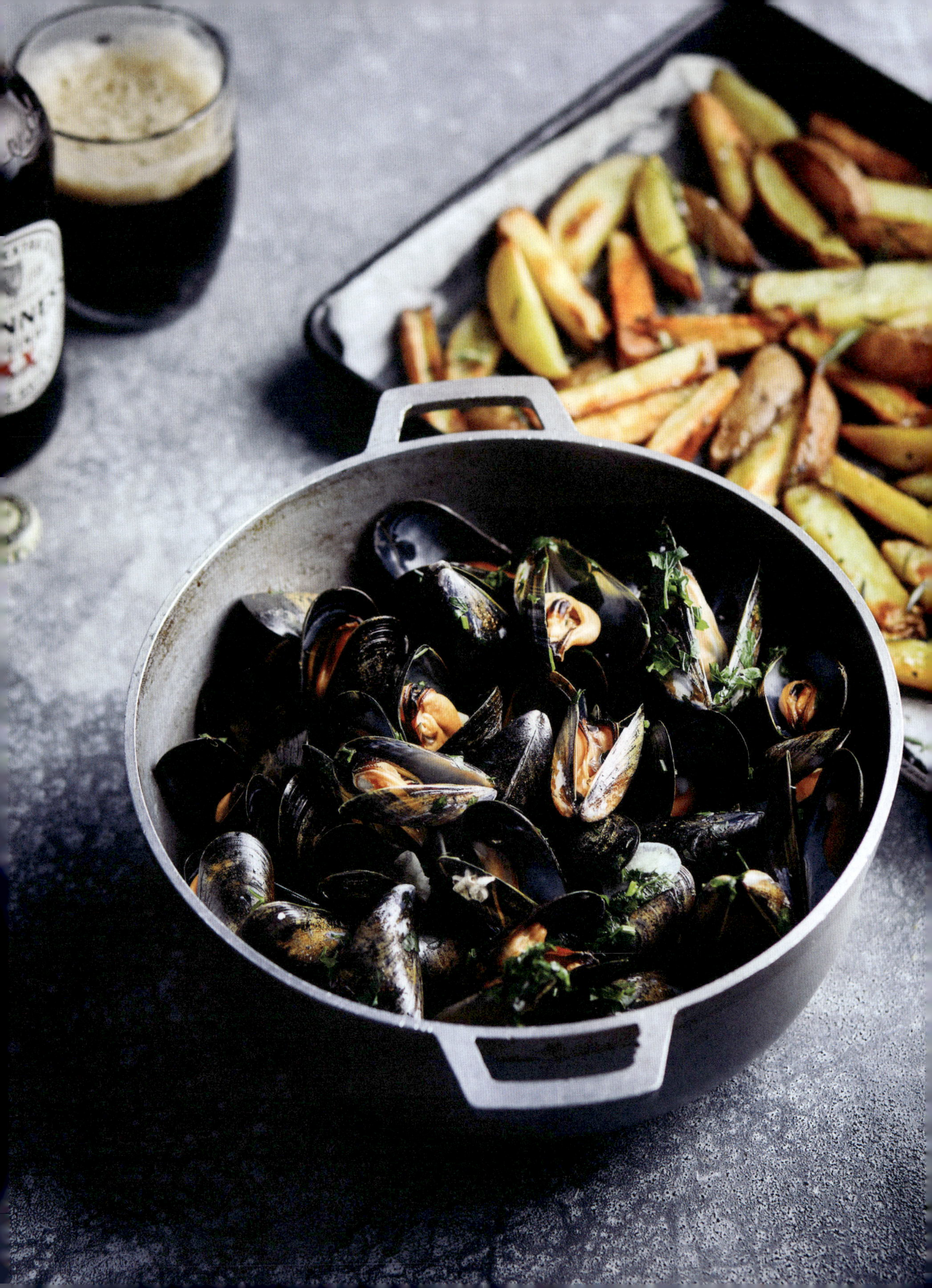

IRELAND

The Song of Wandering Aengus

I went out to the hazel wood,
Because a fire was in my head,
And cut and peeled a hazel wand,
And hooked a berry to a thread;
And when white moths were on the wing,
And moth-like stars were flickering out,
I dropped the berry in a stream
And caught a little silver trout.

When I had laid it on the floor
I went to blow the fire a-flame,
But something rustled on the floor,
And someone called me by my name:
It had become a glimmering girl
With apple blossom in her hair
Who called me by my name and ran
And faded through the brightening air.

Though I am old with wandering
Through hollow lands and hilly lands,
I will find out where she has gone,
And kiss her lips and take her hands;
And walk among long dappled grass,
And pluck till time and times are done,
The silver apples of the moon,
The golden apples of the sun.

W. B. YEATS
You could pick almost any poem by W. B. Yeats (1865–1939). I include 'The Song of Wandering Aengus'. Christy Moore sings a wonderful version of this poem.

Poitín: the Irish moonshine was legalized in 1997. As a distilled spirit made of potatoes, its alcohol content can get to around 90 per cent.

HURLING is regarded as the fastest field sport in the world. It has prehistoric origins and is played with stick and ball.

GAELIC FOOTBALL is the most popular sport in Ireland in terms of attendance.

The Act of Settlement in 1652 effectively barred the Irish from owning land in Ireland, and from membership in the Irish Parliament.

Jamaican Guinness is stronger than the home country version.

The world's oldest working whiskey distillery is **OLD BUSHMILLS** in County Antrim. A landowner was given a licence to distil by King James I on 20 April 1608: 'for the next seven years ... to make, drawe, and distil such and soe great quantities of aquavite, usquabagh and aqua composita, as he or his assignes shall thinke fitt; and the same to sell, vent, and dispose of to any persons ...'

The word **'whiskey'** comes from the Gaelic word *uisce/uisge*, which means 'water'. Distilled alcohol was known in Latin as 'aqua vitae', the water of life. Apparently a chieftain died at Christmas 1405, 'taking a surfeit of Aqua vitae'.

America's Wallgreens pharmacy grew from twenty retail stores to almost 400 during **prohibition,** through legal sales of prescribed whiskey.

Another Irish emblem is the **harp.** As in Wales, artists would travel the country playing harp music, telling stories, reciting poetry to the sound of the harp, visiting and praising patrons and chieftains and bringing with them news.

CAROLAN
The Celebrated Irish Bard.

St. Patrick preaching at Tara.

Many academics now agree that **ST PATRICK** was a Welshman from Banwen, near Port Talbot. Maewyn Succat, (his birth name which means devoted friend) left two pieces of writing in which he tells of being captured by Irish pirates and taken as a slave to work in Ireland as a shepherd for six years. During this time he became increasingly religious, before eventually escaping home, becoming a cleric and deepening his study and understanding of the Christian faith.

Then the story takes a turn: he heard Irish voices calling him. 'We appeal to you, servant boy, to come and walk among us.' Maewyn responded to their request and returned to Erin's Isle, eventually founding more than 300 churches and baptizing over 100,000 people. He died on 17 March 493 or thereabouts.

'There is no sincerer love than the love of food.'

GEORGE BERNARD SHAW

The shamrock was apparently used by St Patrick to teach the Holy Trinity. Another story has him chasing all the snakes in Ireland into the sea.

His walking stick once took root as he was evangelizing, and grew into a living ash tree. The place was named 'Aspatria' (Patrick's ash) and is now a town of just under 3,000 people in Cumbria, north-west England.

Hello/Good day: 'Dia Dhuit' (D-AH GWIT, rhymes with 'twit', 'g' as in God), literally, 'God be with you'.

Reply with: 'Dia is mire duit' (DEAR is moorah gwit) 'God and Mary be with you, too'.

Slainte: 'Cheers!' (shlointah, emphasis on the o).

Please: 'le d'thoil' (lead duh Hull).

Thank You: 'Go Raibh maith agat' (Go rev mahagot).

Yes: 'Ta' (tag).

No: 'Nil' (kneel).

Goodbye: 'Slan', or 'Slan leat' (SLAAN lat, rhymes with 'cat').

Dublin grew out of a Viking settlement of about 841, which was known as 'Dyflin', **'BLACK POOL'** in Gaelic, named after the dark tidal pool where the River Poddle joined the Liffey.

On the table spread the cloth,
Let the knives be sharp and clean:
Pickles get and salad both,
Let them each be fresh and green:
With small beer, good ale, and wine,
O ye gods! how I shall dine.

FROM 'HOW I SHALL DINE' BY JONATHAN SWIFT (1667-1745)

I fell in love over six oysters and a pint of Guinness, a 'Davy Byrnes' 12-euro deal in this Dublin pub mentioned in James Joyce's *Ulysses*. I was proposed to on stage in the National Concert Hall and a few months later married myself a Donegal man. As for the country of his birth, I've been in love with it for as long as I've known it was there. Trefin, where I grew up, is some fifty miles from Rosslare over the Irish sea; Irish Gaelic was always on the radio, and there was the umbilical cord of the ferry which passed our house daily, if the sea conditions allowed. The book I carried around with me wherever I went, alongside Roger Phillips' *Wild Food,* was Soodlum's book of Irish ballads. All of life's trials were packed into this collection: famine, politics, single motherhood, suicide, prostitution, murder, religious persecution, war, disability, witchcraft and love. It opened up the world to a young mind, the Irish repertoire an abundance of riches. And the artists too: the Clancy brothers, Luke Kelly, Rory Gallagher, Thin Lizzie, Christy Moore, the Pogues, the Fureys, Sinéad O'Connor, Mary Coughlan, Van Morrison, Seamus Ennis, and let's not forget the blind harpist with the million melodies: Turlough O'Carolan (born 1670): unending inspiration for any music lover.

It's not romantic folly to say that life here is fuelled by music and books, but the landscape talks its own poetry too: Connemara, crazy country roads over tiny causeways like wild stitches holding together floating patches of land and seaweed, the Galway singing, the folk stories of Tipperary, the mad puck goat of County Kerry, the Sunday carveries, the Shannon in Limerick, sleeping Yeats in Sligo, the bracing winds off Mount Errigle, the dreaming vista off the shore of Gweedore: nothing between you and America but one vast Atlantic Ocean.

We toured there one memorable year in 2006. I've never seen such rain, and I'm from Wales. Turloughs (winter lakes) in every field, with pubs the first, last and only resort. As for food, it's soda bread, roast dinners and mash all the way. And oysters. Next time you have raw oysters, try grated fresh horseradish: a great kick like wasabi which doesn't confuse the sea-fresh taste of the oysters, ideally served on crushed ice and bladderwrack.

So, to the menu. It's going to be honest and hearty. Soda bread, champ, and/or roast potatoes with rosemary and mussels, because I used to pick them from the Irish Sea, watching that ferry heading to and from Rosslare. To drink, the best Guinness cocktail, given to me by Ian Brown of the Stone Roses: Death by Chocolate dessert is the best hot Guinness chocolate dessert you'll ever taste.

IRELAND

'If you have to swallow a frog, try not to think about it. If you have to swallow two frogs, don't swallow the smaller one first.'

'It was a brave man who first ate an oyster.'

JONATHAN SWIFT

IRELAND

Hozier in session for my BBC 6 Music show, Dublin, 2014.

'Statistics show that of those who contract the habit of eating, very few survive.'

GEORGE BERNARD SHAW

ON THE MENU

CHAMP AND COLCANNON

BROWN SODA BREAD

MUSSELS IN WINE WITH CHIPS

ROAST CHIPS

DESSERT

CHOCOLATE AND GUINNESS FONDANTS

COCKTAIL

DEATH BY CHOCOLATE

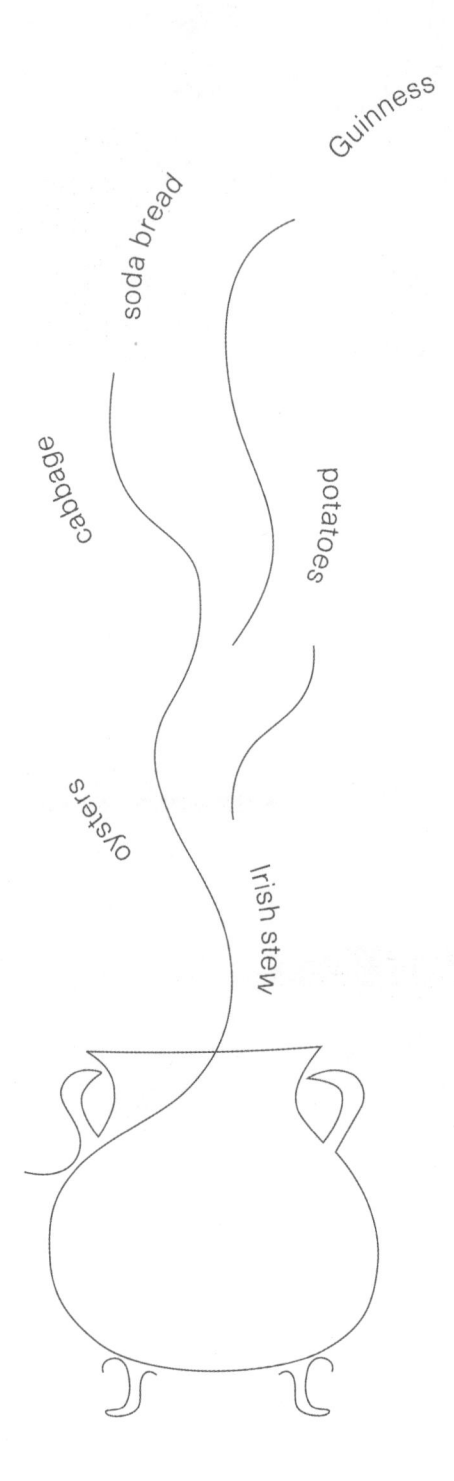

Guinness
soda bread
cabbage
potatoes
oysters
Irish stew

Christy Moore 'Farmer Michael Hayes'

Van Morrison 'Sweet Thing'

Champ and Colcannon

(VG) (GF)

From spring until late autumn, young nettle tops can replace the onion for variation. Try it with chives instead of spring onions; or try adding cheese.

Ingredients

1kg potatoes, cut into even-sized chunks
75ml milk (semi or whole)
75g butter
5 spring onions, finely chopped
salt and pepper

Method

1. Put the potatoes into a large saucepan and cover with cold water. Place over a medium high heat and bring to the boil. Simmer until soft when pierced with a fork, about 15 minutes.
2. Drain the potatoes, reserving some of the water, and add the milk, butter, spring onions and a really good pinch of salt and pepper.
3. Add more cooking liquid until you reach the consistency you prefer for your mash. Taste and season accordingly.

Colcannon

This is a similar side dish. Mash the potatoes as above, don't use cheese, but add around 225g boiled chopped kale or white cabbage to the mashed potato and onion mix. For leek colcannon, use 225g chopped leeks, softened in salted butter again, added to the potato and onion mix.

'It was customary to offer champ to the fairies at Hallowe'en or All Soul's Night (1 November). A bowlful was left on field posts or under hawthorn and whitethorn bushes.'

ALAN DAVIDSON,
THE OXFORD COMPANION TO FOOD

The Gallowglass Ceili Band Jig Selection, 'Lannigan's Ball', 'Smash The Windows'

Brown Soda Bread

(VG)

The Irish climate, neither very hot in summer nor very cold in winter, is more amenable to soft wheats rather than the hard wheats that respond well to yeast. There was plenty of fuel – forest, heather and turf – so you could bake on your fire at home with a bakestone, rather than resorting to communal baking ovens. Both these factors led to the popularity of soda bread, bread whose rising agent is bicarbonate of soda. The secret here is to work quickly, as the soda starts to work straight away. The quicker you get your dough to the heat source, the lighter the end result. No need to knead soda bread, so it's so easy and quick to make.

There are two main types: traditionally the 'cake', a round with a cross cut into the top, which used to be cooked in a casserole over the fire, now most often baked in the oven; and second the 'farl', where the cross in the round cuts right through to make quarters and which is usually cooked on a bakestone/griddle.

On average you cook 20 minutes per side and serve split in half, spread with butter. For the 'Ulster Fry', it's fried up again with ingredients like bacon, sausage or black pudding. This recipe uses wholewheat flour and eggs or sugar for a heartier, heavier loaf.

I like to cook this in a Dutch oven (basically, any thick-walled pot with a lid, like a casserole dish). But don't worry if you don't have one – you could bake this just as well on a tray, as long as you reduce the cooking time by 10–15 minutes.

Ingredients

400g wholewheat flour, plus a handful of jumbo oats
1 tsp salt
1 heaped tsp soda
350ml buttermilk or options, as below

Method

1. Preheat oven to 200°C/gas 6.
2. Mix the dry ingredients in a large bowl.
3. Pour in most of the liquid and using spoon or hands, bring it to a lump, no matter how messy, as fast as you can – if too dry, add the rest of the liquid. Don't knead it. It'll make it heavier, plus the faster you get it to the heat source the better.
4. Make the lump round, plonk it in the Dutch oven which you've greased and sprinkled with more oats, brush the top with butter, cross it deeply with a knife, lid on and shove it in the oven for 50 minutes. Knock it on the bottom – it will sound hollow when ready.

Buttermilk alternatives

I almost never have buttermilk in the house, but swap it for any of the following:

- 350ml hot milk soured with 1 tablespoon of lemon juice. Add the lemon (or vinegar) to the milk and wait till it curdles. It does this in minutes.
- 250ml yoghurt plus 100ml milk (or whey from the Mexican cheese-making)
- 350ml whey
- If you want a vegan version, you could use 350ml of oat milk, again adding a little lemon juice for acidity.

Note:

Soda bread is best toasted if eaten the following day. You can also experiment by adding dried fruit and spices to it.

The Pogues 'A Pair Of Brown Eyes'

Tim O'Brien 'Mick Ryan's Lament'

Mussels in Wine with Chips

GF NV

Ingredients

1.5kg mussels, scrubbed clean and beards removed

25g butter (or oil)

2 cloves garlic, peeled and finely sliced

salt and pepper

200ml white wine

a handful of fresh parsley leaves, roughly chopped

Method

1. Give the mussels a rinse in a sink of cold water. Discard any that do not shut when tapped against the edge of the sink or any that have broken shells. Drain.

2. Heat a large saucepan with a lid over a medium heat. Once hot, add the butter and garlic along with a pinch of salt and stir around over the heat for 2 minutes until softened but not colouring.

3. Tip in the mussels and pour in the wine along with a little bit of salt and pepper. Turn up the heat so that the wine starts to bubble. Stir, then cover with the lid and leave to steam over the heat for 4 minutes, shaking once or twice. Remove the lid and check to make sure the majority of the mussels are opened. If they aren't, return the lid and cook for a further couple of minutes.

4. Stir the opened mussels around in the sauce. Discard any mussels that haven't opened. Sprinkle in the parsley. Taste and adjust the seasoning if necessary, and serve immediately.

Roast Chips

V VG GF DF

Ingredients

800g potatoes, chipped
(or about 4 medium-large potatoes)

5 tbsp olive oil

salt and pepper

generous sprig of fresh rosemary

Method

1. Preheat oven to 220°C/gas 7.

2. Wash and chip the potatoes, dry in a tea towel, then put into a bowl and cover them with the olive oil.

3. Turn the potatoes into a non-stick roasting pan. Sprinkle with salt, black pepper and rosemary leaves, then toss so they don't stick together.

4. Roast for 30–35 minutes, until golden and cooked through, turning them after the first 20 minutes.

Altan 'Dúlamán'

Sharon Shannon 'Blackbird'

Chocolate and Guinness Fondants

VG

I loved the rich chocolate fondant that I tasted in Nobu in the nineties. They served it with green tea ice cream (see Japan chapter). This is so simple, but so, so good. You'll need 4 ramekins.

Ingredients

75g butter
100g dark chocolate
100ml Guinness
2 eggs
50g soft brown sugar
2 egg yolks
50g plain flour

Method

1. Preheat oven to 180°C/gas 4.
2. In a saucepan on a low heat, melt the butter and chocolate.
3. Turn off the heat and allow to cool.
4. Meanwhile, put the Guinness, the 2 eggs and the sugar into a bowl and whisk.
5. Set aside, and meanwhile add the 2 egg yolks to the cooled chocolate and butter mix.
6. Now combine both mixes and add in the flour.
7. Grease the ramekins and share the mix between them.
8. Bake in the oven. They should be done in just under 10 minutes; the centre should still look a little uncooked.
9. Serve immediately in the ramekins.

Death by Chocolate

V VG DF

The cocktail 'Death by Chocolate' was given to me by Ian Brown from the Stone Roses. It should be the eighth wonder of the world. I regularly prescribe it for people who don't like Christmas shopping. Slip into a pub, grab one of these and you'll be shopping all afternoon without stress, though lord knows what ends up under the tree.

Method

Into an empty half-pint glass pour a shot of Tia Maria and a shot of vodka, fill up to the top with cold Guinness from the barrel or a widget can, and serve.

Laoise Kelly 'Lon Dubh/Maidrín Ruadh'

IRELAND

Nuala Kennedy 'Mo Bhuachaill Dubh Dhonn (My Brown Haired Boy)

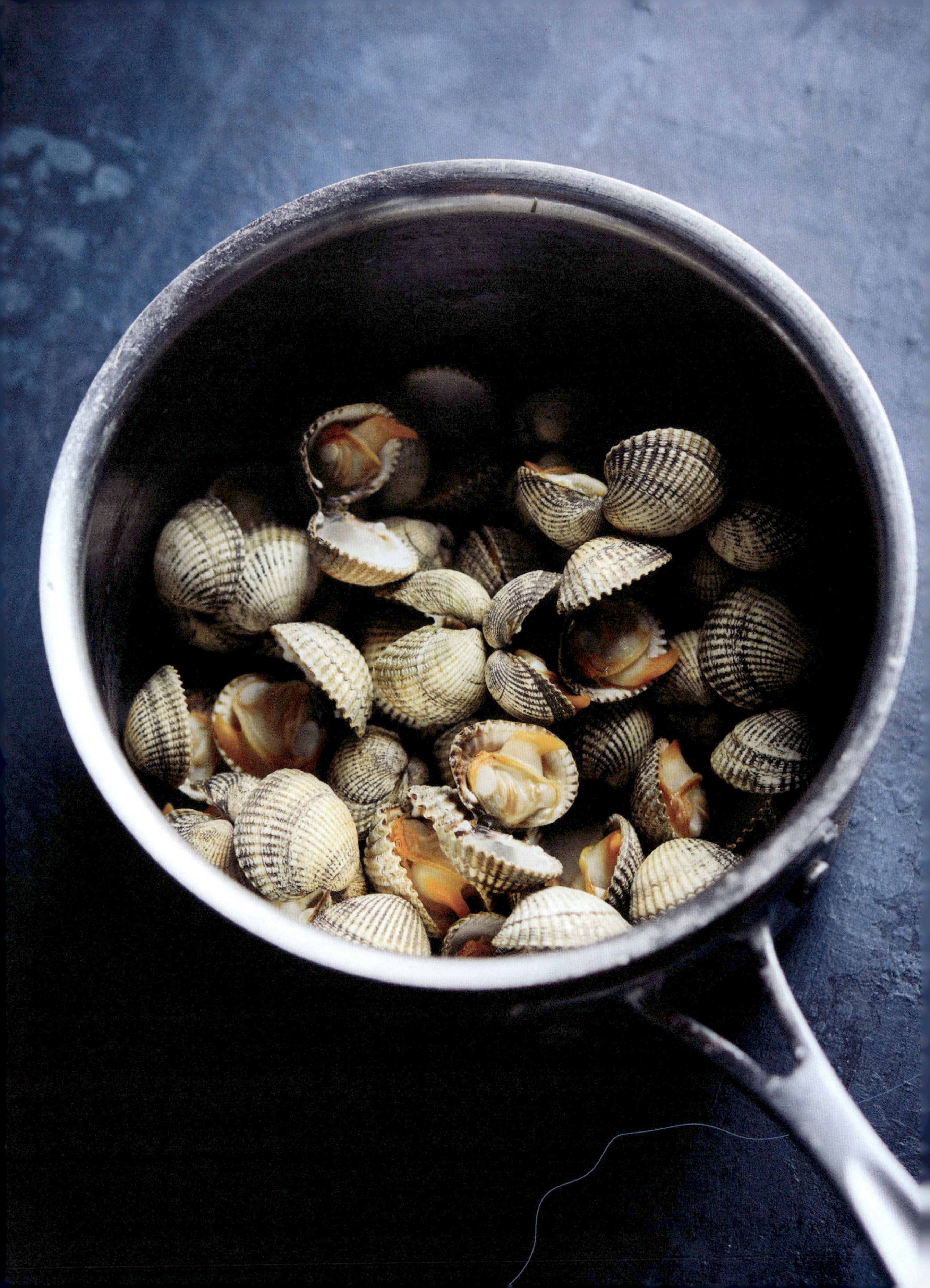

WALES

Mabinogion: The Game of Badger in the Bag

'Lord,' said he, 'may Heaven reward thee, I have an errand unto thee.'

'Welcome be thine errand, and if thou ask of me that which is just, thou shalt have it gladly.'

'It is fitting,' answered he. 'I crave but from want, and the boon that I ask is to have this small bag that thou seest filled with meat.'

'A request within reason is this,' said he, 'and gladly shalt thou have it. Bring him food.'

A great number of attendants arose and began to fill the bag, but for all that they put into it, it was no fuller than at first.

'My soul,' said Gwawl, 'will thy bag be ever full?'

'It will not, I declare to Heaven,' said he, 'for all that may be put into it, unless one possessed of lands and domains and treasure shall arise and tread down with both his feet the food that is within the bag and shall say, "Enough has been put therein".'

Then said Rhiannon unto Gwawl the son of Clud, 'Rise up quickly.'

'I will willingly arise,' said he.

So he rose up and put his two feet into the bag. And Pwyll turned up the sides of the bag so that Gwawl was over his head in it. And he shut it up quickly, and slipped a knot upon the thongs, and blew his horn.

And thereupon, behold, his household came down upon the palace. And they seized all the host that had come with Gwawl and cast them into his own prison.

And Pwyll threw off his rags, and his old shoes, and his tattered array, and, as they came in, every one of Pwyll's knights struck a blow upon the bag and asked, 'What is here?'

'A Badger,' said they. And in this manner they played, each of them striking the bag either with his foot or with a staff. And thus played they with the bag.

Every one as he came in asked, 'What game are you playing at thus?'

'The game of Badger in the Bag,' said they. And then was the game of Badger in the Bag first played.

This excerpt was translated by the extraordinary **LADY CHARLOTTE GUEST** (1877).

CAWL (sounds like cow) is called 'lobscows' in North Wales, A sailor's stew which has similar sounding dishes in countries that have shorelines along the Baltic Sea – Sweden, Germany, Latvia, Lithuania – and which gave Liverpool's Scousers their name.

The original patron saint of lovers is **ST DWYNWEN,** celebrated in Wales every 25 January. Remains of her church are found on the island of LLanddwyn which you can visit when tides allow.

Legend had it that if you scattered breadcrumbs in the water of her well, then laid your handkerchief on the surface, if eels living in the well disturbed it, then your lover would be faithful.

Shakespeare's *Henry V*, Act V scene 1:

Fluellen: I do believe, your Majesty takes no scorn to wear the leek upon Saint Tavy's day.

King Henry: I wear it for a memorable honour; for I am Welsh, you know, good countryman.

Fluellen should of course be Llewelyn, as rarely can an Englishman sound the double 'll's properly. See also **'Flummery',** for Llymru, a jelly dessert made from oats. Flummery is a good word. But it's not my favourite dessert, so we'll pass on that recipe.

Daffodil
in Welsh is 'Cennin Pedr' (Peter's leek)

Patron saint: **ST DAVID** (500–589). Extremely austere, this monastery and church founder didn't drink beer or eat meat and expected his monks to do likewise. A wonderful story I was told about this fellow involved a local chief who tried to **WOO ST DAVID'S MONKS** from the good path by brazenly sending naked women running into the monastic gardens. It didn't work. The monks continued to plough the fields (without animals), as per St David's wishes.

'The whole population lives almost entirely on oats and the produce of their herds, milk, cheese and butter. You must not expect a variety of dishes from a Welsh kitchen, and there are no highly seasoned titbits to whet your appetite.'

TWELFTH-CENTURY TRAVEL WRITER, GERALD OF WALES

'Tamaid a'm twyllodd,' ebe'r pysgodyn'
'I was taken in by a morsel,' said the fish.

'Tew y beiau lle tenau'r cariad'
'Faults are thick where love thins.'

'Wedi yfed syched sydd'
'Thirst comes at the end of drinking.'
(Hangover central).

'Shwmae?'
(Shoaw-m-eye?)
'How d'you do?'

'Iawn?'
(Ee-iah-oo-n)
'Okay?'

'They do not sing in unison like the inhabitants of other countries, but in many different parts ... You will hear as many different parts and voices as there are performers who all at length unite with organic melody.'

GERALD OF WALES

Leeks:

There's a story dating from the early 1600s that St David ordered his soldiers to wear a leek on their helmets in a battle against Saxon invaders. (The battle is also said to have taken place in a field full of leeks.) The Welsh association with this vegetable goes back even further in time, to when people and their druids worshipped trees, plants and other aspects of the natural world. The leek was used as a cure for a cold, a pain reliever in childbirth, and a protector against wounds in battle, lightning strikes and evil spirits. It was also thought to have supernatural powers: if a maiden put a leek under her pillow at night, she'd see the face of her future husband.

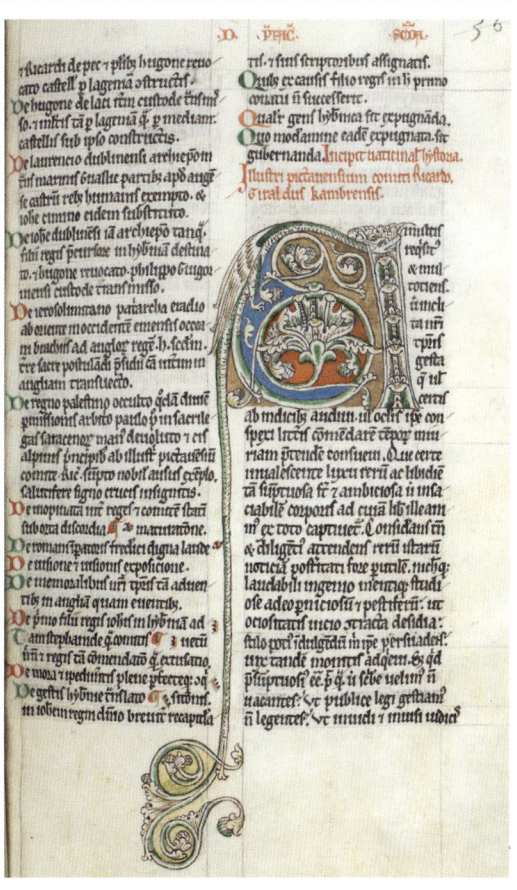

> *'The world is never the same place once a great poem has been added to it.'*
>
> **DYLAN THOMAS**

My history with food from the old sod doesn't begin auspiciously. Grandad Challacombe was affectionately known as Chaco de Faggot de Dung Merchant. (What did his enemies call him?) He used to collect horse manure for his vegetables, and his family sold homemade faggots in Neath market. I also had professional faggot-makers on my maternal grandparents' side. But when I came along, as expected then, it was Mam who was responsible for feeding us. Bicarbonate of soda-boiled vegetables were the order of the day and my mother Pauline, who ate only chicken and chips, didn't like cooking. While the Bay City Rollers played us through the seventies and 'Tainted Love' blasted on the radio in the eighties, we enjoyed Libby's Sunshine Orange, crispy frozen pancakes, stuffed vol-au-vents, potted sandwich spread or meat paste and Vesta curry. Easily the best day of the week was Saturday, when we fetched shop-bought chip butties with rissoles, curry sauce and pickled onions from Dick Barton's. Then came a miracle. In the wake of cheap flights to the Continent, suspicions towards 'foreign' food waned and within our Formica-walled kitchen, round the breakfast bar that shook with the spin of the washing machine beneath, Pauline reconnected with the family's home-cooking roots.

We still ate chips, but Mam's menu started to vary. Welsh classics came out: cawl, laverbread with cockles and bacon, smoked haddock poached in milk or ham with parsley sauce, griddled sprats when the fish man came, home-baked Welsh cakes, bara brith and flapjacks. One year came the hefty and dangerous malt beer of Pembrokeshire – heat with the poker from the fire, serve hot with brown sugar and sit back and wait for it to hit you. But best of all? Her curries, learnt from her friends Madrika and Mrs Boorah. Out went the freeze-dried carrots and hello came whole spices, freshly ground and puffed balls of roti and puri breads. It made us all staunch believers in the satanic art of home cooking. Come the early nineties the transformation was complete, from a straw-bottled, Rosé-wine-guzzling, greens-hating Neath native emerged a herb-growing experimental exponent of feast-making in the heart of the home, and I salute her. Mam's love of cooking hasn't left this family. I learnt to cook, argue, taste and season right there alongside my siblings: it's still chaos at Christmas, knives at dawn as to whose methods are to be used, all keen to be captains of the ship that is the kitchen, the heart of the house, the middle of the action.

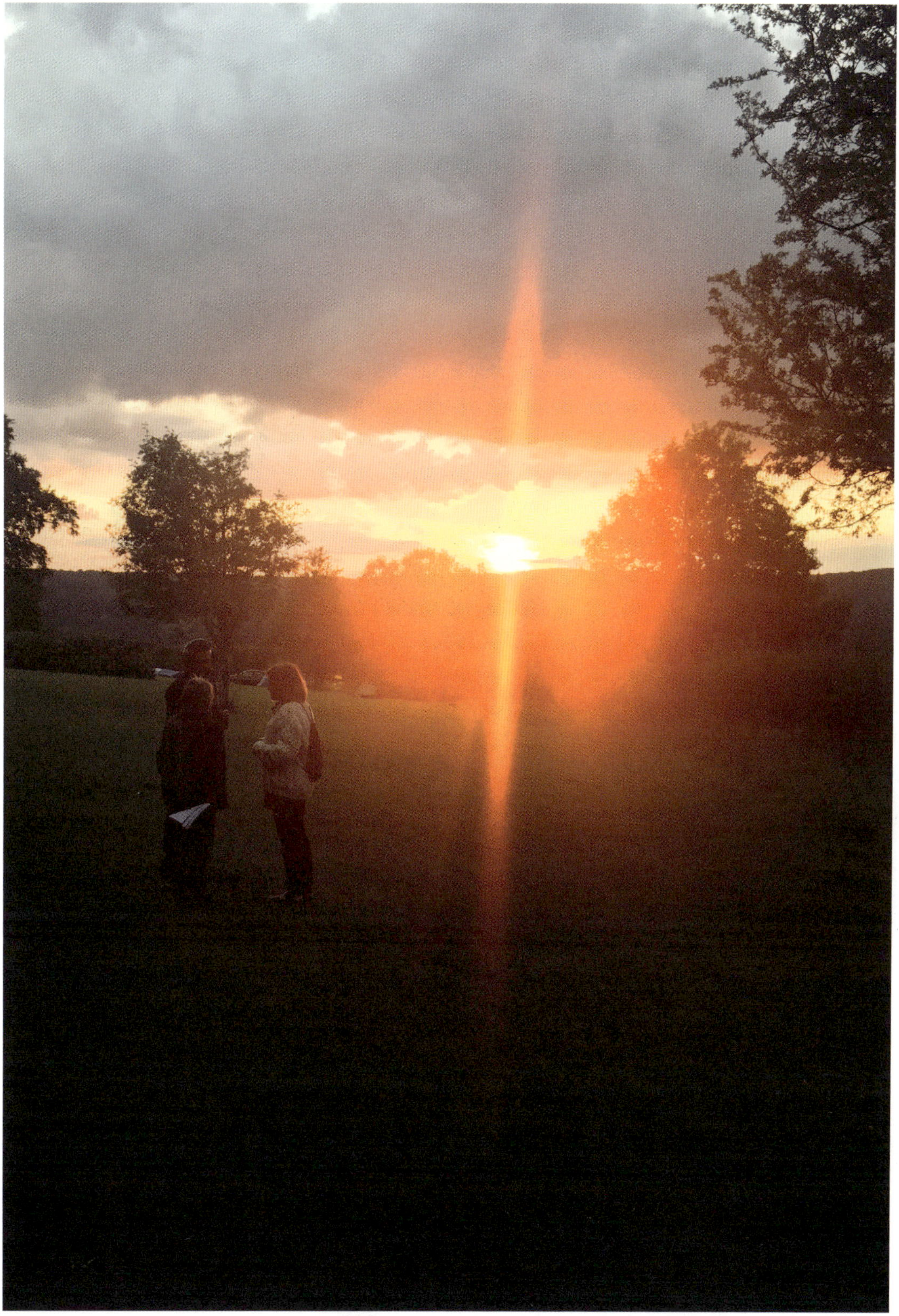

WALES

Roger Phillips

111

WALES

ON THE MENU

FAGGOTS

CAWL

LAVERBREAD AND COCKLES

LEEK AND POTATO SOUP

HOMEMADE BREAD

HEDGEROW SALAD

DESSERT

GRAMMA'S SHERRY TRIFLE

WELSH CAKES

HOMEMADE CUSTARD

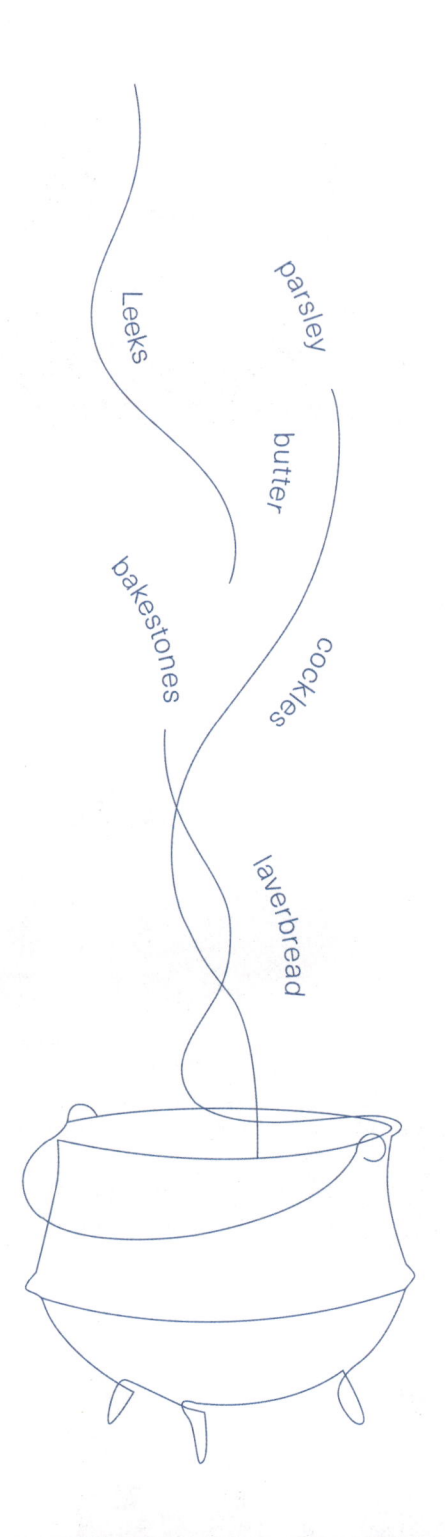

Leeks · parsley · butter · bakestones · cockles · laverbread

Llio Rhydderch 'Castell Rhos Y Llan'

Faggots

DF NV

This is a 100-year-old family recipe, thanks to Aunt Dilys, Nan's first cousin.

Ingredients

225g crustless bread (about a whole large loaf, minus the crusts)
225g onions
1 small Bramley apple
225g pig's liver, minced
85g pork belly or bacon, minced
1 tbsp finely chopped parsley
1 tsp ground mixed spice
salt and pepper
pig's caul if available (about 125g)

Option:
Ask your butcher to mince the liver and pork belly for you. It's fine to mince them together.

For a vegetarian faggot option, head to the England chapter's nut roast recipe (p. 150).

Idea:
If you like fried liver, try it with a squeeze of lemon.

Method

1. Soak the bread in enough water to saturate it – about 250ml. Once soft, beat it with a fork or squeeze with your hands to break up into small pieces and get rid of any lumps. Then squeeze out all the excess water and discard.

2. Grate the onions and apple on the coarse part of the grater, or chop into small chunks in a food processor.

3. Mix the liver, pork belly/bacon, apple, onions, bread, parsley, mixed spice and a generous amount of salt and pepper together – faggots should be highly seasoned. To check for seasoning you can fry a small patty of this mixture on either side in a medium-hot frying pan until cooked through. Taste and adjust the seasoning in the mixture if necessary.

4. Preheat the oven to 220°C/gas 7.

5. Cut the pig's caul into 16 squares. Place a ball of the mixture into each square and tightly wrap the caul around it. Place in a roasting tin, join side down. Repeat with the remaining mixture, placing each faggot close to the others to prevent them from moving around too much. If you can't get hold of caul, put the mixture into a lined roasting tin and cook whole, then cut into squares to serve.

6. Place in the preheated oven and bake for 35–45 minutes or until firm, cooked through and good and brown on top.

Meic Stevens 'Y Brawd Houdini' — Hwntws 'Cwd Cardotyn'

Cawl

(V) (VG) (GF) (DF)

Years and years ago, when cauldrons simmered in the fireplace, you might add vegetables as they became available. And while you were working in the fields, it kept doing its magic, so, when you returned, famished, it was ready to dish out. This version has no meat, but I've included a non-veg additional step at the end.

Ingredients

1 onion, chopped

1 leek, chopped

olive oil

salt and pepper

1 large carrot, chopped

1 large parsnip, chopped

400g swede, chopped

400g potato, chopped

2 sprigs of thyme

1.2 litres of water (plus vegetable stock cube optional)

1 x 400g cooked butter beans, with their liquid (or other peas/beans like pre-cooked chickpeas, kidney beans, black eyed peas, peas or fava beans).

a handful fresh parsley, chopped

Method

1. Put the onions and leeks in a pan with a glug of oil and sauté with a pinch of salt until soft, 10 minutes or so.

2. Stir in the rest of the peeled, chopped vegetables, the herbs and the water, bring to a boil, then turn down heat and simmer until the vegetables are all tender, around 30 minutes.

3. Add the butter beans with the liquid and stir through. Keep at a gentle simmer, season to taste. (At this point it's technically ready, but can be left now at the lowest setting, to wait for you.)

4. Serve in bowls (traditionally wooden ones, with wooden spoons, but hey), sprinkle with chopped parsley. On the table, offer a chunk of cheese and the grater, and the salt and pepper.

*Non-veg option:
Add small pieces of browned lamb (fried up quickly in hot oil before you fry the onion, remove from pan and set aside, adding back in at step 2). Traditionally, cheap cuts like the neck were used, so the longer you simmer, the less tough the meat; taste to see and keep adding water if it gets too thick and risks catching at the bottom.

Option:
To make easy dumplings to go with the dish, see p. 155.

Georgia Ruth 'Codi Angor'

Rhos Male Voice Choir 'Tydi A Roddaist'

Robin Huw Bowen 'Gypsy Waltzes'   Crasdant 'Pibddawns Trefynwy'

Cerys Matthews 'Sosban Fach'

Laverbread and Cockles

GF NV

Buy laver when you see it, in paste form, preferably in glass jars, although it also comes in long-lasting packs now. Laver is seaweed while laverbread is the boiled seaweed. It's also sometimes called Welshman's caviar.

Laver harvesting is thought to be an ancient custom, the seaweed being common around the British and Irish coast. I once tried picking it from the beach and preparing my own. You have to boil it for hours: I made a total mess, so feel no qualms about buying it ready prepared now. I love its distinct texture and taste; it spells holidays to me and is full of minerals and iron.

Ingredients

150g laverbread
30g oats
15g salted butter
100g cockles – fresh cooked and shelled from the market (not pickled in vinegar)*
freshly ground black pepper

Method

1. Mix together the laverbread and oats.
2. Add butter to a large frying pan over a medium heat. Once melted, place the laverbread on one side of the pan and the cockles on the other. Cook for a few minutes so it gets hot right through.
3. Season with pepper and serve with toasted homemade bread and hot tea.

Options:

Add a little more butter and fry an egg in there too, or for non veg, go traditional and fry rashers of bacon first, lose the butter and cook all of above in the bacon fat.

With the oats, the more you add, the more solid the patty you end up with. It really is a matter of preference – some add none at all, some just a handful. Any way you choose, the laverbread will probably stick to the pan and your teeth. But hey, it's sustainable and healthy.

* You can also use fresh cockles. Simply give the cockles a rinse in a sink of cold water. Discard any that do not shut when tapped against the edge of the sink or any that have broken shells. Drain, then cook in a covered pan with a splash of water until they have just opened. Discard any that do not open.

Mary Hopkin 'Aderyn Pur' (live at the Royal Festival Hall, 1972)

Phil Tanner 'The Gower Reel'

Leek and Potato Soup

Vegan option:
Exchange the butter for olive oil, replace milk with vegetable stock.

VG GF

Ingredients

2 large leeks, chopped (a tip to clean: slice leeks longways from just where the white turns to green, so it's easy to open the layers of leek, then run under the tap, to remove any soil)

50g butter

salt and pepper

500g potatoes, cubed

900ml vegetable stock

200ml whole milk

handful of parsley, to garnish

Method

1. Cook the leeks until soft with the butter and a pinch of salt in a large saucepan over a medium heat with the lid on, about 8–10 minutes.

2. Once the leeks are soft, add the potatoes. Pour in the stock and bring to a simmer until the potatoes are completely soft and broken down, roughly 25–30 minutes.

3. Pour in the milk and heat through for 3–4 minutes. Remove from the heat and blitz with a stick blender, or mash with a potato masher to break up the potatoes. It shouldn't be completely smooth; chunks make good texture. Taste the soup and season as necessary. Garnish with parsley (add some cream or more butter if you want added richness), and serve with a black pepper grinder and homemade bread (see recipe opposite).

Yr Hennessys 'Ar Lan Y Mor'

9 Bach 'Pontypridd'

Homemade Bread

VG

You can use different ratios of flours, e.g. only use white strong flour, or use white strong with a portion of ground flax or gram flour or mix up rations of white and wholemeal flours. Experiment with whatever you have.

My thanks to chef Claire Thomson for nudging me into bread baking with her promise that it's 'very, very easy'. I gave it a shot using a handheld mixer (taking the place of hand-kneading) and joined the club. I can now also vouch that making bread like this is indeed a piece of cake. Keep dried yeast in your fridge, and as long as you have water, salt and flour, you're good to go.

Other options when you begin to experiment include adding chopped nuts, seeds, dried fruit or olives. You can use this basic yeast bread recipe to make any shapes, flat breads, pizza base, rolls etc.

Ingredients

300g strong white flour
300g strong wholemeal flour
100g ground flax seed
1 generous tbsp easy-bake yeast
1 tsp sea salt
550g warm water (I use warm water straight from the tap)
melted butter or olive oil, if you fancy, for decoration

Method

1. Mix all ingredients except the butter in a large bowl for a few minutes until they form a dough, not too dry, not too wet. (Use the knead accessory on a hand mixer, or a food processor.) Cover the bowl with a clean tea towel.
2. Leave to rise for 1 hour.
3. Preheat the oven to 180°C/gas 4.
4. Knead again for 2 or 3 minutes and leave it to rise for a further 30 minutes – so it's started to rise but not quite 100 per cent – this way it will have room to grow more in the oven.
5. Place in a loaf tin, slash the top with a knife and, if using melted butter (or olive oil), paint it on the top.
6. Put in the oven for 45 minutes, then raise the temperature to 200°C/gas 6 for a further 15 minutes.
7. Turn the loaf out of the tin and tap the bottom – it should sound good and hollow.
8. Leave to cool on a wire mesh tray.

Bob Delyn 'Pethau Bychain Dewi Sant'

Bois Y Felin 'Milgi Milgi'

Cayo Evans 'Men Of Harlech'

Hedgerow Salad

(VG) (GF)

I pick sorrel from the hedgerows in Pembrokeshire. It's what sailors did when they figured out that scurvy was caused by lack of vitamin C – sorrel is full of it, hence its refreshing citrus taste. Or you can grow it in the garden. Watercress is also found in the streams in West Wales; other options are dandelions (aiming for the young, less bitter leaves); nasturtium and lime (Linden, not citrus) trees that are common in cities and parks in the UK. Again, go for the young leaves and for all these foraged options, wash well before eating. Alternatively, there are so many salad leaf options available now: baby spinach, lettuce, radicchio, chicory. With all of these, nuts – walnuts, cashews or almonds – all work well, especially if you toast them for a few minutes on a hot iron skillet. I use hazelnuts as I recently bought some and they tasted so good, reminding me of cracking them open with my teeth in Swansea woods, which, like opening a beer bottle with my teeth, I don't think I'd try these days.

Ingredients

4 large handfuls of leaves – a mixture of sorrel, nasturtium, dandelion (or watercress) and lime leaves

50g toasted chopped hazelnuts

50g Caerphilly cheese, crumbled (or other crumbly cheese, e.g. feta)

salt and pepper

1 handful nasturtium flowers, wild garlic flowers or other petals, e.g. chrysanthemums

For the dressing

1 tsp mustard, such as Dijon or wholegrain

1 tsp honey (optional)

2 tbsp vinegar of your choosing, such as white wine, balsamic or cider vinegar

6 tbsp olive oil (classic vinaigrette ratio is 3:1 vinegar to oil, but if you like zingyness amend the ratio to suit your taste)

salt and pepper

Method

1. Wash and dry the leaves and place them on a serving plate. Sprinkle with the chopped nuts and crumbled cheese.

2. Put all the dressing ingredients into a jam jar and add seasoning. Shake vigorously to mix.

3. Dress the salad lightly, just before serving. Serve with the flowers scattered over the top.

Options:

- Crumbled pieces of blue cheese go especially well with bitter leaves like chicory or radicchio and walnut.
- Experiment with dressing too: any acidic choice will work: e.g. white wine vinegar, cider vinegar/lemon/yuzu/orange/lime juices, balsamic.
- Also try with different oils, e.g. use sesame oil or walnut oil for a nuttier flavour.
- Add chopped chives.
- Pick dandelion heads/flowers while you're at it, wash, dry, dip in pancake batter and fry like fritters.

Vegan super salads:

1. Green leaves with cooked quinoa, chickpeas, green lentils, almond flakes (or nuts of your choice), parsley, pomegranate, pumpkin and sunflower seeds, charred, blanched broccoli and fennel, and serve with hummus and roasted beetroots.

2. Green leaves with wild rice, avocado, cucumber, peas, mint, parsley, and a mix of all or any of these: toasted caraway, sunflower, flax, sesame and nigella seeds.

These go well with the mustard salad dressing as above or, for a creamier vegan dressing, try adding a tablespoon of miso paste or mashed silken tofu.

A third option is a quick 'ponzu' dressing: a mix of soy sauce, rice vinegar and lime or lemon or yuzu juice.

Cowbois Rhos Botwnnog 'Didl-Dei'

Public Service Broadcasting 'They Gave Me A Lamp' (featuring Haiku Salut)

Gramma's Sherry Trifle

VG

This is my paternal grandmother Gwenddydd Mai's go-to dessert. I remember the taste of the sherry so well – unforgettable to a young child – also the crunch of the almond flakes makes a wonderful partner to the custard and cream. Using a flat dish means more sherry with every serving.

Ingredients

160–180g square trifle sponges, halved (whichever size pack your supermarket sells)
4–5 tbsp good quality raspberry jam (optional)
200ml medium cream sherry
100g amaretti biscuits, crumbled
100g flaked almonds, toasted
300ml double cream
1 egg white
1 tbsp caster sugar
500g custard (for homemade, see opposite)
100g glacé cherries, halved
(optional) angelica, for decoration

Method

1. Sandwich the sponge pieces together in pairs with jam in the middle (if using) and place in the bottom of a wide trifle bowl. Pour over the sherry (enough so that the sponge is soaked). Sprinkle over the crumbled amaretti biscuits along with half of the almonds.

2. Whisk the cream in a bowl until stiff. In a separate, clean bowl with a clean whisk, whisk the egg white until soft peak stage. Add the sugar and whisk until stiff peaks form. Fold the egg white into the whipped cream until completely incorporated.

3. Spoon the custard over the biscuits and almonds. Top with the whipped cream, gently spreading it out. You can chill the trifle overnight at this stage or use it straight away.

4. Before serving, sprinkle over the remaining flaked almonds and if using, decorate with the halved glacé cherries and angelica.

Welsh Cakes

VG

Ingredients

225g self-raising flour
110g butter, cut into small pieces
55g caster sugar
a handful or two of raisins (around 70g, or currants or sultanas – your call)
pinch of grated nutmeg (or ground cinnamon or mixed spice)
1 egg, beaten
1–2 tbsp milk

Method

1. Put the flour and butter into a bowl and rub it in with your fingertips until it's like breadcrumbs.
2. Add the sugar, dried fruit and pinch of spice, then add the beaten egg to the mixture to make a stiff, mouldable dough, adding some milk if necessary.
3. Roll out on a floured board to 1cm thick, then cut into rounds. Your choice which size – I like them small.
4. Cook on a hot griddle for 2–4 minutes on each side until golden brown.
5. Cover a cooling rack with greaseproof paper, and as soon as the cakes come off the griddle, sprinkle with caster sugar.

Vegan Welsh cakes:
Replace butter with vegetable oil, and replace egg by using a binder made with ground chia (or flax seeds): for one egg you need 1 tablespoon of ground chia and 3 tablespoons of water. Put in fridge so it congeals, then use as per egg in the recipe.

Homemade Custard

VG GF

Ingredients

500ml milk (whole or semi-skimmed)
1 tsp vanilla extract or 1 vanilla pod
4 egg yolks
2 tbsp honey (or caster sugar, or soft brown sugar), to taste
1 tbsp cornflour

Note:
It's fine to use up all these extra egg whites in the cream when making the sherry trifle.

Method

1. Heat the milk in a saucepan with the vanilla until it is just about to reach the boil. Remove from the heat and leave to infuse and cool.
2. Whisk the egg yolks, sugar/honey and the cornflour in a bowl. Slowly whisk in the cooled milk. (Remove the vanilla pod if using.)
3. Pour this mixture back into the saucepan used to heat the milk.
4. Stir over a low heat until the mixture thickens enough to coat the back of the spoon. Taste, adding more sugar or honey if needed (or, if using sugar, stirring to dissolve).

Meredydd Evans 'Si Hei Lwli (Lullaby)'

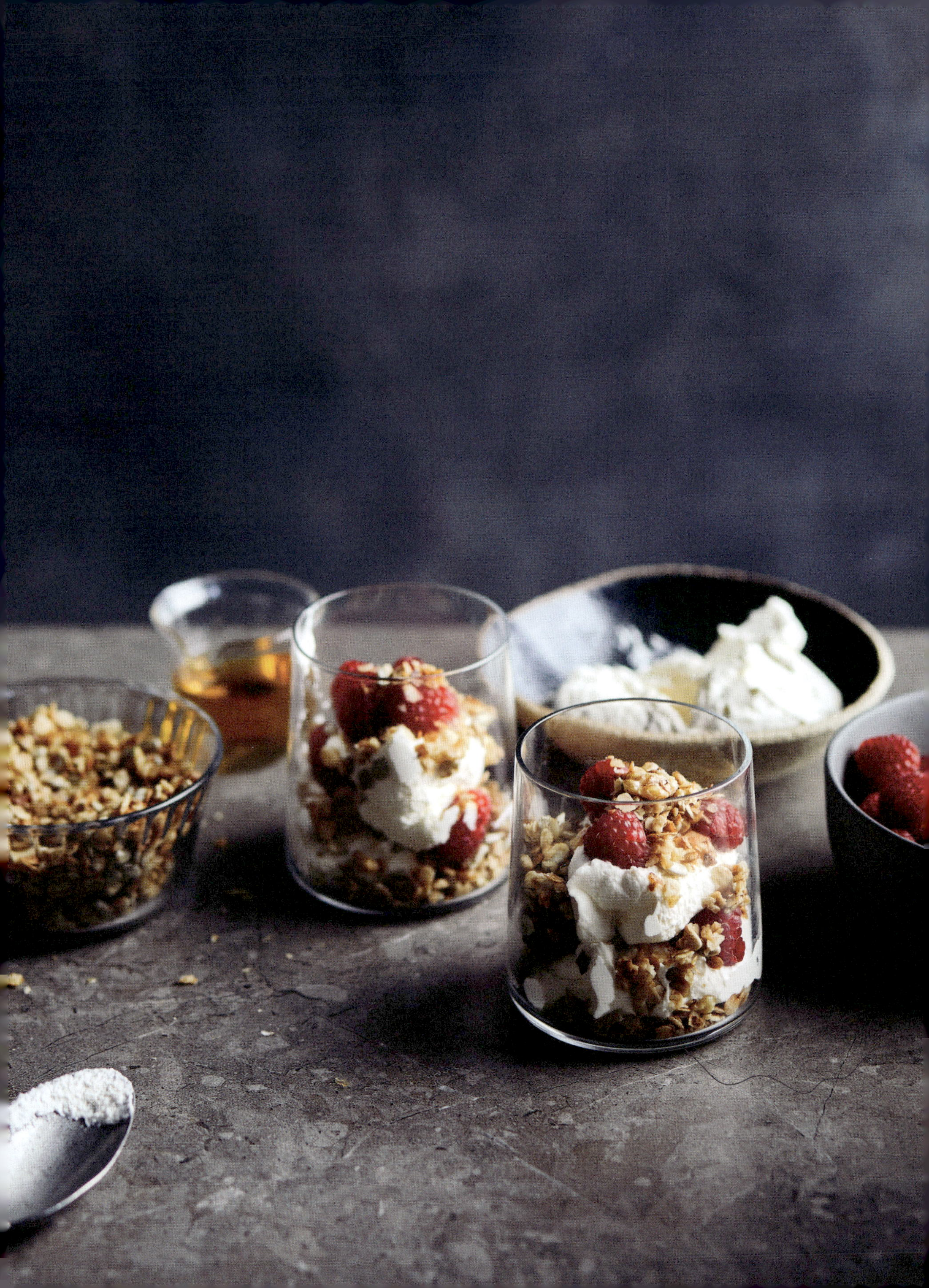

SCOTLAND

Address to a Haggis

Fair fa' your honest, sonsie face,
Great chieftain o' the puddin-race!
Aboon them a' ye tak your place,
Painch, tripe, or thairm:
Weel are ye wordy o' a grace
As lang's my arm.

The groaning trencher there ye fill,
Your hurdies like a distant hill,
Your pin wad help to mend a mill
In time o' need,
While thro' your pores the dews distil
Like amber bead.

His knife see rustic Labour dight,
An' cut you up wi' ready slight,
Trenching your gushing entrails bright,
Like onie ditch;
And then, O what a glorious sight,
Warm-reekin', rich!

Then, horn for horn, they stretch an' strive:
Deil tak the hindmost, on they drive,
Till a' their weel-swall'd kytes belyve
Are bent like drums;
The auld Guidman, maist like to rive,
'Bethankit' hums.

Is there that owre his French ragout,
Or olio that wad staw a sow,
Or fricassee wad mak her spew
Wi' perfect scunner,
Looks down wi' sneering, scornfu' view
On sic a dinner?

Poor devil! see him owre his trash,
As feckless as a wither'd rash,
His spindle shank a guid whip-lash,
His nieve a nit;
Thro' bloody flood or field to dash,
O how unfit!

But mark the Rustic, haggis-fed,
The trembling earth resounds his tread,
Clap in his walie nieve a blade,
He'll make it whissle;
An' legs an' arms, an' heads will sned,
Like taps o' thrissle.

Ye Pow'rs, wha mak mankind your care,
And dish them out their bill o' fare,
Auld Scotland wants nae skinking ware
That jaups in luggies:
But, if ye wish her gratefu' prayer,
Gie her a Haggis!

Robert Burns

YOUR BURNS' NIGHT SUPPER
The first item for your programme of Burns supper is the address to the haggis. Carry your haggis in on a silver platter to the sound of a piper playing a rousing Scottish air. 'Scotland the Brave', perhaps? Your guests clap to the beat. There must be a whisky-bearer to make sure everyone has a drop to toast the haggis. Once in the room, one of the guests recites the poem, knife held aloft, and at the line 'trenching its using entrails', with drama, they pierce the haggis, open up the skin and reveal the delicious insides. At the poem's end, the haggis is raised to the air. Raise a glass to the haggis, then serve with neeps and tatties.

St Andrew was a fisherman born in 6th century BC in Galilee and became one of Jesus' disciples.

His name means valour, and some say he founded the city now known as Istanbul. He was the first Christian in **GEORGIA**, founding the Georgian church there.

He was martyred by crucifixion on an X-shaped cross, as he felt himself unworthy to be crucified on the same shaped cross as Jesus, hence the **SALTIRE.**

You'll find a part of this cross, some of his skull and his little finger in Patras, Greece.

Some **RELICS** reached Fife, and the city of St Andrews was founded.

The Scottish **UNICORN** is a mighty amalgamation of four animals: lion's tail, goat's beard, narwhal's horn and horse's body. It symbolizes masculinity, power, nobility and purity. Its arch enemy is the lion, and both are showcased on the UK's royal coat of arms.

A story goes that the **THISTLE** saved a sleeping army of Scottish warriors from an ambush of invading Norsemen, as one of them stepped on a thistle, yelped and woke the slumbering natives.

Legend has St Andrew answering the prayers of the king of the Picts, **OENGUS** (820–834), when fighting the Angles.

A cross of clouds appeared in the blue skies above the battle field. Despite being inferior in number, emboldened by this divine interruption, Oengus' army were victorious and Andrew was appointed **PATRON SAINT** of Scotland.

St Andrews is also the patron saint of Barbados, Romania, Russia and Ukraine.

The white saltire on the blue of the **FLAG** symbolizes the white cloud cross in the blue skies, which appeared that day to Oengus and his men.

Stirling Castle news
Everyone drank ale* from morning to night in the 1500s: each servant was given a daily allowance of a 'joug' (1.7 litres) and it was consumed with every meal, even by the children, as it was considered safer than water or milk as germs were killed by the brewing process.

*It had a low alcohol content.

Whisky/Whiskey is an alcoholic drink made by fermenting grain mash. The Guild of Barber Surgeons in Edinburgh held the monopoly on the production of this aqua vitae or 'water of life' in the early sixteenth century. It would have been a much harsher drink then, as it was raw alcohol and not aged. Whisky is spelled 'whisky' in Scotland and 'whiskey' in Ireland, the added 'e' apparently to distinguish the Irish spirit as a superior product, distilled three instead of two times and in a specific type of still.

Only a quarter of Scotch Whisky distilleries are owned by Scottish companies. The first one in India was founded in the 1820s.

It wasn't the Scottish who were the first to turn oats into porridge – apparently this is credited to the **GREEKS.** Porridge was also found in the stomachs of 5,000-year-old bog bodies.

'Bees that hae honey in their mouths, have stings in their tails.'

Oats became popular in Scotland because they grew despite the low temperatures and high humidity. Ancient universities had holidays called **'MEAL MONDAY'**, which allowed students to return to their farms to help harvest the crop.

'It's a sair feicht for half a loaf'
(Life is hard and it's tough to even get small recompense.)

'Enough's as gude as a feast'
(From a 1707 pamphlet about moderation and drinking, meaning you shouldn't have more than you need.)

Samuel Johnson in his dictionary of 1755 defined **OATS** as:
'A grain, which in England is generally given to horses, but in Scotland appears to support the people.'

The Scotsman's retort was 'That's why England has such good horses, and Scotland has such fine men.'

I hopped on board a schooner in Oban at the age of twenty-one, having made friends with some of the crew in a pub in the old port. We sailed around Barra, South and North Uist, Benbecula, Harris and Lewis. I set to work cleaning the crab and scallops caught by the divers on board and when the weather got rough and the galley chef sick, I found myself in charge of the kitchen. Close to three decades on, I still dream of the Outer Hebrides, and have never returned for fear of bursting that bubble. In my mind these islands stretch into turquoise seas; coastal fields are marked by ancient stone walls in stripes of yellow (from the buttercups) and white (from the daisies), pocked with long-haired red Highland cattle. I sense the freshness even now writing this in London: the light of the skies, the sweet touch of Lewis shortbread.

Even the names of Scottish food sound, if not poetic, certainly lyrically distinctive: clapshot, bannocks, cock-a-leekie soup, Cullen skink, Rumbledethumps, clootie dumplings, stovies pie, Cranachan. These are good old recipes to fill the stomachs of those born to this astonishing landscape, with its fifty shades of grey rocks and skies, craggy lines, pine trees and cutting winds. Visiting Scotland is intense, like a slap in the face: a feast for the eyes, the ears and nose. I love it. We toured a lot there – Glasgow's King Tut's Wah Wah Hut, Barrowlands, Inverness, Aberdeen, the underground caves in Edinburgh, the floors littered with centuries-old oyster shells. I have admired Glasgow's eye for art, eaten fish suppers in Kirkcaldy, mince and tatties in Dundee and lobster in Scalloway, Shetland. Shetland is closer to Norway than to mainland Scotland, and the accent in Whalsay has a loud Scandinavian bent. Then Orkney, though closer to the mainland, but culturally so distinct, with its fiddling, that sing-song accent, Skara Brae, the Ring of Brodgar where Billy Connolly apparently loved to run naked.

Back on the mainland, I recently walked in J. M. W. Turner's footsteps and entered Sir Walter Scott's house, with his library, all dark wood and inspiration in a castle looking out over the river Tweed. Inverness, the Scottish highlands, pine jelly and, yes, Robert Burns must make an appearance. The oldest Burns club in the world was founded in Irvine in 1826 by Burns's friends. He'd landed there to learn about growing linseed and settled in 1781 aged twenty-two. I adore Burns, sympathetic to all God's creatures, to lice and mice, and his 'a man's a man for a' that' is an early voice raised against slavery. A farm labourer who broke the class barriers and left an eternal legacy, despite dying at thirty-six. Here's a verse from his 'The Shepherd's Wife', a poem/song where the wife tries to tempt her husband home from work with various promises: you'll have to read the whole poem to find out what clenched the deal. Clue: it's predictable.

Ye'se get a panfu' o' plumpin parridge,
And butter in them, and butter in them,
Ye'se get a panfu' o' plumpin parridge,
Gin ye'll come hame again een, jo.

Some hae meat and canna eat,
And some wad eat that want it,
But we hae meat and we can eat,
And sae the Lord be thankit.

BURNS NIGHT, SELKIRK GRACE

'The proper drinking of scotch whisky is more than indulgence. It is a toast to a civilization, a tribute to the continuity of culture, a manifesto of man's determination to use the resources of nature to refresh mind and body and enjoy to the full the sense with which he has been endowed.'

**DAVID DAICHES,
SCOTCH WHISKY: ITS PAST AND PRESENT**

SCOTLAND

'Here's tae us. Wha's like us? Damn few, and they're a' deid!'

TRADITIONAL TOAST

'Two negatives make a positive, but only in Scotland do two positives make a negative: "aye, right!"'

FRANKIE BOYLE

SCOTLAND

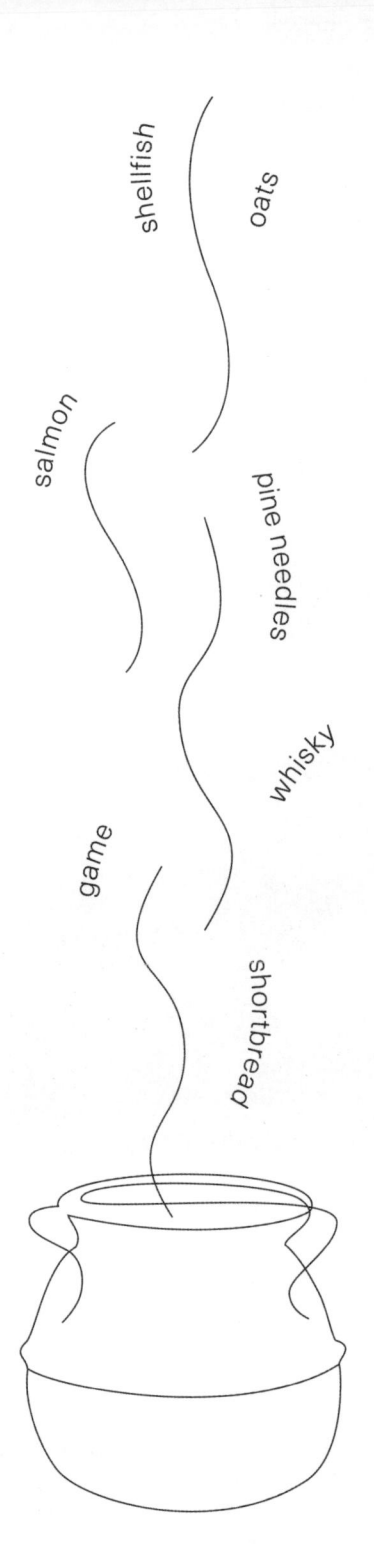

ON THE MENU

NEEPS

TATTIE SCONES

HAGGIS (VEGAN)

HOME HAGGIS (NON-VEG)

COCK-A-LEEKIE SOUP

DESSERT

CUMNOCK LOAF

CRANACHAN

AYRSHIRE SHORTBREAD

DRINK

WHISKY

SCOTTISH SPRING WATER

shellfish, oats, salmon, pine needles, whisky, game, shortbread

Jimmy Shand 'Dashing White Sergeant'

Red Hot Chilli Pipers 'Flower of Scotland'

Neeps

V VG GF

Ingredients

1 swede, chopped (approx. 500g)

blob of butter (approx. 50g, to taste), or oil if vegan

50ml potato cooking water (or use cream for creamier option)

salt and pepper

Method

1. Boil the swede in water with a pinch of salt until soft, then pour off all but about 50ml of water and mash with the butter. Add a little of the cooking water if necessary.

2. Season well with loads of black pepper.

Tattie Scones (potato scones)

V VG

Traditional with breakfast – to me they taste good at any time of day. You need a ratio of 4:1 mashed potatoes to flour. This recipe makes 12 pieces (from 3 rounds).

Ingredients

200g potato, boiled (I don't peel, but you can remove skins once boiled if you want)

blob of butter (approx. 50g), or oil if vegan

salt and pepper

50g self-raising flour

extra flour for floured surface and for adding if needed

Method

1. Mash potatoes in a bowl and season (option: add a blob of butter).

2. Pour in 50g flour and mix to make a dough.

3. On a generously floured surface, work it, adding flour when you need, until you can roll it out approx. 5 mm thick.

4. Heat a bakestone or thick iron pan, lightly greased with butter (or oil if vegan).

5. Use a saucer, cut around the saucer to make rounds, put rounds in pan, and with a knife mark with a cross.

6. Cook each side for approx. 2–3 minutes, until golden.

Option:

Slather with butter while still hot, or serve with smoked salmon, garnished with soured cream and sprigs of dill.

Simon Howie's Scottish Dance Band 'Reels, Tricky But Catchy – Leveneep Head/Jessie Stuart's Welcome In Dufftown /D. Ridley's Compliments To Jim Halcrow/Lynn's Reel'

Saltfishforty 'Old Joe Clark' (live)

Julie Fowlis 'Puirt A Beul Set: Ribinnean Riomhach'

John Findlater 'The Orkney Style Of Courtship'

Haggis (Vegan)

(V) (VG) (GF) (DF)

(If you don't have a muffin tin, use ramekins or a baking dish/loaf tin.)

Ingredients

1 medium onion, peeled and finely diced
oil for sautéing, greasing and brushing
1 medium carrot, finely diced
100g mushrooms, finely diced
100g jumbo rolled oats
½ tsp fine sea salt
2 tsp freshly ground black pepper
1 tsp ground coriander seeds
1 tsp nutmeg
1 tbsp miso paste
200ml vegetable stock
3 tbsp sunflower seeds
250g cooked beluga lentils (or puy lentils if beluga are unavailable)

Method

1. Preheat the oven to 180°C/gas 4.

2. Sauté the onion in a little oil with a pinch of salt until softened and translucent. Add the carrot and mushroom and continue to cook for a further 5 minutes. Remove from the heat and leave to cool.

3. Put the oats, seasoning and spices into a food processor. Stir the miso into the stock and add to the mixture along with the sunflower seeds and onion/carrot/mushroom mix. Pulse briefly to break everything down a little, keeping a rough texture. Stir the lentils through at the end, making sure they are evenly distributed. Taste and adjust the seasoning if needed.

4. Grease a 12-hole muffin tin with oil and divide the mixture between the holes. Flatten down the tops with the back of a spoon. Cover tightly with a layer of baking paper, topped with foil.

5. Place onto an oven tray and into the preheated oven. Bake for 20 minutes then remove the foil, brush the tops with a little oil and bake for a further 20 minutes or until lightly browned on top and firmed up enough to hold their shape, but still with a little give in the middle.

6. Serve whilst warm with the traditional haggis accompaniments: neeps and tatties, basically mashed swede with butter, and mashed potatoes.

Home Haggis (Non Veg)

GF DF NV

A simpler version than traditional, so no boiling up lungs. (Use ramekins or a baking dish/loaf tin if you don't have a muffin tin.)

Ingredients

1 medium onion, chopped
oil for sautéing and greasing
200g lamb's liver, washed
400g lamb mince
1 tsp fine sea salt
1 tsp freshly ground black pepper
1 tsp ground coriander seed
1 tsp ground nutmeg
200ml water
200g pinhead oats

Method

1. Preheat the oven to 180°C/gas 4.

2. Sauté the onion in a little oil with a pinch of salt until softened and translucent. Remove from the heat and leave to cool.

3. Meanwhile, put the liver, mince, seasoning and spices into a food processor and roughly pulse until the liver is broken down and everything is mixed together. Add the onions, 200ml of water and the pinhead oats and pulse a few more times to mix through, making sure everything is evenly distributed throughout the mixture.

4. Grease a 12-hole muffin tin with oil and divide the mixture between the holes. Flatten down the tops. Cover tightly with a layer of baking paper, topped with foil.

5. Place onto an oven tray and into the preheated oven. Bake for 20 minutes then remove the foil and bake for a further 15–20 minutes or until lightly browned on top.

6. Serve whilst warm with the traditional haggis accompaniments: neeps and tatties, basically mashed swede with butter, and mashed potatoes.

Dolly Parton with Mairead Ni Mhaonaigh and Altan 'Barbara Allen'

John Pritchard and Joan Sutherland 'Spargi D'Amore Pianto', from *Lucia di Lammermoor*, Act II, Scene 2, by Donizetti

Cock-a-Leekie Soup

DF **NV**

One-pot wonder.

Ingredients

400–500g chicken thighs, bone in, skin removed
2 tbsp olive oil
2 leeks (approx. 500g once trimmed), chopped
1 stalk celery, diced
sprig fresh thyme, or ½ tsp dried thyme
small bunch of fresh parsley, chopped
1L vegetable or chicken stock
75g pearl barley
4 prunes, stones removed, chopped (optional)
salt and pepper

Method

1. Brown the chicken pieces on all sides in the oil in a large pot, over a medium heat.
2. Add the leeks, celery and a good pinch of salt, soften for a few minutes.
3. Add the thyme, half the parsley, stock and the pearl barley to the pan. Bring to a simmer, then put on lid and simmer for 45 minutes. Stir occasionally.
4. Add the prunes, if using, 5 minutes before serving.
5. Taste and season. You can serve as is, or take out the chicken, remove the bones, then put the meat back in the soup.
6. Sprinkle with the rest of the parsley and serve.

Cumnock Loaf

VG

You hear a lot about bad neighbours and not enough about the best. John MacArthur is one of the latter. This recipe was given to me to share by John's mum, Jean MacArthur (born in the former mining community of New Cumnock, Ayrshire, 90 years ago), via her cousin, Rita Tyson. My huge thanks to all three – our London lives are sweetened now that I have the following two recipes. Bursting with plump raisins, Cumnock Loaf is a two-step waltz to heaven. More so buttered and served with a cup of tea.

Part One

110g soft brown sugar
110g butter
200ml water
300g raisins
1 tsp baking soda

Put the above ingredients into a saucepan, bring to the boil, then reduce the heat and simmer for 5 minutes. Allow to cool, but while still warm proceed to Part Two.

Part Two

225g self-raising flour
1 beaten egg

Add the flour and egg to the still-warm ingredients from Part One and mix thoroughly. Pour the batter into a 450g loaf tin lined with greaseproof paper and bake for about one hour at 170°C/gas 3. Test until a knitting needle or knife blade comes out clean.

The Corries 'A Man's A Man'

Aly Bain and Tom Anderson 'Come Agen Ye're Welcome/Da Corbie An' Da Craw'

Cranachan

VG GF

Some people mush the oats in the cream, but this cold, gloopy texture doesn't do it for me. Toasting the oats adds a lovely taste, but even better is using the oats to make granola – its crunch puts cranachan back into the top league.

Ingredients

100g oats
75g seeds and nuts
1 tbsp coconut oil or coconut cream (or butter)
pinch of sea salt
2 tbsp honey
250g fresh berries (raspberries or blackberries; frozen work too)
300 ml double cream (Greek yoghurt works here too)
3 tbsp whisky

Method

1. Preheat oven to 150°C/gas 2.
2. Mix the oats, seeds and nuts, coconut oil or coconut cream, salt and a heaped tablespoon of honey in a bowl, then spread thinly on a sheet of grease-proof paper or foil in a roasting tray.
3. Roast for 10 minutes until golden brown.

Whisky Cream
Whip up the cream, then add the whisky and 2 tablespoons of honey.

To serve
Serve the cream, the roasted oat mix (granola) and berries whichever way you fancy: layered in pots (do this just before serving so that the granola retains its crunch) or, as was traditional, in separate heaps on a plate for people to build their own. Any leftover granola is good for breakfast and will keep for up to two weeks.

Ayrshire Shortbread

VG

New Cumnock delivers us another recipe. This time from Papa John Cunningham, Jean's dad and John's grandfather, a baker by trade. The secrets to light Scottish shortbread are here revealed.

Ingredients

225g butter
85g icing sugar
200g plain flour
85g cornflour
1 level tsp baking powder

Method

1. Preheat the oven to 180°C/gas 4.
2. Cream butter and sugar, then mix in the remaining ingredients.
3. Roll out to about 5mm thickness and cut into whatever shape you like with a pastry cutter. Prick each one 4 or 5 times with the tines of a fork.
4. Put on a baking tray and bake until golden brown, roughly 5–10 minutes.
5. Remove from the oven and sprinkle with caster sugar once cooled.

The Rose In The Heather / Does This Train Go To Bellshill / Trip To Kilkenny

Trevor Morrison 'Hirta' Eddi Reader 'Ae Fond Kiss'

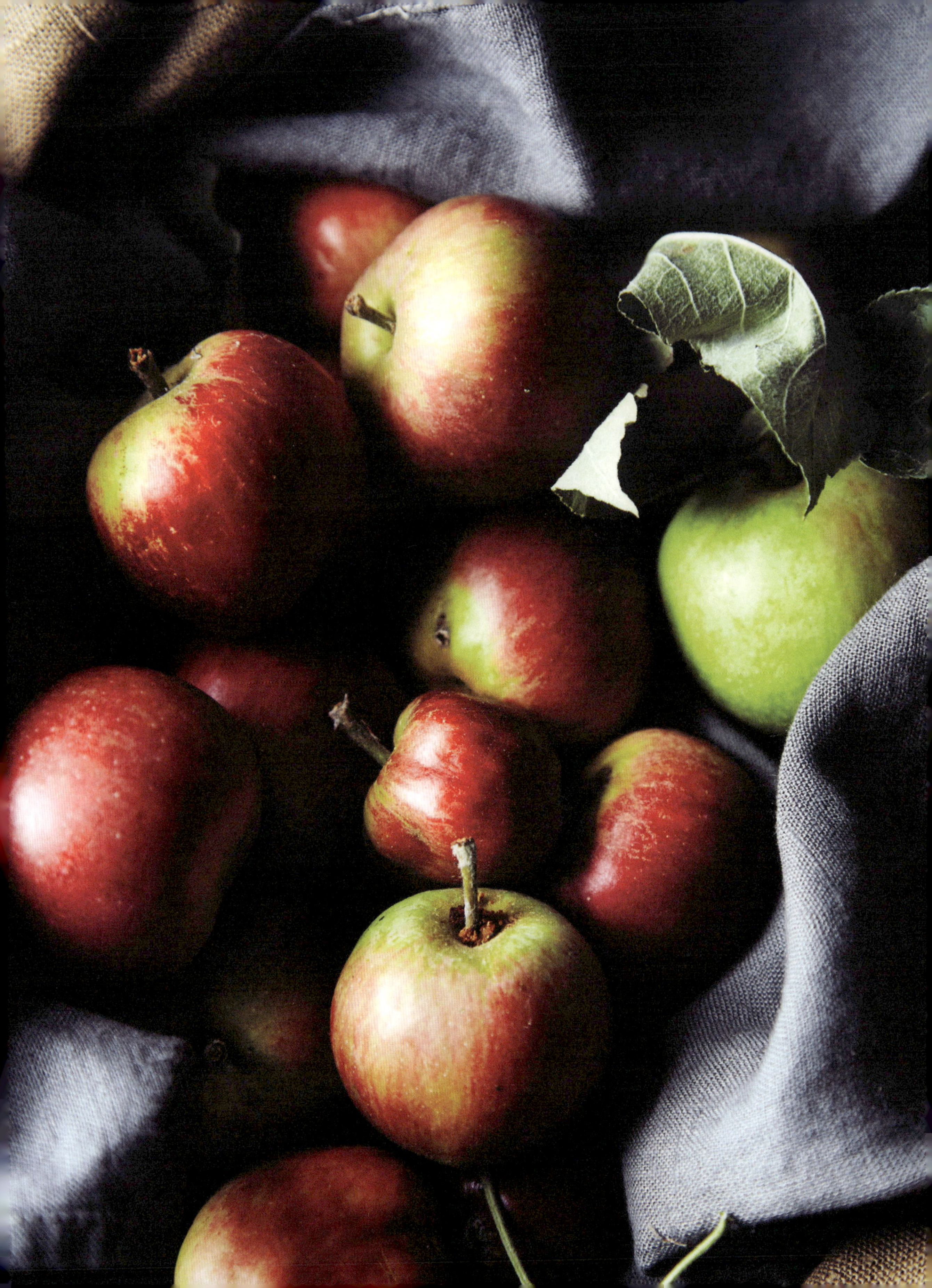

ENGLAND

'All Nature Has a Feeling'

All nature has a feeling: woods, fields, brooks
Are life eternal: and in silence they
Speak happiness beyond the reach of books;
There's nothing mortal in them; their decay
Is the green life of change; to pass away
And come again in blooms revivified.
Its birth was heaven, eternal is its stay,
And with the sun and moon shall still abide
Beneath their day and night and heaven wide.

'Autumn'

The thistledown's flying, though the winds are all still,
On the green grass now lying, now mounting the hill,
The spring from the fountain now boils like a pot;
Through stones past the counting it bubbles red-hot.

The ground parched and cracked is like overbaked bread,
The greensward all wracked is, bents dried up and dead.
The fallow fields glitter like water indeed,
And gossamers twitter, flung from weed unto weed.

Hill-tops like hot iron glitter bright in the sun,
And the rivers we're eying burn to gold as they run;
Burning hot is the ground, liquid gold is the air;
Whoever looks round sees Eternity there.

JOHN CLARE (1793–1864)
The son of two illiterate parents born in Peterborough, Clare worked as a manual labourer but found time to write and publish several volumes of poetry. In later life he suffered delusions and he spent the last twenty years of his life in an asylum. You can still visit his cottage in Cambridgeshire.

ENGLAND

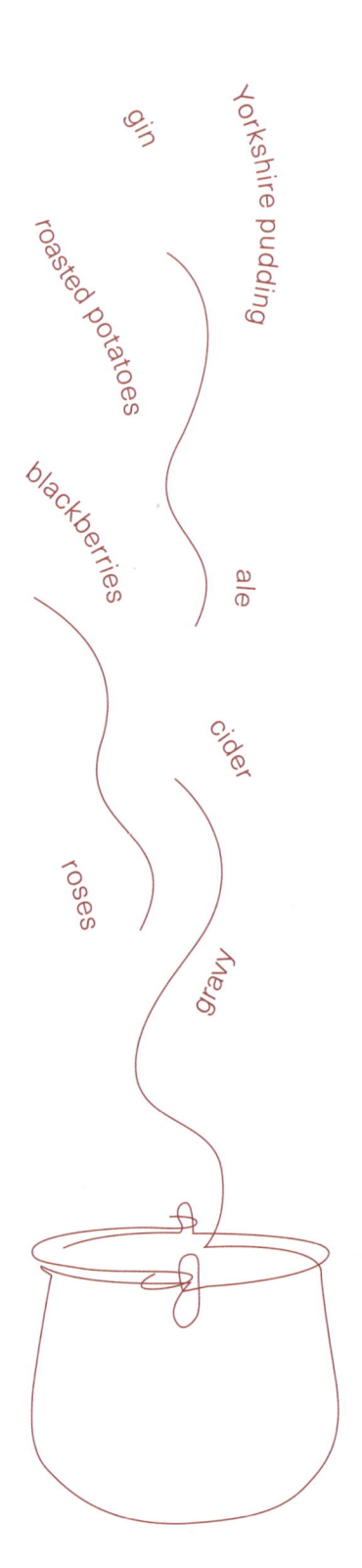

gin — Yorkshire pudding — roasted potatoes — blackberries — ale — cider — roses — gravy

England was introduced to garlic, onions, leeks, cabbages, peas, celery, turnips, radishes, asparagus, rosemary, thyme, bay, basil, walnuts, sweet chestnuts, cultivated apples (rather than crab apples), grapes, **MULBERRIES AND CHERRIES** by the Romans. Which makes you wonder what we ate before they arrived.

JUNIPER BERRIES are used to make gin, but are not berries but rather modified female seed cones.

The invention of gin is often credited to Dutch physician Franz de le Boë in the mid seventeenth century, (though the earliest reference to 'jenever' appears in the 13th century).

To classify as a gin, juniper should be the first flavour you taste.

Gin drinking became really popular in England between 1695 and 1735 – a period known as the gin craze.

Gin was distilled legally in residential houses in the early eighteenth century – sometimes flavoured with turpentine as well as juniper.

The word **'tanked'** as in drunk, comes from the 'tankards' that were used to drink ale.

We used to eat on square plates. Hence **'square meal'**. And we didn't wash them, just turned them over for the cheese course.

A **SUBTLE ENGLISH SOUP** made by a fourteenth-century royal chef included: chestnuts, egg yolks in wine, ground pork liver, ginger, cloves and saffron.

'Mind your ps and qs' comes from **PINTS AND QUARTS,** pub ale measurements.

ST GEORGE (c.256–303 CE)

wasn't the first patron saint of England. That was St Edmund, who died fighting the Vikings in 870. His head was famously found in the depths of a forest (where the Vikings had thrown it) because a wolf drew attention to it by crying out *'Hic, hic, hic'* ('Here, here, here' in Latin).

St George wasn't English, he was a high-ranking officer, of Greek descent, in the Roman army, who was tortured to death for refusing to recant his Christian faith.

He didn't slay a dragon.

He most likely never even visited England.

We have the Crusaders to thank for the association with St George: they loved him, and used his name to bring luck with their missions.

Edward III made him patron saint in 1350 and used the red cross on white associated with George for his Royal Standard.

It is his cross that forms the national flag of England, and part of the Union Jack.

St George is also the patron saint of Genoa, Georgia, Malta and Gozo, Portugal, Romania, Aragon and Catalonia. He is venerated by Jews and Muslims – a popular guy – although some in England feel they would like Edmund back.

The rose was adopted as an emblem during the Wars of the Roses (1455–1485) between the royal houses of Lancaster (red rose) and York (white). The Tudor Rose symbolically unites England by using both colours.

In medieval times there were 'Fastes' on Fridays, Saturdays and sometimes Wednesdays: this meant no meat, and during Lent, no butter, eggs or other dairy.

According to Victorian journalist and author Margaret Dods, 'The French take the lead of all European people in **SOUPS AND BROTHS...** the Scotch rank second, the Welsh next, and ... the English, as a nation, are at the very bottom of the scale.'

The name 'sandwich' first appeared in the late 1700s when a French writer wrote about John Montagu, the Earl of Sandwich, eating meat between slices of toasted bread as he didn't want to have to leave the **gambling table** to eat. The name stuck.

England has fish and chips, pasties, pies, pigs in blankets, Guernsey bean jars, eggy bread, Eton mess, toad in the hole, singing hinnies (northern flat cakes named for the sizzling sound as they cook), ploughman's lunch, pickled onions, spotted dick, jellied eels and liquor, bubble and squeak, devils on horseback and tikka masala. And Sunday lunch (meat or no meat), as long as it comes with that quintessential English side, Yorkshire pudding. A friend from Sheffield taught me to cook it in one pan. Bangers and mash? Another great dish.

I first came to London aged sixteen. We fed the pigeons in Trafalgar Square and stared at Big Ben. I remember it being grey and smelling of dust and traffic; I didn't fall for its charms until later. Now I call it home, and love being a small fish in a big pond, one of thousands like me who, to quote Dylan Thomas, got off the bus and never got on again. My neighbourhood is a cultural wonderland – walk up its streets and eat Spanish, Swedish, French, Thai, Mexican, American, Ethiopian, Chinese, Japanese, Moroccan, Portuguese, Turkish – and English.

One of life's great pleasures is scrumping, and there are still opportunities for the wild eater even in central London. Keep an eye open for cherry and apple trees, grape leaves, nettles, young dandelion leaves in the park, hazelnuts, bay leaves for spicing stews, rosemary, lime/linden leaves and elderflower trees.

2017 was a year of abundance for berries. A cherry tree near my house was heavy with fruit: I put the local children on my shoulders and we grabbed as many as we could. One passer-by asked, 'Aren't they poison?' I replied, 'They're cherries!' And then they told me they'd rather buy them in Tesco.

I was given Roger Phillips's *Wild Food* as a ten-year-old in eighties Britain, immediately loving the idea of knowing what was edible in the world around me. Nettle soup is delicious, costs nothing and is simple to make. I first used the recipe in Roger's book and offer my own version in this chapter. There's wild garlic too come early spring (good to use in pesto and flat breads), rosehips for making tea, and you can use rose petals for garnish, fresh or crystallized. All sorts of flowers can be eaten or presented with food for decoration: daisies, chrysanthemums, sunflowers, courgettes/marrows and clover are just some. Hawthorn berries can be nibbled, spitting out the seeds, and outside the big cities are field mushrooms to look out for after the rain – gather quick before they ruin. Delicious with salted butter on toasted homemade bread. (Stating the obvious here, double check you've got the right species of mushroom before eating.) You can also collect sticky grass, aka sticky willy/goose grass/cleaver, to eat, wilting it in some butter or oil like you do with spinach. Pick the young leaves and stems before they fruit.

It was Sunday lunch and a pint of ale that I missed the most when living abroad. Brunch is not the same. Eggs Benedict doesn't cut the mustard like roast potatoes, especially for a hangover: a plate of potatoes and a pint of ale and you're centred again.

It's a nostalgic menu I propose here, much of it inspired by this scrumping in and around England. I'm not roasting potatoes in duck or goose fat, but you can. The mighty potato! I have a painting of potatoes in my house. What would life be without them? I'm also including a gin idea here, for a little dose of the clear stuff, another product inextricably entwined with England, although it may actually have been invented by the Dutch.

*'The strawberry grows underneath the nettle,
And wholesome berries thrive and ripen best
Neighbour'd by fruit of baser quality.'*

SHAKESPEARE, *HENRY V,* **ACT 1, SCENE 1**

ENGLAND

'I cannot stand people who do not take food seriously.'

OSCAR WILDE

'One cannot think well, sleep well, love well, if one has not dined well.'

VIRGINIA WOOLF,
A ROOM OF ONE'S OWN

> 'You never know what's more than enough until you know what's enough.'
>
> **WILLIAM BLAKE**

> 'The art of cooking as practised by Englishmen does not extend much beyond roast beef and plum pudding.'
>
> **PEHR KALM, FINNISH BOTANIST,** *KALM'S ACCOUNT OF HIS VISIT TO ENGLAND ON HIS WAY TO AMERICA IN 1748*

Food-related rhyming slang

Rub a dub – pub
Ruby Murray – curry (or just … ruby)
Syrup of figs – wig
Vera Lynn – gin
Rosie Lee – tea
Plates (of meat) – feet
Mince pies – eyes
Butchers (hook) – look
Bubble and squeak – Greek

ON THE MENU

EVERYDAY VEGAN BREAKFASTS (SUMMER AND WINTER)

NETTLE SOUP

NUT ROAST

VEGAN MUSHROOM GRAVY

YORKSHIRE PUDDING AND PANCAKES

GREEN LENTIL SHEPHERD'S PIE

STORE-CUPBOARD SOUP WITH DUMPLINGS

DESSERT

BAKED APPLES

DRINK

SLOE GIN

FURTHER LIQUOR EXPERIMENTS

Everyday Vegan Breakfasts

Smoothies

Buy packets of frozen fruit, e.g. mangoes, raspberries, blackberries. Liquidize a packet with enough water or fresh fruit juices to make the constituency you prefer, adding a scoop (about 50g) of pea or chickpea flour for added protein and sustenance. You can add a whole fresh banana, 2 teaspoons of chia seeds, 1 teaspoon of cocoa nibs (they can be bitty – some like them and some don't).

Super Bowls

Adding oats to smoothies is a revelation, giving you endless great vegan breakfast options: for these super bowls, to 250g frozen fruit add 3 handfuls of oats (about 60g) and enough coconut or almond milk to give a good consistency (about 200 ml) and blend. Then serve with your choice of fresh or dried fruit, whole nuts and seeds, e.g. fresh mango slices, pineapple, pomegranate seeds, blueberries and raspberries, almonds, cashews, pistachios, walnuts, pine nuts, chia, sunflower, pumpkin, sesame seeds (all pre-toasted if you want) cocoa nibs, desiccated or fresh coconut, kiwi fruit, goji berries, dates, dried cranberries, honey or agave syrup …

Winter

Porridge cooked with water served with a choice from the above nuts, seeds and fruit. (Any leftover porridge can be used to make homemade bread).

Nettle Soup

VG **GF**

Use rubber gloves and scissors to pick and prepare the nettles. Once the nettles are cooked, they'll no longer sting. 400g of nettle leaves is about ¾ of a full carrier bag.

Ingredients

1 onion, peeled and diced

25g butter

olive oil

salt and pepper

1 large potato or 2 medium potatoes, peeled and diced

1L vegetable stock (or water with organic stock cube)

400g nettle leaves, ideally the youngest, smallest leaves you can find, washed

75ml double cream

Method

1. Sauté the onion along with the butter, a dash of oil and a good pinch of salt in a large saucepan over a medium heat until soft, about 10 minutes.

2. Add the potatoes and stir around in the butter. Pour in the stock and bring to a simmer. Simmer for 15–20 minutes (this will depend on how small you've chopped your potatoes) or until the potatoes are completely soft and starting to collapse.

3. Add the nettles and a pinch of salt and cook for a further minute, or until the leaves have wilted. Remove from the heat, pour in the cream and blitz until smooth with a stick blender or in a blender.

4. Taste and adjust the seasoning as necessary. Reheat gently before serving.

Vegan:
Use olive oil in place of butter, adding 2 stalks of celery and a clove of garlic, all finely chopped, to the onions. Leave out the double cream and add some vegan cream or yoghurt as desired.

Ian Dury 'Apples'

Sian Phillips 'When Most I Wink Then Do Mine Eyes Best See' (Shakespeare's Sonnet 43)

Nut Roast

(V) (VG)

Ingredients

- 1 tbsp vegetable oil, plus extra for greasing
- 25g butter (or oil if vegan)
- 2 large onions, diced
- 120g mushrooms, diced
- 4 sprigs thyme, leaves only
- 2 tbsp chopped sage leaves, 2 whole for garnish (if you have some)
- 1 tbsp plain flour
- 150ml apple juice, cider or white wine
- 75g cooked chestnuts, roughly chopped
- 120g fresh breadcrumbs
- 120g hazelnuts, roughly chopped
- 1 egg, beaten (leave out if vegan)
- salt and pepper

Method

1. Preheat the oven to 180°C/ gas 4. Grease a medium ovenproof dish, loaf tin or roasting tin.

2. Fry the onions in the butter and oil along with a good pinch of salt for 10 minutes, or until softened completely, in a large frying pan over a medium heat.

3. Add the mushrooms, thyme and chopped sage and continue to cook for 4–5 minutes, or until they're also soft.

4. Sprinkle in the flour and stir to mix through. Cook for 30 seconds, then slowly pour in the apple juice, stirring as you pour (if using cider or white wine, allow to bubble for a couple of minutes). Once mixed well, remove from the heat, stir in the chestnuts, breadcrumbs and hazelnuts (or whatever nuts you want to use) and leave to cool until just warm.

5. Once the mixture has cooled, add the beaten egg (if using), season well and mix, making sure everything is evenly distributed.

6. Tip into the greased tin/dish and lay the whole sage on top for decoration. Bake in the oven for 40–45 minutes, or until firm to the touch. If at any point the nut roast looks like it is browning too quickly, cover with foil.

7. Serve with all the usual roast trimmings.

Option:
If you have any leftover sage leaves, fry in butter or oil until crisp.

Nick Drake 'Saturday Sun'

Max Richter 'Three Worlds', voice of Virginia Woolf from *Words:* Mrs Dalloway

Vegan Mushroom Gravy

(V) (VG)

If you can't get hold of dried shiitake mushrooms, any dried mushrooms will do. But they do need to be dried rather than fresh, so that you achieve a depth of flavour and umami richness. Once you've mastered the basics of this gravy, you can play around with the flavours. Try adding a teaspoon of wholegrain mustard or redcurrant jelly, changing the herbs used or adding a little horseradish for a bit of a kick.

Ingredients

750ml vegetarian dashi or vegetable stock (or a mix of stock and wine)

6–8 medium dried shiitake mushrooms (about 25g)

1 tbsp olive oil (or 25g butter if vegetarian)

1 medium onion or 2–3 shallots, very finely diced

salt and pepper

1½ tbsp plain flour

1–2 tbsp soy sauce

1 tsp Dijon mustard

½ tsp Marmite (optional)

1 tsp finely chopped thyme or tarragon leaves (optional)

Method

1. Heat the stock until steaming, then remove from the heat and add the mushrooms. Leave to one side while you get on with the rest of the recipe.

2. Heat a medium saucepan over a medium heat. Add the oil, then stir in the onion along with a pinch of salt and cook until very soft (about 10 minutes).

3. Sprinkle the flour into the pan and stir around for a minute or two. Pour in a little of the stock through a sieve, stir to mix. Continue adding the stock, bit by bit, until it is all incorporated. Strain the mushrooms.

4. Add the mushrooms, soy sauce, the mustard, Marmite and herbs, if using, and stir well. Bring to a gentle simmer, then keep simmering until thickened to your liking.

5. Taste and adjust the seasoning as necessary. You may need an extra tablespoon of soy sauce, especially if you haven't used the Marmite suggested.

6. Serve warm.

The Kinks 'Village Green'

David Bowie 'Uncle Arthur'

Yorkshire Pudding and Pancakes

VG

This can also be used as a pancake batter. If you've time, chill the mix in the fridge before you use it. It can be left overnight.

Ingredients

150g plain flour
4 eggs
pinch of salt
200ml milk
vegetable oil (for greasing)

Method

1. Preheat the oven to a very high temperature (250°C/gas 9)
2. Whisk the ingredients in a bowl.
3. Generously grease a flat roasting pan or muffin tin with vegetable oil, to about 1–2 mm, and put in oven until piping hot.
4. Take the tin out of the oven, pour in the mixture, and put straight back into the oven.
5. Turn down to 220°C/gas 7 and roast (trying not to open the door) for 15–20 minutes, until puffed up and golden.

Tip for Sunday roasts:
If you are roasting a whole chicken, or other birds, spatchcock by cutting open along the back (not breast side), and then squashing it so hard it lies flat.

Roast in a tin until the juices run clear (about 45 minutes, smaller birds will take a lot less) with options like whole cloves of garlic, rosemary, potatoes and other root veg. The resulting meat is really moist, it reduces roasting time, it'll fit in a smaller oven, and there's less washing up.

George Formby 'Andy The Handyman'

Kathryn Tickell 'Walking To Dances (Northumbrian Voices)'

Green Lentil Shepherd's Pie

(V) (VG)

Ingredients

200g green lentils

900ml water

600g potatoes (about 5–6 potatoes) diced

25g butter (or vegetable stock if vegan)

a splash of milk (optional)

sea salt and freshly ground black pepper

a splash of vegetable oil

1 large onion, finely chopped

2 cloves of garlic, finely chopped

2 large carrots, chopped

100g mushrooms, chopped

1 vegetable stock cube

½ tsp of thyme

a squirt of tomato purée

1 tsp soy sauce

1 tsp Marmite

1. Preheat the oven to 180°C/ gas 4.
2. Put the lentils into a saucepan with 900ml of water to cover them, bring to the boil, then reduce the heat to a simmer and cook until soft (around 45 minutes, depending on the lentils you are using). Turn off the heat and keep the cooking water when done.
3. Put the potatoes into another saucepan, simmer until cooked (approx. 15 minutes).
4. Pour off most of the potato cooking water (keep this water) and mash the potatoes. Add butter and milk (or olive oil if vegan), season to taste and set aside.
5. In a large casserole, fry the onion and garlic in oil with a pinch of salt on a medium heat for 10 minutes, until softened and beginning to brown.
6. Add the carrots and mushrooms and fry for a few minutes.
7. Add the cooked lentils plus the stock cube, thyme, tomato purée, soy sauce and Marmite. Adding some of the potato cooking water if the lentil mix is getting too dry, simmer for 5 minutes.
8. Taste and season accordingly. I love a lot of freshly ground black pepper. Add water or reduce to get a good consistency. It should not be too watery.
9. Spoon the mash on top of the lentils and bake in the oven for 30 minutes.

Vera Lynn 'We'll Meet Again'

Anne Shelton 'A Nightingale Sang In Berkeley Square'

Store-cupboard Soup with Dumplings

VG

Soup

Ingredients

1 onion, chopped
2 tbsp olive oil
2 cloves of garlic, grated
250g red lentils
1 bay leaf
salt and pepper
1.2 litres vegetable stock, or boiling water and 2 stock cubes
1 x 400g tin of tomatoes

Method

1. In a large pan fry the onion in the oil for 5–7 minutes, until coloured.
2. Add the garlic and fry for another 1–2 minutes.
3. Add the lentils and stir around in the oil, then add the bay leaf and a good grinding of black pepper. Add the stock, bring to the boil, then turn down the heat, put a lid on the pan and simmer for 20 minutes until the lentils are soft.
4. Add tomatoes, season, stir well, and keep simmering on low while you make the dumplings.

Dumplings

(Ratio of suet 1:2 flour)

Ingredients

60g vegetarian suet
120g self-raising flour
1 egg, beaten
40–50ml milk
pinch of salt

Method

1. Mix the ingredients in a bowl, adding nearly all the milk – you're not looking for a stiff dough but a gloopy mess, so if you need to, add the rest of the milk.
2. Turn up the heat a little so the soup is quietly bubbling, then scoop a tablespoon of the mix into the soup and repeat.
3. Put on a lid and leave for 6 minutes, then take the lid off and turn over the dumplings – they should be fluffed right up like clouds. Put the lid back on, turn down the heat if it's looking like the soup is sticking, and cook for another 6–7 minutes.
4. Serve the soup and dumplings with handful of fresh parsley leaves, chopped, and (optional) add a dollop of yoghurt/cream/grated cheese.

Red Soup
Add any red vegetables you have to the above store-cupboard base, e.g. chopped carrots, red pepper, fresh tomatoes, sweet potatoes. Simmer until soft, then blend and season well before serving.

Green Soup
Use the same base of oil, onion, garlic and stock, but omit the lentils and tomatoes, and instead use any chopped green veg, including salads: lettuce, celery, courgette, cucumber, cabbage, spinach, spring onions, chard, kale etc. with an option to add a handful of breadcrumbs and/or potatoes to make it heartier; you can also try adding a pinch of caraway seeds. Simmer until soft and blend, season well, then serve.

'The History Of Timon Of Athens, The Man Hater', Purcell, by Wolfgang Katschner

Baked Apples

VG GF

Ingredients

50g mixed dried fruit (e.g. chopped dates and dried apricots, also raisins, currants, sultanas)

3 tbsp brandy (optional)

30g chopped nuts and seeds in any combination or just one kind, e.g. walnuts, pecans, almonds, hazelnuts, peanuts, pumpkin seeds

4 whole apples, any variety, eating or cooking, e.g. Granny Smith, Braeburn, Pink Lady

grated nutmeg or ground cinnamon

2 tbsp honey or soft brown sugar

1 tbsp lemon juice/zest of lemon (optional)

50g melted butter (use oil if vegan)

Method

1. Soak the fruit in brandy in a bowl for as long as you have, even overnight. (Miss this step if not using alcohol.)

2. Preheat the oven 180°C/gas 4.

3. Toast the nuts in a thick iron pan for a few minutes (they will release an aroma and start to turn golden).

4. Use a corer or a knife and teaspoon to remove the apple core and pips, keeping the bottom of each apple intact. Once cored, if they don't stand up straight in a roasting pan, cut a sliver off their bottom.

5. To the bowl with dried fruit, add your spice of choice, the honey, the nuts (keep a handful for garnish), the lemon juice and/or zest if using.

6. Stuff the mix into the hole at the centre of each apple.

7. Pour melted butter into these holes, dribbling it over the apples.

8. Bake until soft: a small to medium apple will take around 30 minutes (up to 45 minutes for larger and cooking apples).

9. Serve on plates, spooning over the juices from the pan, with the rest of the chopped toasted nuts, and some yoghurt, cream or ice cream.

John Renbourn 'The Trees They Do Grow High'

Fairport Convention 'Matty Groves'

Sloe Gin

(V) (VG) (GF) (DF)

I had the pleasure of joining Sheila Dillon and wild barman Andy Hamilton on BBC Radio 4's *The Food Programme* recently. We walked around the fields of our campsite near Monmouth picking herbs and plants to infuse in various spirits. If you do the same, follow the Country Code or plant your own blackthorn tree. You're making your own brand of liquor. My mother did the same when we were little. Here is her sloe gin recipe.

Ingredients

Approx. 450–500g ripe sloes (this fills about a third of a litre bottle), picked just after the first frosts, i.e. any time when they are ripe – that is, not rock hard. They grow on the blackthorn, common on the coast of Pembrokeshire.

1 litre gin

200g caster sugar (you can use less or more, depending on how sweet you want the final drink)

Method

1. Wash the sloes, then dry them and prick each one with a clean needle.
2. Put the sloes, gin and sugar into a large sterilized jar, such as a Kilner. Seal tightly and leave in a dark place.
3. Shake as you pass by for the first week (every other day or so), then every week thereafter.
4. It'll be ready in about 2 months.
5. You can strain the sloe gin through a muslin and decant into a smaller sterilized bottle – it keeps for years and apparently gets better as it ages. Ours never lasted that long.

Further Liquor Experiments

My favourite addition is pine needles. What is gin made from, after all? It already has a pine base, so adding more works very well, giving it a wonderful wintry taste.

You can try any other fruit or vegetable, e.g. blackberries, plums, zest of lemon or lime, celery, cucumber.

Also try spices like peppercorns, chillies, ginger, lemongrass, thyme. A sprig or two of roasted rosemary is delicious added to a bottle of gin and left to infuse. You can also try using vodka, brandy, rum or tequila the same way.

Note:

You can freeze sloes, then you don't have to pick them before using to make sloe gin.

Alan Haven Theme from *A Jolly Bad Fellow*

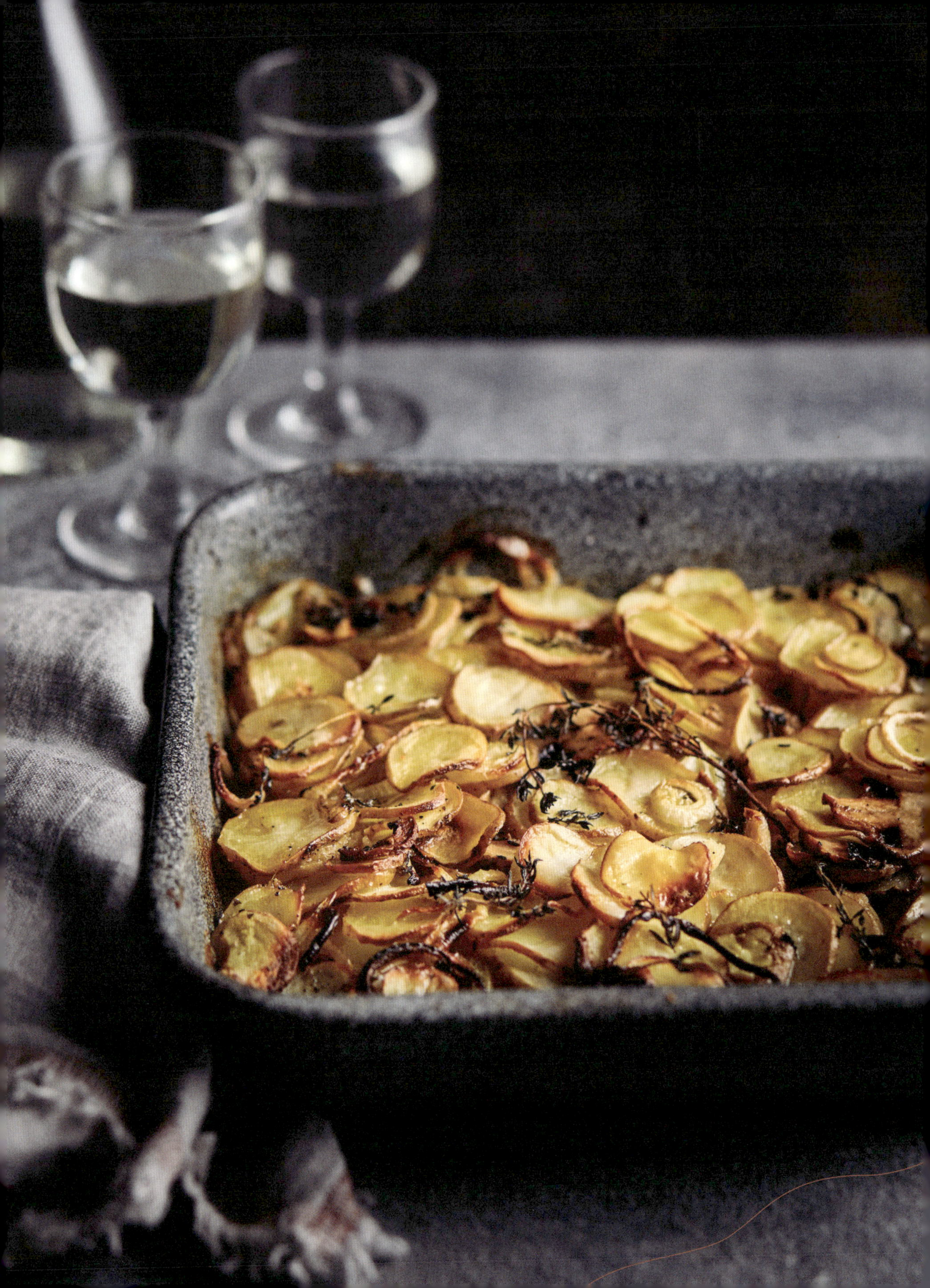

FRANCE

I

We aren't serious when we're seventeen.
–One fine evening, to hell with beer and lemonade,
Noisy cafés with their shining lamps!
We walk under the green linden trees of the park

The lindens smell good in the good June evenings!
At times the air is so scented that we close our eyes.
The wind laden with sounds–the town isn't far–
Has the smell of grapevines and beer . . .

'Novel' *by Arthur Rimbaud (Translated by Wallace Fowlie)*

I

On n'est pas sérieux, quand on a dix-sept ans.
–Un beau soir, foin des brocks et de la lemonade
Des café tapaguers aux lustres éclaitant!
–On va sous les telleuils verts de la promenade.

Les telleuils sentent bon dans les bon soir de juin!
L'air est parfois si doux, qu'on ferme les paupière
Le vent chargé de bruits–la ville n'est pas loin–
A des parfum des vigne et des parfum des bières . . .

Green

Here are some fruits, flowers, leaves and branches
And then here is my heart which only beats for you
Don't tear them with your two pale hands,
I hope my humble gifts seem sweet to your beautiful eyes.

I arrive still covered in dew,
which the morning wind froze to my face
Let my weariness rest at your feet,
Dream of dear moments and relax.

Let my head rest on your young chest
Still singing from your last kisses;
Let the great storm blow over
So that I may sleep a little while you rest.

From 'Romances sans paroles' *by Paul Verlaine*
Published in 1874 and written when he was
travelling with Arthur Rimbaud.

Voici des fruits, des fleurs, des feuilles et des branches
Et puis voici mon coeur qui ne bat que pour vous.
Ne le déchirez pas avec vos deux mains blanches
Et qu'à vos yeux si beaux l'humble présent soit doux.

J'arrive tout couvert encore de rosée
Que le vent du matin vient glacer à mon front.
Souffrez que ma fatigue à vos pieds reposée
Rêve des chers instants qui la délasseront.

Sur votre jeune sein laissez rouler ma tête
Toute sonore encore de vos derniers baisers;
Laissez-la s'apaiser de la bonne tempête,
Et que je dorme un peu puisque vous reposez.

The love bridge in Paris covered with padlocks, the Jewish/gay quarter, Le Marais, the bookshops, Sacré-Coeur, picnics by the Seine. Perhaps only Venice rivals Paris for romance. So two poems this time, from the notorious poet lovers, **PAUL VERLAINE**, an absinthe drinker and alcoholic (1844–1896) and wild, libertine **ARTHUR RIMBAUD** (1854–1891) who was just sixteen when he was summoned to Paris by the older Verlaine: 'Come dear, great soul, we call you, we await you.'

JOAN OF ARC (1412–1431)

was born into a peasant family and was illiterate; she believed God had chosen her to lead France to victory against the English during the Hundred Years War. Her vision came true: she led the troops that freed the besieged town of Orleans in 1429, reportedly wearing white armour and riding a white horse. That Jeanne d'Arc achieved this just nine days after her arrival, following months of siege by the English, was perceived to be miraculous, and a huge strategic and morale boost for the French.

Not so many months later, however, the Maid of Orleans was captured by her enemies – the Anglo-Burgundian forces – and tried for witchcraft, heresy and dressing as a man and was burned at the stake in 1431 aged just nineteen. King Charles, whom she'd helped immeasurably, did nothing to negotiate her release. Joan was canonized in 1920.

The **Croissant** possibly originated in the form of the Austrian *kipferl.*

The **COCKEREL** is the national animal, which originally came about to make fun of the Celtic French, known as Gauls, as *gallus* means cockerel in Latin.

The **Eiffel Tower** was built to commemorate the centenary of the storming of the Bastille, the turning point of the French Revolution, on 14 July 1789.

Visit **Honfleur** on Bastille Day to see people running along the cannons at the marina, to see how far they can get before falling off.

A story goes that **FRENCH FRIES** were invented in Belgium, when small fish were difficult to find; they fried potatoes shaped like fish, and ended up inventing the chip.

THE FIVE 'MOTHER SAUCES'

are the godheads of French cuisine and many a professional kitchen today. Codified in 1903 by the 'king of chefs and chef of kings', chef and culinary writer Auguste Escoffier, they are refined from an earlier list by **Marie-Antione Carême**, b.1784:

BECHAMEL
Flour heated with butter or cooking fat and whisked with milk to make a thick white sauce.

VELOUTÉ
Flour heated with butter or cooking fat, whisked with stock (traditionally veal).

ESPAGNOLE
Browned roux (cooked longer) with beef, veal or chicken (brown) stock, tomato purée, browned *mirepoix* (this can be used when cooking boeuf bourguignon).

SAUCE TOMATE
Tomatoes cooked down to a thick sauce, to which roux can be added, classically flavoured with salt pork and *mirepoix*.

HOLLANDAISE
Emulsion of egg yolks, melted butter and lemon juice.

MIREPOIX
Mix of chopped vegetables like onions, carrots and celery, slowly cooked in fat so they don't brown or caramelize but sweeten, which then become a base for stews and, with added liquid, stock. In the same vein as Spain's *sofrito*, Italy's *soffritto*, Portugal's *refogado*, German's *Suppengrün* and the Polish *włoszczyzna*.

BOUQUET GARNI
A bundle of tied-up herbs for adding to stews and soups, e.g. thyme, bay leaf, parsley and sage.

PETIT FOURS
Small bite-sized sweets, literally, 'small oven', which, like Boulangère potatoes, were a way of not wasting the heat of the fire – bakers put them in to cook as the ovens cooled.

MISE EN PLACE
Getting ingredients chopped and kitchen prepped and ready for cooking.

National flower is the iris, as in the **Fleur-de-lis,** also the symbol of the French monarchy.

'Les haricots ne sont pas sales'
a phrase used when times are so hard, you can't afford the salted meat/salt to season your greens. Say 'Les haricots' fast and you get 'Zydeco' – that accordion-led music from Louisiana. Clifton Chenier is 'king of Zydeco.'

> *'The French like to say that their food stems from their culture and that it has developed over centuries ... We foreigners living in France respect and appreciate this point of view but deplore their too strict observance of a tradition which will not admit the slightest deviation in a seasoning or the suppression of a single ingredient.'*
>
> **ALICE B. TOKLAS**

France is just a hop, skip and a jump away, and the minute you get there you taste still-warm baguettes fresh from the ovens and view exquisite offerings in pâtisseries. How can two neighbouring nations have developed such different attitudes to food? Cross the Channel and for the most part you're likely to be able to find freshly cooked local food in bistros and restaurants. Compare this to the microwaved-from-frozen-identikit menus in pubs and food outlets that are often the prevailing choice outside the major cities of the UK. Living in Pembrokeshire I'd watch Arctic lorries drive up to our neighbouring fishing village, buy up all the lobsters and crab and drive back over the Channel to be cooked up by the French and Spanish. Things are changing, but I'm still fascinated by why our taste developed the way it did, and how the French retain their deep connection with food, drink, and the regions and land that produce it. Perhaps there are some answers in the very famous medieval recipe collection *Le Viandier*, begun as early as 1300 and added to as years went by. Much of *Le Viandier* is attributed to the master chef of the King of France, Guillaume Tirel, aka Taillevent, (c.1310–1395). It became the cornerstone of French gastronomic tradition. It offered a kind of medieval haute cuisine and was full of the spices used at the time in the palace kitchens, including some quite surprising ones, such as the wonderfully named 'Grains of Paradise' (a West African native plant from the ginger family).

How about these dishes offered for invalids: pullet mash, dew water, Flemish caudle, barley gruel, perch mash, capon white fish, fish cumin dish. More recipes included in *Le Viandier* were: bright green eel soup, lamprey in galantine, frumenty, subtlety of a swan re-clothed, fish jelly, herons, cranes, cormorants, spoonbills, chicken cumin dish, ragout of small birds, subtle English soup.

It's a million miles from my first memory of food in France, from the early eighties: 'Give them ravioli and tell them to shut up,' said my father, somewhere in a service station in France. We'd pack into a Peugeot estate, four siblings in the back seat, always starving. I've never eaten ravioli again. But there were magical times too. Lyons: dark, late, with winged creatures swarming around the lamplights over the black river. Still hungry, almost crying in the hope that a restaurant would still be open. Most kitchens said '*Non*.' Then one took pity on us. We were served a classic boeuf bourguignon, in a side room plush with burgundy velvet.

Alors, a table. Our French feast. A bottle of great French wine, preferably Bordeaux, a Margaux. Oh, and the music! Even the most mainstream French radio stations pump out a great mix of styles: jazz, blues, pop and world music. Try FIP radio, one of the best in the world.

FRANCE

'La moutarde lui monte au nez.'

(MUSTARD RISING TO THE NOSE, I.E. TO GET ANGRY)

'On ne fait pas d'omelette sans casser des oeufs.'

(YOU CAN'T MAKE AN OMELETTE WITHOUT BREAKING EGGS)

'Age is something that doesn't matter unless you're a cheese.'

FROM THE BOARD OF THE PORTOBELLO ROAD FRENCH CHEESE SHOP

FRANCE

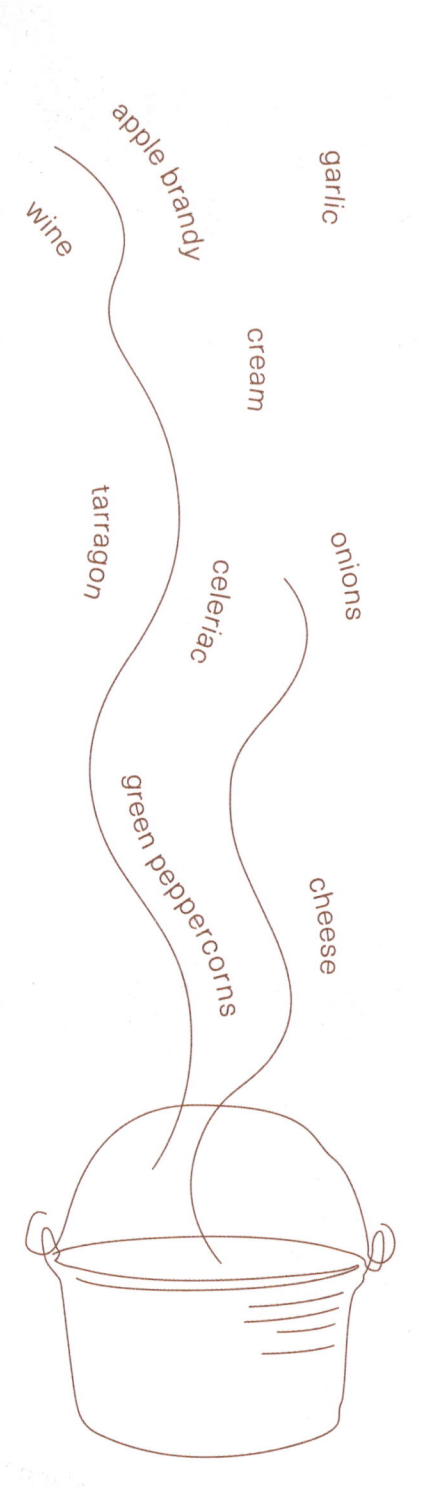

Ingredients swirling from pot: wine, apple brandy, garlic, cream, tarragon, celeriac, onions, green peppercorns, cheese

ON THE MENU

SAUTÉED SCALLOPS WITH LEMON

GREEN BEANS

EGGS EN COCOTTE

POTATOES DAUPHINOISE

POTATOES BOULANGÈRE (VEGAN)

CELERIAC MASH

DESSERT

POACHED PEARS

DRINK

HOT CHOCOLATE

Jacqueline Taïeb '7 Heures Du Matin'

Emily Loizeau 'Je Suis Jalouse'

Sautéed Scallops with Lemon

GF NV

Time it right, and you'll see carts of freshly landed coquilles Saint-Jacques plump with coral and white meat in fishing villages around Honfleur, Normandy. Eat them in a nearby restaurant, cooked simply with butter and herbs.

Ingredients

12 scallops, roes attached
flavourless oil, e.g. vegetable or sunflower
salt and pepper
50g butter
½ lemon
handful of fresh parsley leaves, roughly chopped

Method

1. Preheat a large heavy-based frying pan over a high heat. Pat the scallops dry on both sides with kitchen paper.

2. Once the pan is really hot, add a dash of oil, then add the scallops, keeping a note of what order they went into the pan. A good trick is to start at the 12 o'clock point of the pan and work around in a clockwise pattern. Season the scallops but do not touch them for 1½ minutes.

3. After 1½ minutes, turn the scallops, starting with the first scallop to enter the pan. Cook for a further 1½ minutes, adding the butter to the pan for the remaining 30 seconds, spooning the butter over the scallops as they cook.

4. Remove from the heat and squeeze over the lemon juice (watch out, the pan may spit a bit). Spoon the lemony butter over the scallops. Divide between warmed plates, spooning over the lemon butter. Sprinkle with parsley and serve immediately.

Serge Gainsbourg 'Aux Armes Et Cætera'

Zaz 'Paris Sera Toujours Paris'

Green Beans

VG GF

Top and tail about 250g of fresh green beans (de-string them if necessary). Blanch them in boiling water for 2 minutes, then drain and shake dry. In a frying pan, sauté the beans in unsalted butter, adding chopped fresh herbs like tarragon or chives, thyme or parsley, and season with salt and pepper.

Eggs en Cocotte

VG GF

This recipe works with pretty much anything you like. I love it with sautéed mushrooms at the bottom. But you can try it with smoked salmon, tarragon, chives, wilted spinach, sautéed tomatoes, grated courgettes, feta cheese – the list is endless. My ramekins have lids that keep the whites of the eggs soft; another option is to pour enough boiling water into the roasting tin so that it comes halfway up the ramekins. If you do this you may need to cook them for about 2 minutes longer.

Ingredients

butter, for greasing

handful of chopped mushrooms

small bunch of fresh tarragon, chopped

4 large eggs

salt and pepper

4 tbsp double cream

Method

1. Preheat the oven to 180°C/gas 4 and butter four ramekins generously.

2. Sauté the mushrooms for 2–4 minutes.

3. Place the ramekins in a small roasting tin. Put a tablespoon of mushrooms and a sprinkling of tarragon in the bottom of each one. Break an egg into each ramekin, season well with salt and pepper, then pour a tablespoon of cream over each egg.

4. Place in the preheated oven and bake for 10–12 minutes for runny yolks. For a more set yolk, cook for a couple of minutes longer. Serve immediately.

Thousand 'Le Nombre De La Bête'   Renaud 'Héloïse'

Django Reinhardt 'Minor Swing'

Juliette Gréco and Melody Gardot 'Sous Les Ponts De Paris'

Potatoes Dauphinoise

(VG) (GF)

Named after the Dauphiné region where it originated.

Ingredients

25–50g melted butter, for greasing and drizzling on top
600g potatoes, sliced
1 clove of garlic, finely chopped
salt and pepper
220ml milk (semi-skimmed or whole)
sprig of fresh rosemary (or thyme)

Method

1. Preheat the oven to 180°C/gas 4. Grease a small roasting tin with some of the butter.
2. Layer the sliced potatoes in the tin, sprinkling the garlic in between the layers, and season with salt and pepper.
3. Pour on the milk and lay the sprig of rosemary/thyme on top.
4. Place in the preheated oven. After 20 minutes, drizzle the remaining butter over the top layer of potatoes.
5. The potatoes are done when easy to pierce with a fork, after about an hour.

Option:
Add grated cheese or/and cream and sprinkle nutmeg between the layers of potato before putting into the oven.

Potatoes Boulangère (vegan)

(V) (VG) (GF) (DF)

'Baker's' potatoes, named for the bread ovens where they would be slow-cooked.

Ingredients

6 tbsp olive oil, for greasing and drizzling on top
600g potatoes, sliced
1 onion, sliced thinly
4–6 button mushrooms, sliced thinly
1 clove of garlic, finely chopped
salt and pepper
220ml vegetable stock (or water with a stock cube, dissolved)
sprig of fresh thyme

Method

1. Preheat the oven to 180°C/gas 4 and grease a small roasting tin with the oil.
2. Layer the sliced potatoes in the tin, onion and mushrooms, sprinkling the garlic in between the layers, and season with salt and pepper.
3. Pour on the stock and lay the sprig of thyme on top.
4. Roast in the preheated oven for 1 hour, or until the potatoes are soft when pierced with a fork. Cover with foil if the potatoes start to colour too much before they are cooked through.

Option:
Use 100g of sliced firm tofu (smoked or unsmoked) or 100g of crumbled silken tofu, and layer it under the potatoes and onions for added protein and creaminess.

Edith Piaf 'Non, Je Ne Regrette Rien'

France Gall 'Le Cœur Qui Jazze'

Celeriac Mash

(VG) (GF)

Ingredients

2 celeriac, peeled, roughly chopped, and put straight into cold water with the added juice of ½ a lemon to prevent discoloration

butter, to taste

salt and pepper

Method

1. Drain the chopped celeriac and put it into a saucepan. Cover with water and bring to the boil. Once boiling, turn the heat down to medium and cook until soft (just like potatoes).
2. Drain, then mash the celeriac, adding butter and seasoning to taste.

Options:
Add cream, add 1 tablespoon of mustard or boil with a chopped clove of garlic. You can also boil with a sprig of herbs like thyme or rosemary. For a celeriac and potato mash, exchange one celeriac for the same weight of potato and mash them up together.

Remoulade:
Grated raw celeriac with mayonnaise is delicious: to 1 peeled, grated celeriac, sprinkled with the juice of ½ a lemon, add 1 tablespoon of mustard, 5 tablespoons of mayonnaise, 1 tablespoon of crème fraîche and 1 tablespoon of chopped fresh parsley.

Hot Chocolate

(VG)

There's an anonymous quote that reminds me of drinking the large bowls of hot chocolate you get as a child for breakfast in France. It was like putting your head in the stuff: 'Forget love, I'd rather fall in chocolate.'

Ingredients

large bars of chocolate, milk, white and dark

1 pint of milk

honey or sugar (to taste)

shot of brandy or whisky (optional)

Method

1. Using a sharp knife or grater, shave chocolate bits from the bars in the ratio of your choice so you end up with a large handful of shavings.
2. Bring a pint of hot milk to almost boiling (or steam, if you have the appliance).
3. Pour the milk into a mug until two-thirds full. Sweeten it to your preference, then add a handful of chocolate shavings.
4. Serve with a teaspoon.

Option:
Add a shot of liquor such as whisky or brandy to the sweetened hot milk.

Brigitte Bardot 'Je Danse Donc Je Suis'

Jane Birkin 'Fuir Le Bonheur De Peur Qu'il Ne Se Sauve'

Poached Pears

(VG) (GF)

Such an easy dessert: basically you're making mulled wine and poaching pears in it. It fills the house with such a lovely festive perfume, and is worth doing even if you don't much like pears.

Ingredients

4 pears
1 bottle of red wine, Merlot, Cabernet, Rioja . . . (I know), i.e. 750ml (you can substitute a cup or two of water if you want to be a bit more thrifty)
50g honey or soft brown sugar
2 bay leaves
1 tsp vanilla extract (or 1 vanilla pod)
4 cloves
1 cinnamon stick (or a 5cm strip of cassia bark)
1 star anise (or nutmeg, if you don't have anise)
200g crème fraîche
100g toasted walnuts, chopped
fresh mint

Method

1. Peel the pears using a potato peeler, leaving the stalk and bottom intact.

2. Put the wine (and water, if using), honey, bay leaves and spices into a saucepan, add the pears and place on a low heat.

3. Turn the pears carefully from time to time so that all sides are covered and they take on the ruby red colour of the wine. The longer you cook them, the darker they become. If you're in a hurry, ripe pears can be eaten after 20 minutes, but it's best to cook them for longer.

4. Take out the pears and ramp up the heat to reduce the liquid until it becomes a syrup.

5. Slice off the bottom of each pear to make them level and stand them on a serving plate. Pour over the syrup, serve with crème fraîche, walnuts and sprig of mint.

MC Solaar 'La Belle Et Le Bad Boy'

Jean Ferret 'La Vipère Du Trottoir'

Charles Trenet 'La Mer'

Charlotte Gainsbourg et son sixtette 'Oxalis'

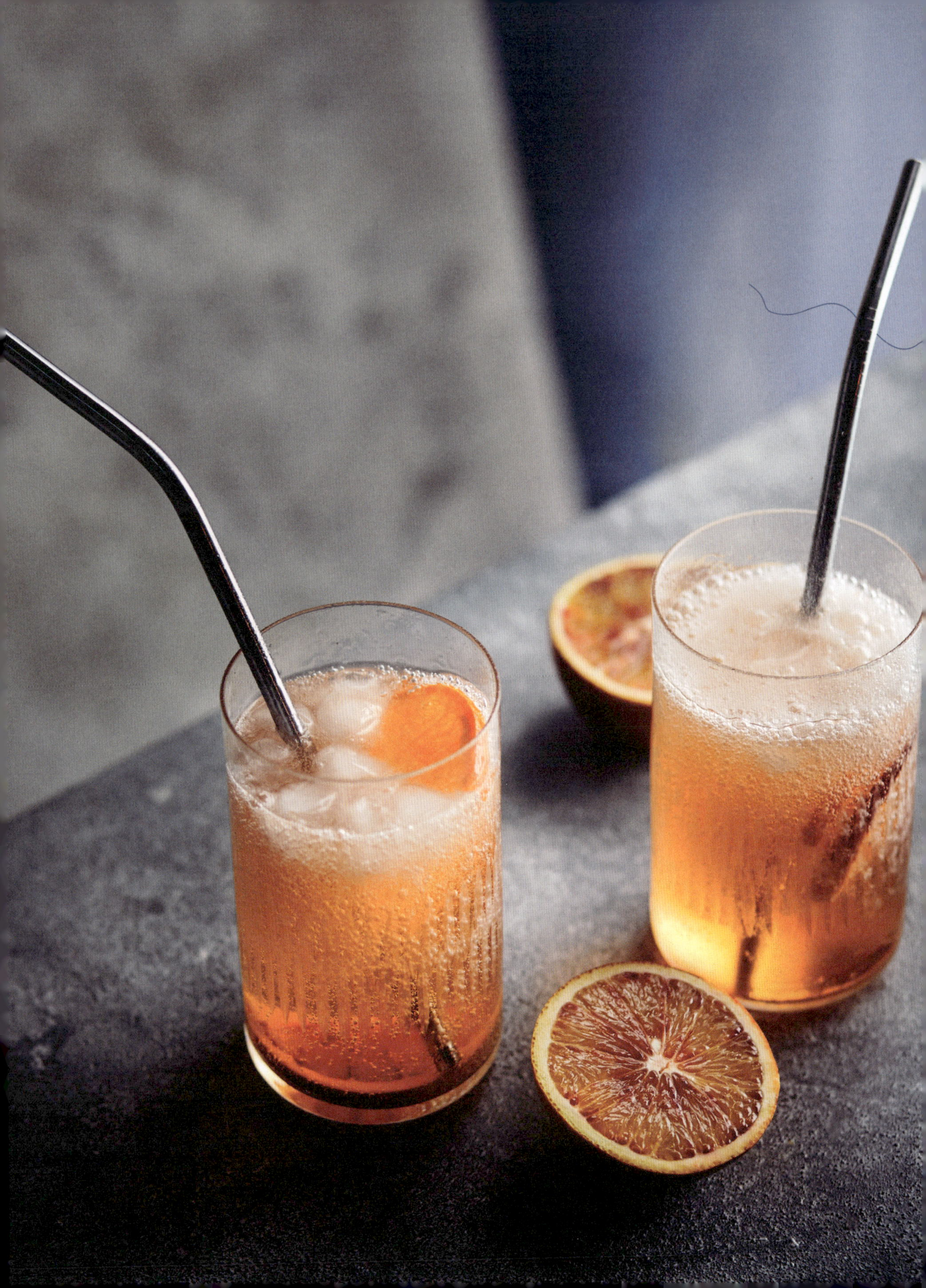

ITALY

from Celebration

So drink a whole gallon of wine, Maecenas,
celebrating your friend's escape, and we'll quench
the flickering lamps at dawn: keep far away
the noise and anger.

Leave the cares of state behind in the City:
Cotiso's Dacian army's been destroyed,
the dangerous Medes are fighting each other,
in grievous battle,

our old Cantabrian enemies are slaves,
subdued, in chains, at last, on the Spanish coast,
and now the Scythians, their bows unstrung, plan
to give up their plains.

A private citizen for now, don't worry
yourself, overmuch, what troubles the people,
and gladly accept the gifts of the moment,
and forget dark things.

Horace

'No poem was ever written by a drinker of water,' wrote the Roman poet **HORACE (b.65 BC)**. Interesting how this the rock 'n' roll 'crazy/tormented/tragic' artist myth continues to resonate down the centuries. Another of his lines echoes loudly: one picked up again in the early part of the twentieth century by Wilfred Owen: 'Dulce et decorum est pro patria mori'. In this poem by Horace, 'Celebration', we recognize another familiar characteristic: our ability to try and set aside troubles, with good company, food and drink.

ST FRANCIS OF ASSISI (1181–1226)

'Start by doing what's necessary, then do what's possible, and suddenly you're doing the impossible …'

He called creatures 'brothers and sisters', and spoke of the world around him as 'brother sun, sister moon, sister birds …'

ST CATHERINE OF SIENA (1347–1380)

started having visions at the age of seven. 'Build a cell inside your mind, from which you can never flee,' she said, and resisted attempts to marry her off, becoming a Dominican nun instead. She wrote letters (more than 300 have survived) and is respected as an early Tuscan writer, known for her twenty-six prayers and a treatise, 'The Dialogue of Divine Providence'.

The oldest continually operating educational institution in Europe is the University of **BOLOGNA,** founded in 1088.

There's no such thing in Italy as Bolognese sauce. The meat dish we now call Bolognese is **'RAGU',** and some don't even make it with tomatoes.

The famous Austrian dish, **SCHNITZEL,** is thought to have been originally Italian, a variant of the Italian veal dish *cotoletta alla Milanesa.*

FORKS

Italy was the first European country to use forks. In the seventeeth century the wealthy would bring their own to dinner in a box, though this practice was considered rather effeminate at first.

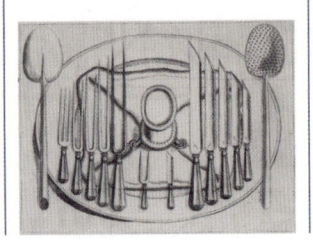

Popular description of Bologna: la dotta, la grassa, la rosa – 'Learned one' for the university, 'fat one' for the rich food, 'red one' for the red tiles of the city.

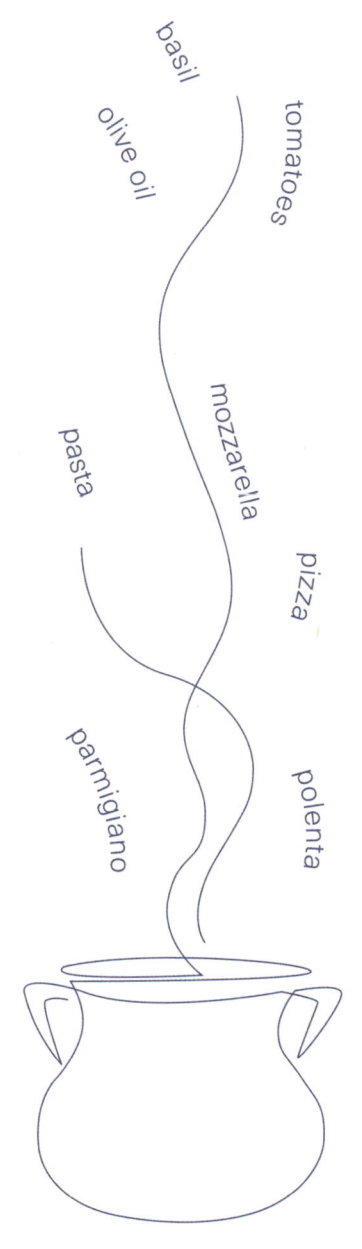

basil · olive oil · tomatoes · pasta · mozzarella · pizza · parmigiano · polenta

The tomato plant belongs to the solanaceae family, which also includes: tomatillos, potatoes, peppers, tobacco, aubergine, chillies, physalis, goji berry, and the deadly nightshade, **BELLADONNA.**

Tomatoes only arrived in Italy in the sixteenth century, from the Americas. The name comes from the Aztec language 'Nahuatle'.

Polenta and grits are both made from dried corn ground into pieces: fine, medium or coarse (stoneground). To cook polenta in the 'authentic'/'traditional' northern Italian way, you'd be male and you'd be cooking it outside in a copper pan with a wooden stirrer, over a wood fire.

Eighteenth-century folk feared the tomato, and called it the **'POISON APPLE'**, as people seemed to get sick after eating them. (It was the acidic tomato juices reacting with the lead in the pewter plates.)

A German name for tomato translates as 'wolf peach'. Other names are Jerusalem apple or love apple ...

'Col. Johnson announced that he would eat a tomato on the steps of the county courthouse at noon ... That morning, in 1820, about 2,000 people were jammed into the town square ... The spectators began to hoot and jeer. Then, 15 minutes later, Col. Johnson emerged from his mansion. The crowd cheered ... he spoke to the crowd about the history of the tomato ... He picked a choice one from a basket on the steps and held it up so that it glistened in the sun ... "To help dispel the tall tales, the fantastic fables that you have been hearing ... and to prove to you that it is not poisonous I am going to eat one right now" ... There was not a sound as the Col. dramatically brought the tomato to his lips and took a bite. A woman in the crowd screamed and fainted ... he raised both his arms, and again bit into one and then the other. The crowd cheered and the firemen's band blared a song ... "He's done it," they shouted. **"HE'S STILL ALIVE!"'**

excerpt from the Salem County Historical Society: *The Story of Robert Gibbon Johnson and the Tomato*

> 'They eat the dainty food of famous chefs with the same pleasure with which they devour gross peasant dishes, mostly composed of garlic and tomatoes, or fisherman's octopus and shrimps, fried in heavily scented olive oil on a little deserted beach.'
>
> **LUIGI BARZINI, *THE ITALIANS* (1964)**

Those 'gross peasant dishes' sound delicious – all that fresh seafood in garlic with olive oil and tomatoes. It is hard to think of Italian food without tomatoes. Like the accordion, which was only patented in 1829, and is now found at the heart of so many folk traditions, tomatoes spread like wildfire despite only arriving on European shores from the Americas in the sixteenth century. Nowadays, flat bread topped with tomatoes – the pizza – is synonymous with this boot-shaped land and snacked on all over the world.

But it's not a completely modern invention: flat breads and toppings have been popular for centuries, especially in the Middle East, and the Romans called theirs *panis focacius* (focaccia bread). Naples is regarded as the place of origin for the modern pizza: the peasants started adding tomato to their yeast-based flat bread in the late eighteenth century.

There's a quote, attributed to film director George Miller, which pretty much sums up my experience of Christmas in Naples with my great friend Andrea: 'The trouble with Italian food is that five or six days later you're hungry again.' We ate for hours, having nine or ten courses: nuts, breads, olives, salami, salads, vegetables, pasta, fish, meat, cheese, nuts, fruit, desserts, sweets, coffees, limoncello... and still we went out afterwards and had Campari and Prosecco in local bars and clubs; well, the young men and I did. I was allowed along as visiting guest, while the rest of the women were left to clean the kitchen. Perhaps this is their particular family tradition or one specific to Naples, but it was pretty impressive – not the split in sexes, but the feast and the rituals – and I was glad at that moment to be alive, heading out into the frosty Naples night.

I love the tradition of Italian food. Out of the apparent chaos and drama of traffic and speech comes this oasis of ritual. Expectancy and tradition go hand in hand. We were recently in Milan and the waiter took great delight in pointing out where our order did not tally with social norms: choice of wine, choice of order and food. Creamed mash potato is apparently fine, a request for chipped potatoes elicited a loud harrumph, red wine with fish is a total no, and so on. I've included a traditional feast meal order below. I've always thought it's good to know the rules, then break them.

South Wales has a close connection with Italy: many Italian families arrived from the 1890s onwards to work in the mines, and when this industry went into decline their descendants opened cafés and ice-cream parlours and these are now an integral part of South Wales valley culture and history. These family-run businesses provided warm and welcoming places for the locals. In the nineties, I'd arrive home post-tour, drop my bags then head straight out to an Italian called La Puccinela in Cardiff. (Alas, it is no longer there.) It was run by Andrea, who pretty much became a member of my family, and kept me grounded during those touring years. After the fuss and noise of months away singing and promoting, it was always hard to settle back in. The tour bus would reach your house, you'd step out; it drove away. And that was it. I felt institutionalized. On tour you were rarely alone – you had a tour manager to direct your every move, and an itinerary to map them out for months ahead. So, like a whelk out of a shell, wide eyes all blinking in the cold street, the door opened on a cold house and a silent TV. Thank God for Puccinela's, the heat and noise of the kitchen was easy company. I simply sat in my corner and watched, or when it was quiet, I'd hang in the kitchen. Andrea taught me to cook Neapolitan style: marinated lamb chops in garlic and lemon juice flash grilled on charcoal (these ribs were excellent for teething babies and loved by my son John), fish, squid, pasta with simple tomato sauce. Everything fresh. We'd go fishing sometimes (thanks Dave Lewis), and we'd cook them straight up in the restaurant: sea bass in paper packets, mussels with black pepper. I even caught some mudbugs from the River Kennet, and we cooked a rice dish like paella with them. And by the by, never, ever eat cheese with a fish dish: not Parmesan, not anything, according to Andrea. But yes to limoncello: there was always a bottle homemade and ready in the coldest part of the fridge.

As for my daily use of Italian flavours now? An obsession with trying to recreate the best Spaghetti Vongole at home, as tasted in Venice this year in a workmen's café. Holy moly: the taste sensation was unforgettable. Seems to me that simple is always best in most cases. Like Italian tomato sauce, which some cook simply with tomatoes, no onion, no anchovy, no bay leaf, no nothing: just good fresh ripe tomatoes. Andrea introduced me to handmade buffalo mozzarella. We used to bring it back on the plane in boxes from Naples: it 'milks' as you cut it. Simply serve with fresh slices of tomatoes, fresh basil leaves and olive oil. What a starter, a whole ball of milky heaven . . .

ITALY

'Take a rest, a field that has rested gives a beautiful crop.'

OVID

'Life is a combination of magic and pasta.'

FEDERICO FELLINI

'Everything you see I owe to pasta.'

SOPHIA LOREN

*'Chance is always powerful.
Let your hook be always cast;
in the pool where you least
expect it, there will be a fish.'*

OVID

ORDER OF FEAST

APERITIVO
DRINK WITH SNACKS, e.g. OLIVES, NUTS

ANTIPASTO
SALAMI, HAM, SMALL BRUSCHETTA

PRIMO
PASTA, RISOTTO, SOUP

SECONDO
MEAT OR FISH DISH

CONTORNI
(SIDE DISHES SERVED WITH SECONDO BUT NOT ON SAME DISH, VEGETABLES LIKE ROAST POTATOES)

INSALATA
SERVING OF SALADS
CHEESE AND FRUIT

DESSERT
CAKE, OR GELATO, RUM BABA IN NAPLES, SORBET

CAFFE
(NEVER CAPPUCCINO IN THE AFTERNOON)
USUALLY ESPRESSO

DIGESTIVO
GRAPPA OR LIMONCELLO TO HELP DIGESTION AFTER A MEAL

ON THE MENU

HOMEMADE PASTA

SPAGHETTI AGLIO E OLIO

LEMON SPAGHETTI

TINNED TOMATO SAUCE

FRESH TOMATO SAUCE WITH BASIL

SPAGHETTI VONGOLE

CONTORNI

ROCKET AND PARMESAN

WILD GARLIC PESTO

ROASTED ZUCCHINI AND GARLIC

DESSERT

RASPBERRY 'GELATO'

DRINK

CAMPARI SPRITZ

Ornella Vanoni 'Il Mio Posto Qual'è'

Sophia Loren 'Mambo Bacan'

Cooking Pasta

Factor about 100g dried pasta per person. Bring a large pan of well-salted water to a rolling boil.

Add your choice of pasta and cook, watching it doesn't boil over. After 5–6 minutes, try a piece. If it is halfway soft, not soggy, and still with a 'bite' in the middle, it's ready; if not, continue for another 2 minutes. Drain, keeping some of the cooking water aside. Now it's ready for ending the cooking process in a big frying pan with your chosen flavourings: garlic, butter, chilli, clams, mushrooms, lobster, mussels.

Seems to me, the key to great pasta dishes like vongole lies in finishing off the cooking of the pasta in the large frying pan in the cooking sauces – garlic, chilli and clams – and it being served straight out of this pan.

Homemade Pasta

For 4 people, put 400g flour and 4 eggs in a food processor, adding a little water if you need to, so that it forms a ball of dough. (You can always follow a ratio of 100g of soft-wheat flour to one room-temperature egg in this recipe.) This doesn't take long. Traditionally, pasta was made by hand on a flat table, so if you don't have a food processor, make the flour into a kind of nest, crack in the eggs and work slowly to make a dough.

Remove from the processor, and knead for 5–10 minutes until elastic. Form into a smooth ball, dusting with flour if too sticky (it shouldn't stick to your hands), or add a little more water if too dry.

At this stage, if you don't want to use the pasta right away, you can cover in clingfilm and leave in the fridge, or even freeze.

If you are cooking immediately, portion the dough into smaller, workable pieces, dusting where necessary, and roll out into desired shapes using a pasta machine. Dry the pasta, ideally using a pasta rack, or wherever you can if not.

While the pasta is drying, bring a pan of salted water to the boil. Cook the pasta for an average of 2 minutes (depending on thickness).

Drain, then return to your pan with the sauce of your choice. If you need to thin the sauce then use some of the pasta cooking water.

Option:
Wholewheat flour pasta is so good – try with a porcini mushroom sauce.

Tony Muréna 'Indifférence'

Marino Marini and His Quartet ''E Calosce'

Spaghetti Aglio e Olio

V VG DF

Ingredients

2 cloves garlic, finely chopped

2 dried chillies (bullets or similar) or dried chilli flakes to taste (½ tsp)

50–75 ml pasta cooking water

fresh parsley, finely chopped

400g pasta, almost cooked, as on p. 183

salt, pepper

Method

1. In a large frying pan, fry garlic and chilli flakes for a few seconds but avoid burning; then add 50 ml pasta cooking water and chopped parsley, heat and stir to develop the flavours.

2. Add the pasta and finish cooking pasta in this juice. (Add more water if needed to finish the pasta.)

3. Serve sprinkled with fresh chopped parsley, with a chunk of parmesan and a grater and a pepper mill.

Lemon Spaghetti

VG

Ingredients

400g pasta

2 tbsp olive oil

½ clove garlic, smashed or finely grated

75–100g pecorino, grated (or similar hard cheese)

juice of ½ to 1 lemon

fresh parsley, finely chopped

Method

1. Cook pasta until al dente (you won't be finishing it off in a sauce this time) in rolling salted water.

2. Drain.

3. Heat olive oil hot in a large pan, add the garlic and fry for a few seconds.

4. Add the pasta, add 75–100g grated pecorino and the lemon juice.

5. Stir, taste, add more lemon juice if needed.

6. Serve immediately with the chopped parsley.

Option:
Vegans can omit the cheese and instead add some pre-toasted pistachio nuts. Also throw into the mix some basil or baby spinach leaves.

Rocket and Parmesan

VG GF

Ingredients

wild rocket (approx 70g)
parmesan or grana padano (around 50g): shaved

Cover the rocket with cheese and serve: offering balsamic vinegar and olive oil, salt and pepper.

Wild Garlic Pesto

VG GF

At the end of March or April, collect wild garlic leaves to make pesto as an alternative to fresh basil leaves. Here's a recipe I picked up at the Cheltenham Gold Cup (thanks Sue).

Ingredients

75g wild garlic (or basil) leaves
50g pecorino or Parmesan
50g pinenuts (very lightly pre-toasted if you've time)
1 small garlic clove
olive oil
pinch of sea salt

Method

Blend everything together, adding enough olive oil to make the right consistency. Serve with cooked pasta, bread, salads, boiled potatoes, mozzarella …

Tinned Tomato Sauce

V VG GF DF

Tinned tomatoes have a deeper flavour and can deal with the onion better, but still best to use just a little, and very finely chopped.

Ingredients

50g onion (¼ small onion, very finely chopped)
1 clove garlic, finely chopped
1 tin tomatoes
fresh basil (if you have it)
sea salt

Method

1. In a saucepan, on a medium heat, fry the onion for 5–10 minutes with a pinch of salt until soft and translucent, add the garlic, and fry for a few seconds until getting soft, but not changing colour.

2. Add the tomatoes (for a smoother sauce, you can pass them through a sieve first), cook for 15 minutes, add basil leaves, and cook another 5 minutes. If you're pressed for time, you can serve with the pasta at this point, but if you've time, for a more intense flavour, cook for 45 minutes total.

3. In a large pan, heat 1 tablespoon olive oil, add the sauce, add 400g almost cooked pasta, adding a little (2 tbsp) pasta cooking water if needed. Finish cooking the pasta in the sauce, taste and season.

4. Serve garnished with fresh basil, black pepper, a chunk of parmesan and a grater.

Carla Boni 'Mambo Italiano'
Roberto Murolo 'A Canzone È Napule'
Pink Martini 'Una Notte A Napoli'

Fresh Tomato Sauce with Basil

V VG GF DF

There's something about the lightness of fresh tomato sauce cooked with basil. I much prefer it to the richer tomato sauces slow-cooked with onion. The combination of fresh basil and tomato is right up there for me, just as for pineapple with chilli, or biscotti with Vin Santo.

Ingredients

5–6 fresh ripe tomatoes (pierce skin with knife and sit in boiling water for a minute, then plunge into cold)
1 clove garlic, finely chopped
2 leaves basil, torn into pieces
2 tbsp olive oil
pinch sea salt
pinch soft brown sugar (optional)

Method

1. Halve tomatoes, squeeze out seeds into sieve over a bowl, retain juices.
2. Peel off the skins and chop into small pieces. Add to the juices in the bowl.
3. In a saucepan, on medium, gently fry the garlic for a few seconds until softening but not going brown.
4. Add the tomatoes, cook for 15 minutes (you can pass the sauce through a sieve at this point if you want it smoother), add basil leaves and cook another 5 minutes.
5. Add salt (and sugar) to taste, cook for another 5 minutes.
6. In a large pan with the olive oil, add the sauce and the almost cooked pasta (see above), add a little pasta cooking water (2–3 tbsp) if needed. Finish cooking the pasta in this sauce.
7. Serve garnished with fresh basil, black pepper, a chunk of parmesan and a grater.

Option:
If you've got very ripe, flavoursome tomatoes, you don't even need to cook them to make the 'sauce'. Skin, deseed and chop the tomatoes, marinade with the garlic and basil for 30–60 minutes, then add to the large pan with the almost cooked pasta at step 5.

ITALY

Angelo Petisi and His Mandolin Orchestra 'Tarantella Parigina'

Enrico Caruso 'La Danza'

Spaghetti Vongole

DF NV

Oh vongole, vongole. Food of the gods. Once we waited for three hours for a kitchen to reopen just to taste this classic. Was it worth it? Yes, and trying to recreate this seemingly simple dish with the complex favours at home has become my holy grail.

Ingredients

900g clams
3 tbsp olive oil
100ml white wine
2 cloves garlic, finely chopped
chopped parsley
400g spaghetti, almost cooked

Method

1. Soak fresh clams in cold water for 1–2 hours to rid of grit, discarding broken ones. Drain.
2. In a large pan add 2 tbsp olive oil and ½ the finely chopped garlic.
3. Fry gently for a few seconds, don't burn, then add the white wine and clams and cover until the clams open (it won't take long).
4. Discard the ones that don't open.
5. Pour off the juice, set clams and juice aside.
6. In the pan, on a medium heat, add the rest of the garlic, 2 tbsp olive oil, add the clam juice and then the cooked pasta.
7. Let the pasta finish cooking in the juice.
8. Add the clams and the chopped parsley, heat through, serve with lemon wedges and pepper.

If you can only get shelled clams, use 400g pasta, 90g cockles shelled, and I would add tomato sauce to the recipe. It's not the classic vongole, but it's still good.

In a large frying pan on a medium heat, add 2 tbsp olive oil, 1 clove chopped garlic and the shelled clams and gently fry for a minute. Add a generous glug of white wine, stir for a few seconds, then add 100ml tomato sauce and the almost cooked pasta. Let the pasta finish cooking in the juice. Add the chopped parsley, serve with lemon wedges and pepper.

Roasted Zucchini and Garlic

V VG GF DF

Another side dish I often ate with Andrea's family was zucchini (courgette) and garlic.

Ingredients

2 small zucchini/1 large 250g, cut into thick juliennes
1 clove garlic, finely chopped
2 tbsp olive oil
rock salt
chopped parsley

Method

1. Lay zucchini on a greased tray and roast at high heat: 240°C/gas 9 for 15–20 minutes, then cool.
2. In the meantime, finely grate/smash the garlic and sit in the remaining oil.
3. Once cooled, cover the zucchini in the garlicky oil, sprinkle rock salt and finely chopped parsley
4. Serve hot or cold.

Luciano Pavarotti 'Funiculì Funiculà'

Joe Barbieri 'Zenzero E Cannella'

Hugo Montenegro and His Orchestra 'The Good, The Bad And The Ugly'

Campari spritz

V VG GF DF

Campari spritz is popular in the Venice region. Mix 2:1 Prosecco to Campari, top with soda water and serve with ice cubes and a slice of fresh orange.

Raspberry 'Gelato'

VG GF

Ingredients

300g frozen raspberries
200g yoghurt
juice ½ lemon
2–3 tbsp honey

Method

Blend all the ingredients together and serve immediately.

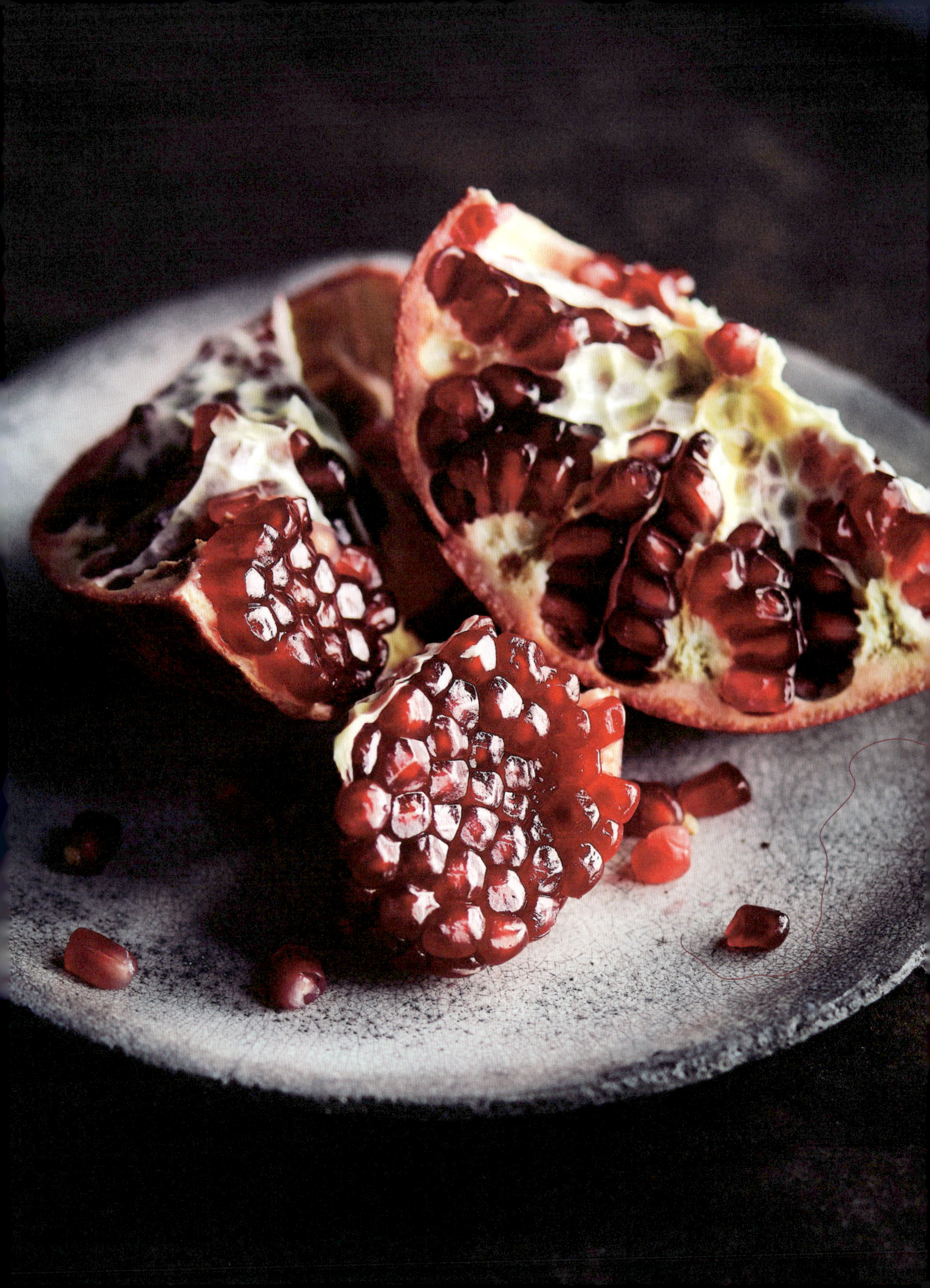

MIDDLE EAST

Every City is a Dulcimer

There is the rising up from light's embrace,
you can see in a summer field
or in a child dancing.

Every city is a dulcimer that plays its chorus
against our ears.

If I don't ever complete a sentence
while we are together, accept my apologies

and try to understand this sweet thought:

Birds initially had no desire to fly,
so God sat close to them playing music.

When He left, they missed him so much
their great longing sprouted wings
and they took to the sky.

Listen, nothing evolves us like love.

From The Gift *by Hafiz*
(translated by Daniel Ladinsky)

HAFIZ (c.1320-1389)
Poetry holds a special place in Iranian culture, and the poets we could choose from are immense: Ferdowsi, Saadi, Rumi (who is bizarrely one of the bestselling poets in the US). I'm going to go with a poem by Hafiz (also spelled Hafez), one of the great Sufi masters, who remains popular both in the East and West, finding firm fans in both Goethe and Queen Victoria. Hafiz writes about love, life, music, food, intoxication and God in such a natural way, it fills your heart.

ZOROASTER

(*c*.1500–1000 BC), founder of Zoroastrianism, the first monotheistic religion. Zoroaster is often portrayed wearing white, carrying what looks like a bundle of sticks – a priest's 'baresman' – and with a finger pointing upwards as if teaching.

Zoroaster was thirty when he had visions of spirits who taught him about the concepts of truth and lies. He decided to begin a lifetime's pursuit of these teachings and encouraged people to take responsibility for their own deeds, to shun polytheism, to stop taking hallucinogens, to give up on animal sacrifice and shun the class system, earning him enemies in the process.

The key symbol of Zoroastrianism is fire.

The Zoroastrian philosophy gives a purpose to humankind: to seek truth (Asa) through thinking constructive thoughts, talking positively and doing good deeds, with an active participation in life. In a nutshell:
THINK GOOD, DO GOOD.
In Iranian food culture, Zoroastrian teachings have had a huge influence on food and its importance to overall well-being.

Pliny claimed that **PYTHAGORAS** and his 'love of wisdom' was influenced by Zoroastrian thinking. There is also a theory that the Three Wise Men, the magi of Christmas, were Persian Zoroastrian priests.

RHUBARB

is used in sweet and savoury dishes in Iran. For a change, try cooking the stalks on the barbecue. It's a close relative of garden sorrel.

Ancient Greeks called Iran 'Persia', but the **FARSI**-speaking people called it 'Iran'. In 1935 the Iranian Government made an official request to be always referred to as Iran. However, since the word 'Persia' is so connected with the cultural side of Iran, and its associations with pioneering advances in science and architecture, many Iranians still use it.

Greek historian **HERODOTUS,** writing on the on 430 BCE Persian community in Susa:

'Of all the days in the year, the one which they celebrate most is their birthday. It is customary to have the board furnished on that day with an ampler supply than common. The richer Persians cause an ox, a horse, a camel, and an ass to be baked whole and so served up to them: the poorer classes use instead the smaller kinds of cattle. They eat little solid food but an abundance of dessert, which is set on table a few dishes at a time; this it is which makes them say that "the Greeks, when they eat, leave off hungry, having nothing worth mention served up to them after the meats; whereas, if they had more put before them, they would not stop eating." They are very fond of wine, and drink it in large quantities.'

The **TULIP** is the national flower of Iran.

Persian inventions: **BACKGAMMON,** the 'fridge' (*yakhchal*, used to keep ice cold in the desert), and quite possibly wine.

Historically **SHIRAZ** was a wine-making region, and the earliest firm evidence of wine-making dates back to 5400 BC. Shiraz was known as Iran's wine capital, and in the ninth century was famous for producing some of the finest wines in the world. It is thought that it is a sweet wine, made of dried grapes and related to Marsala wine, or sherry.

Tehran means 'warm slope'.

The English word **'PARADISE'** comes from a Persian word meaning 'enclosed garden'.

The earliest known reference to Shiraz – city of poets, literature, wine and flowers – appears on clay tablets dated to 2000 BC. The Shiraz we buy in the UK isn't produced in Iran, but is just wine made of dark-skinned **SYRAH** grapes.

MIDDLE EAST

A thumbs-up in Iran is equivalent to our giving the middle finger.

Between 80 and 90 per cent of the world's **SAFFRON** comes from Iran; the stigmas and styles of the *crocus sativus* are hand-harvested. This 'red gold' sometimes sells for more than its equivalent weight in gold.

TAH-DIG
Perisan rice with saffron and crusty base

The monkey could not dance, and blamed it on the floor being crooked.

(PERSIAN SAYING)

You can trace the word **KEBAB** right back to prehistoric times to a proto-Afro-Asiatic language, spoken, it is believed, some 12,000–18,000 years ago, where 'kab' meant to burn or roast. There's also an interesting theory behind the evolution of the kebab: medieval Turkey and Persia had built-up areas where space was tight and firewood lacking. Cooking ground-up meat over smaller grills would have been more practical than the alternative of roasting big cuts of meat over open fires.

Kebab is mentioned by our Moroccan explorer, **IBN BATTUTA,** as a breakfast served with naan bread in thirteenth-century India.

ARAK is an alcoholic drink similar to Pastis or Ouzo, known in Iran as Aragh Sagi.

Doogh is a diluted yoghurt drink, often with added mint (very similar to lassi), although sometimes it's carbonated.

Iran is one of the world's largest exporters of pomegranates, **'anar',** and the second largest producer. Oil is its leading export.

I begin writing this chapter on a train from Hull, tired and hungry. The non-meat offer on board is a hummus sandwich. It's damp and cold, like the sandwiches and dressing rooms I've spent much of my adult life in. I get a grump on. Provisions left for bands in dressing rooms are known in the trade as the rider. And while we're here let's talk about that. While the press might gleefully print stories of demands like 'Versace towels' (Kanye West), 'vitamin water for bathing dogs' (Mariah Carey), 'twenty white kittens' (Mariah again), 'M&Ms with the brown M&Ms taken out' (who knows, who cares), in reality the jobbing musician gets sandwiches and a kettle, if lucky. Besides, if you've bothered to read the small print, you know that the costs of riders get taken out of your gig profits anyway. Most musicians take a long while to realize they foot the bill for recording studios, limos, flights, videos – and any parties thrown in their honour – not that it wasn't fun at the time – just saying. In Germany you might get 'Schweinefleisch und Käse', corners curling up, and black bread on the side, but essentially you can bet your bottom dollar, if you're eating in a dressing room, dinner will be pre-filled cold bread, i.e. a nasty excuse for food. No. I don't like sandwiches, and yes, this is a First World problem. Of course, once you experience trillions (and I mean trillions) of streams of your music, you might start to be able to afford catering. Boom. Goodbye sandwiches, hello to catering and hot meal options.

Let's go back to the story. On that train from Hull to London, it's late at night, and I'm in that horrible state of mind, wanting to teleport home, wishing precious hours away, so I try and turn things around. Yes, the train is warm and quiet, and yes, there's a glass of red wine in hand, and I put a fresh green chilli in with the hummus and kick my mind to the direction of the Fertile Crescent, known as the cradle of civilization, that crescent-shaped area which covers parts of Iraq, Syria, Lebanon, Jordan, Israel, Palestine, Iran, Cyprus and Egypt. Then I ponder the food of the Middle East: kebab, tabouleh, kibbeh, pita, Baba Ganoush. It's the food of the moment; not just to eat in restaurants around the world, but also to be tried at home, thanks to the likes of Claudia Roden, Yotam Ottolenghi and Yasmin Khan. My local shops show clear signs of this embrace: herbs – huge bunches of herbs – making a mockery of the spindly packets that we've been used to until now in our supermarkets. I love this about the cuisine. Sit down in any Lebanese restaurant in west London and you're served with fresh food: a bowl of raw carrots, peppers and celery. Grab some and serve, and bang, there's your first nod to this food when channelling it at home. Bring on the Spice Bazaar of Istanbul, and those precious commodities which have been trundling down the high roads of the world for so long, get them straight into your kitchen. Whole spices ready to roast, to release a puff of aromatics in your grinder, the cumin, cardamom, cloves, cassia bark, saffron.

I don't need to point out here that the Middle East covers a vast area of the earth – seventeen countries including the above-mentioned Fertile Crescent – but also Saudi Arabia, Oman, Kuwait, Turkey – and close to 380 million people. I'm taking the luxury of picking out dishes I return to again and again at home as a place to start, and for the added interest, poetry and salutations, I'll home in on Iran.

'Will rests on the magnitude of those who will it.'

EARLY ARABIC PHILOSOPHER

Runic inscription in the marble of the upper balcony of Hagia Sophia, engraved some 1,100 years ago by a Viking soldier.

ON THE MENU

- SPICE MIXES
- LABNEH
- KUKU SABZI
- FALAFEL
- CACIK
- TAHINI SAUCE
- TABBOULEH
- FUL MEDAMES
- SHAKSHUKA
- PILAF
- HUMMUS

DESSERT

ROAST RHUBARB WITH YOGHURT

DRINK

CHAI
BLACK SWEETENED TEA

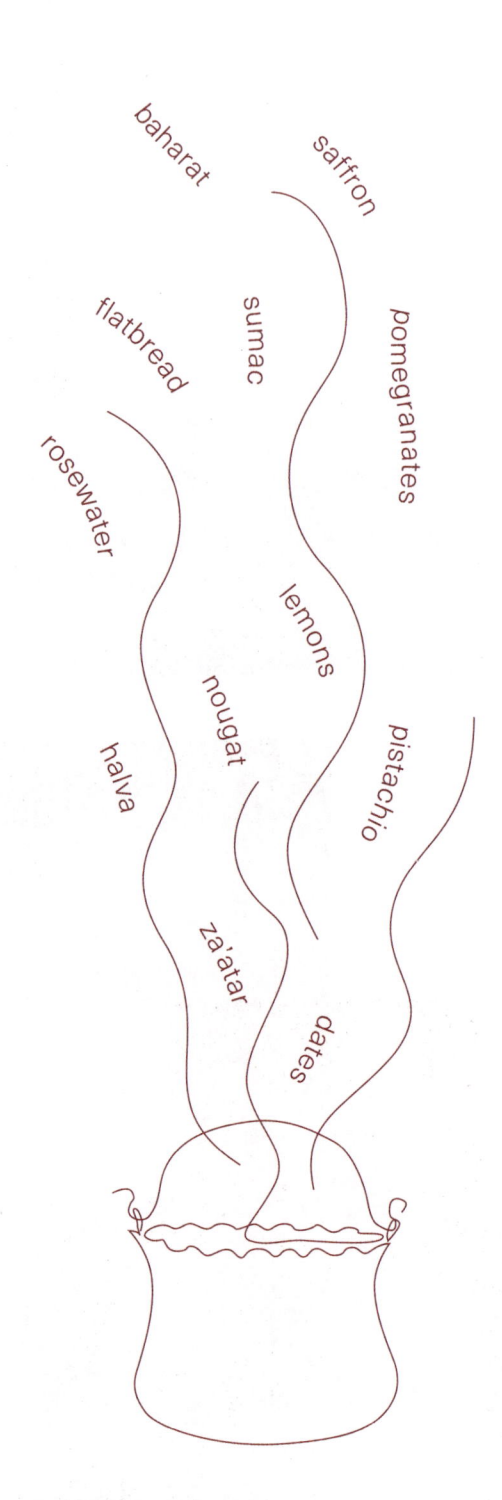

baharat · saffron · flatbread · sumac · pomegranates · rosewater · lemons · halva · nougat · pistachio · za'atar · dates

Fereidoon Farrokhzad 'Aashianeh'

Leila Forouhar 'Yek Nafas Atre To Bas'

Spice Mixes

(V) (VG) (DF)

Baharat

Baharat is a heady mix of aromatic spices, much like India's garam masala, that works well added in small amounts to finish off a dish, but it's also used as a rub for meats. As with all spice mixes, ratios vary: increase and decrease as your taste dictates.

Toast, then grind: ½ tsp each of peppercorns, cardamom seeds, cassia bark, nutmeg, cumin seeds, coriander seeds, dried chilli flakes or paprika, ¼ tsp cloves, ¼ tsp allspice/pimento berries. Mix together.

Za'atar

Arabic for 'thyme', and also the name for a green herb mix. Try a mix of any of these: dried thyme/marjoram/oregano in a 1:1:1 ratio with sesame seeds and sumac. Alternatively, you can add fennel seeds in the same proportion and even a sprinkling of caraway seeds.

Blend together: 2 tsp sesame seeds (toasted), 2 tsp sumac, 2 tsp dried thyme or marjoram or oregano (or a mix of these three), a pinch of salt.

Options:

- Mix with 2 tablespoons of olive oil and brush on to homemade bread before baking.
- Use a pinch to flavour salads.
- Roll balls of *labneh* in it.

Vegan snack:
Fresh flatbread, or pita, with slices of tomato and sweet onion, sprinkled with *za'atar* and seasoned.

Labneh

(VG)

1. Grab a clean old T-shirt or piece of muslin or J-cloth and strain a large pot of natural yoghurt (mixed with ½ tsp of salt) through it. Tie it around the kitchen tap overnight.

2. Next morning, screw up the cloth to squeeze out the remaining liquid, then open to reveal something that resembles cream cheese.

3. You have the option to make this into little balls to use straight away or store in olive oil, or to roll in *za'atar* and store in oil.

4. Serve with toasted pitta bread (it's half the calories of traditional cream cheese), or add to your *shakshuka* (see p. 203).

MIDDLE EAST

Googoosh 'Ma Be Ham Mohtajim'

Kuku Sabzi

VG DF

Fresh herb frittata is called *kuku sabzi* in Iran (*sabzi* means 'herbs' in Farsi). It's foolproof, dramatic with its bright green colour, and a great way of using up tender greens and herbs. Traditionally it's served at Nowruz, the Iranian New Year, in March. The greens symbolize rebirth and the eggs fertility. The door to this wonderful world was opened to me by a frequent guest on my 6 Music radio show, Yasmin Khan, whose cookbook *The Saffron Tales* is a total joy.

Ingredients

250g fresh greens (any combination of parsley, coriander, dill, chives, mint, tarragon, spinach, callaloo and other tender greens will work, clean, dry and chopped finely)
½ tsp ground turmeric
6 eggs, beaten
1 tbsp plain flour
2 tbsp olive oil, plus extra for the pan
½ tsp sea salt
freshly ground black pepper

Method

1. Mix all the ingredients together in a bowl.
2. Cover the bottom of a non-stick frying pan with oil and place on a medium heat.
3. Pour in the mixture, then cover the pan and cook for 10 minutes on a low heat.
4. Finish under a hot grill for 5 minutes.
5. Serve with ground black pepper and a pinch of sea salt, hot or cold, with yoghurt or *labneh* (see p. 197).

Options:

- Sprinkle with walnuts, fresh slices of chilli.
- Experiment by frying a chopped clove of garlic, spring onions or leeks, before adding the egg and herb mix at step 3.
- Or add chopped nuts, and 1 teaspoon of barberries or cranberries.

Kourosh Yaghmaei 'Gol-e Yakh'

Behrad Aria and Mohammad Nouri 'Jan E Maryam'

Falafel

(V) (VG) (GF) (DF)

A superb vegan option, with taste and texture and easy to make. You can make them with uncooked, soaked chickpeas, but I prefer using fava beans (shelled or unshelled) which you use uncooked after soaking overnight. Fava beans are like small broad beans, and some were recently found in sites in northern Israel (the Galilee area) and have been carbon-dated to some 10,000 years ago, making them the world's oldest domesticated fava bean farms, and perhaps even predating the Neolithic farming of wheat and barley products in this particular region.

Makes 12 small falafel.

Ingredients

150g dried fava beans, soaked for 6–8 hours or overnight (uncooked)
½ an onion, chopped (80g)
2 cloves of garlic, chopped (option to pre-toast before blending)
50g–75g bunch of fresh herbs (any assortment – coriander, mint, parsley)
1 tsp cumin seeds, toasted and ground
1 tsp coriander seeds, toasted and ground
¼ tsp cayenne pepper (or dried chilli flakes)
freshly ground black pepper
vegetable oil, for deep-frying
generous ½ tsp sea salt

Method

1. Blend all the ingredients (apart from the oil) together until they form a paste you can mould.
2. Fill a small saucepan about a third of the way up with vegetable oil (about 2–3cm deep).
3. When you flick some water and it sizzles, it's ready. Keep the heat on medium.
4. Scoop out and make small falafel, approx. 2–3cm, in the palm of your hand.
5. Fry the falafel for about 2 minutes on each side, or until golden all over. (Adjust the heat if they are cooking too fast or too slowly.)
6. Drain on kitchen paper and add salt.

Option:

Chickpea falafel are made in exactly the same way as above. If you use 150g of uncooked chickpeas, soaked overnight, it makes about 15 falafel.

Nooshafarin 'Gol-e Aftab Gardoon'

Giti 'Bote Aayaar'

Cacik

(VG) (GF)

This is a refreshing yoghurt side dish. The consistency can be varied from thick to thin, by adding water. Your call, but I don't dilute mine with any water.

Ingredients

200ml yoghurt
⅓ of a cucumber (or 2–3 small Turkish ones), seeds taken out, half-peeled and grated
1 small clove of garlic, finely chopped
20g fresh dill, finely chopped
20g fresh mint, finely chopped
salt and pepper, to taste
olive oil and a pinch of toasted ground cumin seeds, to serve

Method

1. Put all the ingredients (apart from the oil and cumin) into a bowl and mix together.
2. Drizzle with olive oil and a pinch of toasted ground cumin, and serve.

Tahini Sauce

(V) (VG) (GF) (DF)

Double these ingredients if you need more.

Ingredients

1 clove of garlic
generous pinch of salt
4 tbsp tahini
4 tbsp lemon or lime juice
4–8 tbsp water

Method

1. Grind the garlic to a paste with a pinch of salt in a pestle and mortar.
2. Add the tahini, mix, then add the lemon juice.
3. Gradually add the water to get to the thickness you prefer, like cream.

Mohammad Nouri 'Biya Bar-e Safar Bandim'

Tabbouleh

V **VG** **DF**

I like a ratio of herbs to wheat of 4:1.

Ingredients

25g medium bulgar wheat
200ml boiling water
50g fresh parsley, finely chopped
50g fresh mint, finely chopped
1 chopped tomato, deseeded and chopped (and skinned if you like)
2 spring onions, or ¼ of a medium onion, finely chopped (basically you need equal amounts of onion and tomato)
juice of ½ lemon
1 tbsp olive oil
2 pinches of *baharat* (see p. 197)
salt and pepper
handful of pomegranate seeds

Method

1. Soak the bulgar wheat in the boiling water, then cover and leave to soften for 15–20 minutes.

2. Drain in a sieve, squeezing out excess water. Put it into a bowl and mix with the herbs, tomato, onions, lemon juice and oil. Sprinkle over the *baharat* spices and season to taste. Throw on the pomegranate seeds and serve.

Ful Medames

V **VG** **GF** **DF**

Originating in ancient Egypt, this vegan dish has become popular across so many Middle Eastern and African countries, and has become a firm family favourite.

- 2 tins cooked fava beans, or 250g dried fava beans, soaked overnight then boiled in 1 litre water until soft (45–60 minutes or more).
- Fry 1 medium finely chopped onion, with 2–3 cloves, chopped garlic and 2 tsp toasted ground cumin, in oil.
- Add 1 split fresh green chilli, or/and ½ tsp chilli or paprika (your call).
- Add 500ml water, and simmer for 15–30 minutes, letting flavours develop. Mash some beans with potato masher, taste and season generously. Simmer until you get the ideal consistency: a very thick stew. Stir in the juice of ½ lemon just before serving and cover surface of the beans with 1¼ finely chopped sweet onion, a generous handful of chopped fresh coriander(or parsley), finely chopped tomato, a drizzle of olive oil, a pinch of paprika and ground cumin.

Options:

It's not traditional, but I fry a little vegetable oil and sizzle a pinch of asafoetida and whole cumin seeds to add to the mix near the end of cooking, or, failing that, a little pinch of Mexican epazote herb. Both asafoetida and epazote are said to reduce intestinal gas.

Serve with: wedges of lemon, hard-boiled eggs (optional) and flat bread or rice.

Klonk 'Miserlou'

Shakshuka

VG **DF**

This means 'mixture' in Tunisian Arabic and you have the option to add onions, peppers or potatoes to this, but I like to keep it simple, the way my Israeli neighbours prepared it. They had a gas ring outside, prepped the dish in individual terracotta dishes, and served it with homemade bread and tahini sauce.

Ingredients

10–12 fresh tomatoes, skinned, seeded and finely chopped (or 2 x 400g tins of tomatoes)

2 tbsp olive oil

1 clove of garlic, finely chopped

¼ tsp cayenne pepper

4 leaves of fresh basil

4 eggs

¼ tsp cumin seeds, toasted and ground

Method

1. Sit the tomatoes in boiling water until they split, then remove the skins, deseed and chop.

2. Heat the oil in a frying pan on a medium heat, then add the garlic and cook for 1 minute. Add the tomatoes (fresh or tinned) and the cayenne, cover the pan and turn down to a simmer for 20 minutes. Add a little water if it looks too dry.

3. Make 4 holes in the sauce, put a leaf of basil into each one, then crack an egg into each. Season, then cover the pan and cook for 4–6 minutes, or until the eggs are cooked to the desired consistency.

4. Sprinkle with the cumin, and serve with a ball of *labneh* (see p. 197) or crumbled feta, or tahini sauce (see p. 201) and homemade toasted bread.

Erkin Koray 'Timbili'

Mehrpouya 'Dokhtare Shab'

Pilaf

V VG GF DF

This aromatic dish has ancient origins all over the world, including *pilao* in Indian cooking, and has many regional variations. It's a cousin to paella but differs from it, as pilaf is cooked with a lid, uses aromatic spices and is cooked in a broth flavoured with garlic and onion. It is totally versatile, as you can add any vegetables, peas or pulses that you have or that are in season – though using celery, peppers, tomato and smoked paprika would nudge it towards jambalaya territory. For the major flavouring here we are looking at the *baharat* spice mix: cardamom, allspice, cinnamon, clove, sumac. This dish is all about these aromatics, great side by side with yoghurt. Basmati rice is best for its light grains, but long-grain is fine. As usual I'm using brown basmati rice.

Ingredients

1 onion, finely chopped
2 tbsp vegetable oil
salt and pepper
2 cloves of garlic, finely grated
1 stick of cinnamon/cassia (optional)
4 cardamom pods, crushed
2 bay leaves
5 allspice/pimento berries
220g brown basmati rice
100g grated courgette, chopped kale or seasonal chopped vegetables
100g cooked chickpeas/fresh broad beans or peas
600ml vegetable stock
½ tsp sumac (if you don't have any, use ½ tsp grated lemon zest)
2 pinches of *baharat* spice mix (see p. 197)

Method

1. In a large frying pan, fry the onion in the oil with a pinch of salt for 7 minutes, until soft and beginning to colour.

2. Add the garlic, then the cinnamon, cardamom, bay and allspice/pimento berries, and fry on a low heat for 2 minutes.

3. Add the rice and stir to absorb the flavours.

4. Add the vegetables, chickpeas/beans and stock, bring to the boil, then reduce the heat and simmer for 35–40 minutes with the lid on the pan. (If you use white rice, it'll be ready quicker, so taste and see.) At this point, the rice should be ready and the liquid should all have been absorbed – if not, take the lid off and turn up the heat until the liquid has gone.

5. Now add more layers of flavour: ½ teaspoon of sumac, 2 pinches of *baharat* spice mix, salt and pepper to taste, a drizzle of olive oil, (or make a dent in the middle and melt a blob of butter in it).

6. If you like sweetness, add a handful of fresh pomegranate seeds, chopped apricots or dates; if you like chilli, add fresh slices of chilli and garnish with chopped herbs.

Options:

I have some dried black limes that I picked up at a Christmas fair in Marylebone last year. They are used to add a deep citrus flavour to dishes which are cooked with meat, especially chicken dishes, but I use mine when cooking rice, and they work in this one. If you see any, buy them – black or yellow ones. Smash one with a rolling pin so the skin breaks open and put it into the pan when you add the rice. Squeeze the dried lime when close to serving: it really is quite fascinating just how much flavour these little dried fruits hide.

You can also serve with a bowl of *cacik* (see p. 201).

If cooking with meat: add small pieces of browned meats at step 4, or serve the dish covered with pieces or slices of roasted or braised meats, pouring some of the juices on the rice.

Shohreh 'Omadi'

Hummus

(V) (VG) (GF) (DF)

Ingredients

200g chickpeas, soaked overnight, boiled until soft and cooked through (they will take 45 minutes to 2 hours – depending on age or size, watch they don't cook dry)

2 heaped tbsp tahini

2 tbsp olive oil

1 clove of garlic

juice of 1 lemon

6–8 ice cubes, or more, depending on size, or 75–100ml water

¼ tsp salt

pinch of toasted, ground cumin seeds (or paprika), to garnish

Method

1. Blend all the ingredients together (apart from the cumin seeds), keeping some oil and chickpeas for garnish, and adding the ice cubes 2 at a time until you get the creamy consistency you desire. (If you don't have ice cubes, add water, little by little, to the blender until the hummus is good and creamy.)

2. Make a hole in the middle, turning the bowl around a spoon, then pour in some olive oil, add the reserved chickpeas and garnish with toasted ground cumin or paprika.

Roast Rhubarb with Yoghurt

(VG) (GF)

Rhubarb first came to Europe in the fourteenth century along the Silk Road. It was once known as Turkish rhubarb and was more expensive than opium. It is a member of the knotweed family, which I used to eat in the woods behind our house in Swansea, where the young, juicy stems grew in abundance. It is popular in Persian cooking as an addition to savoury stews, and also cooked on charcoal grills with sugar. I like it roasted, as it doesn't stew down to a mush. Don't eat the leaves.

Ingredients

juice of 1 lemon or ½ orange

2 tbsp honey

250g rhubarb, topped and tailed and cut into finger-size portions

yoghurt

Method

1. Preheat the oven to 180°C/gas 4.

2. Mix the citrus juice with the honey, and drizzle it over the rhubarb in an ovenproof dish.

3. Cover with foil and roast for 10–15 minutes, until soft.

4. Serve with strained yoghurt, chopped dates and pistachio nuts.

Selda Bağcan 'Sivas Ellerinde Sazım Çalinir'

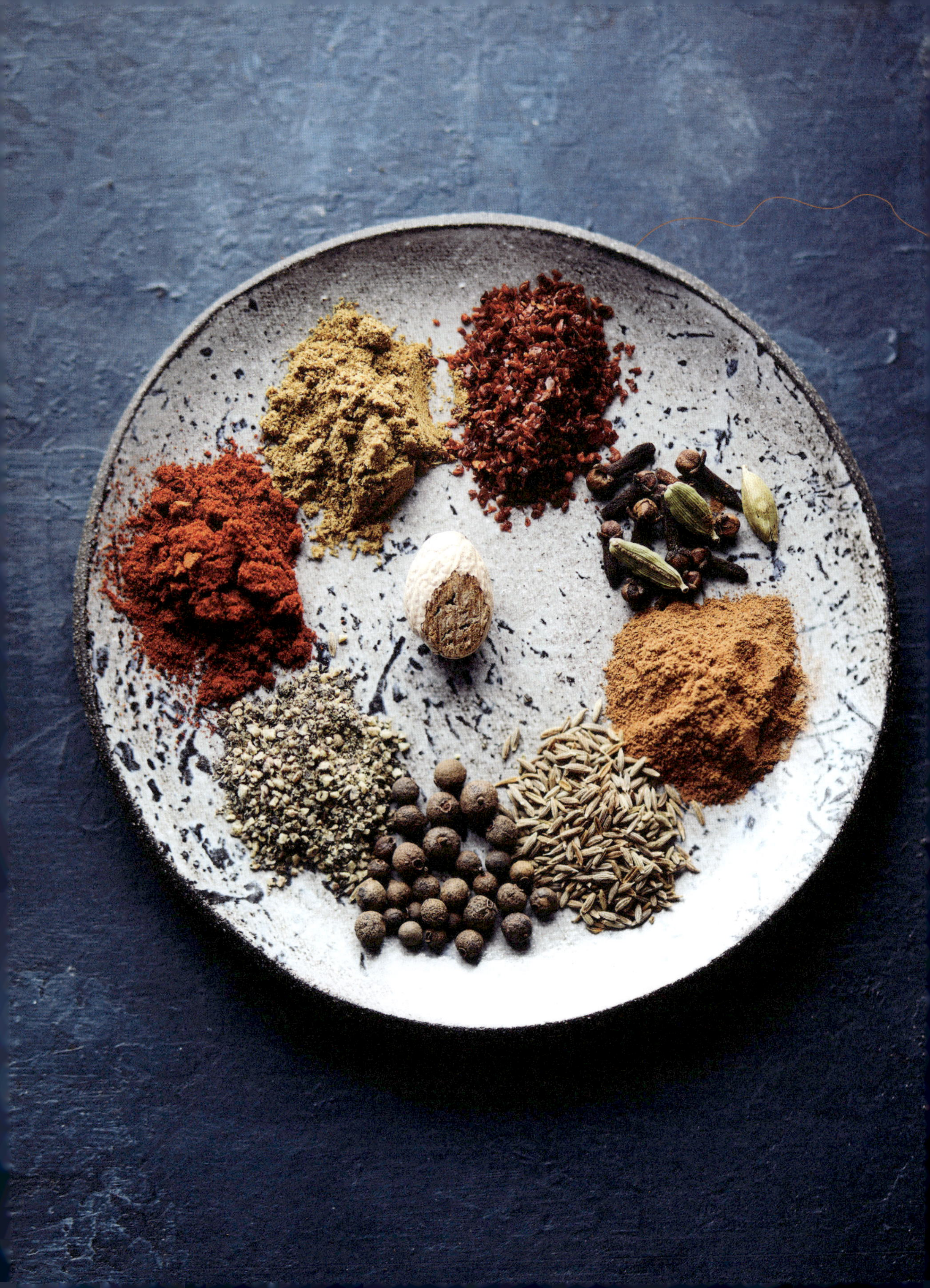

INDIA

Where the Mind is Without Fear

Where the mind is without fear and the head is held high;
Where knowledge is free;
Where the world has not been broken up into fragments by narrow domestic walls;
Where words come out from the depth of truth;
Where tireless striving stretches its arms towards perfection;
Where the clear stream of reason has not lost its way into the dreary desert sand of dead habit;
Where the mind is led forward by thee into ever-widening thought and action
Into that heaven of freedom, my Father, let my country awake.

From Gitanjali ('Song Offerings')
1912 (translated by Tagore)

We return to **RABINDRANATH TAGORE** for a poem. He is considered one of the greatest writers and thinkers in modern Indian literature; a reformer and critic of colonialism. He won the Nobel Prize for Literature in 1913 and was knighted in 1915, but surrendered the honour in the wake of the Amritsar massacre of 1919, when 400 Indians were shot by British troops.

I've picked a poem about open minds and enlightenment. It was his vision for his country to be free, and its people free of fear.

A pillar from 3000 BC can be found in Sarnath, where **LORD BUDDHA** taught the Dharma to five monks. At the top of the pillar are four lions. Below them are four animals: an elephant, representing Queen Maya's inception of Buddha, when she saw a white elephant entering her womb in a dream; a bull, representing desire during Buddha's time as a young prince; a horse, representing Buddha's leaving of the royal life and palace; and another lion, to represent the **NIRVANA** Lord Buddha attained.

CHILLIES are not indigenous to India but to Mesoamerica, including Mexico. They only arrived in India in the fifteenth or sixteenth century, brought there by Portuguese navigators. Before then, **BLACK PEPPER** was used to spice up dishes.

Mohandas Karamchand **GANDHI** (1869–1948) known as Mahatma 'Great Soul'. Gandhi fought for Indian independence from British rule and for the rights of the Indian poor. After studying in Britain and spending time in South Africa, he returned to India and began supporting the disenfranchised. He organized the famous salt march to the sea, in protest at the British salt laws which forced Indians to pay for heavily taxed British salt instead of being able to harvest their own. Gandhi and his wife were imprisoned for protesting about Indian soldiers coming to aid Britain in the Second World War while still being subjugated at home. India gained independence from Britain in 1947, but the Mountbatten Plan split her into two independent states along religious lines, the second state now known as Pakistan. This Partition set off mass killings on both sides. Gandhi was shot three times in January 1948 on his way to a prayer meeting in Delhi, and a crowd of a million or more mourned his death.

Gandhi was a rebellious teenager. He tried meat and alcohol and was married by the age of thirteen, leaving his father's deathbed to sleep with his wife. When the child of this union died, he took it as divine retribution and changed his whole life.

KRISHNA, from Sanskrit, meaning black or dark, described sometimes as the 'dark blue colour of monsoon clouds', and according to scholars, lived on earth between 3200 and 3100 BC. He is beloved as a god to millions and represents love and compassion.

There are twenty-two officially recognized languages in the Constitution of India, but hundreds of languages are spoken there, including Bengali, Gujarati, Odia, Punjabi, Tamil. **HINDI** is spoken by roughly 260 million people and **URDU** by some 65 million.

Some words with Indian origins are in everyday use in the UK:

Blighty, bandana, bungalow, bangle, cheetah, chit, chutney, cummerbund, cushy, dinghy, dungaree, gymkhana, jodhpur, juggernaut, jungle, loot, punch, pyjamas, pukka, thug, tickety-boo, toddy, typhoon, veranda.

'Do everything you have to do, but not with greed, not with ego, not with lust, not with envy but with love, compassion, humility and devotion.'

KRISHNA

'There are three gates to the self-destructive hell: lust, anger and greed.'

KRISHNA

SHAMPOO in Hindi means 'rub'. A Bengali named Sake Dean Mahomed and his Irish wife opened the first British shampooing shop in Brighton in 1814, shampooing itself being a relatively recent practice for us in Britain.

ABRAM WOOD and family, who were descended from people who had left Rajasthan, saved the Welsh tradition of playing the national instrument of Wales (the triple harp) in the eighteenth century.

The national flower is the **Lotus.**

'Mango is dropped in milk, mashed banana added, and then some sugared milk sweets are mashed into this. The sloshing sound echoes in the silence. Even ants return, shedding tears onto the empty plate.'

These words were written as a child by Rabindranath Tagore, born in 1861. This Bengali philosopher and poet collected menu cards wherever he travelled, loving pies as well as the more traditional cuisine of his native Kolkata.

A third of the 1.3 billion population of India are vegetarians, and so it's a great place to visit for anyone trying to reduce the amount of meat in their diet. Notwithstanding the health advantages (both for the planet and your own personal health) and the economics of a more plant-based diet, the overriding reason I eat so much Indian food is because it is, to my taste buds, the most tantalizing food in the world. We recently visited Odisha, on the Bay of Bengal, and I felt as though I'd landed in food heaven, eating *sambar*, *idlis*, *dosa*, coriander and coconut chutneys at every meal. I've carried fresh chillies around with me since I was a teenager, and if our family has a staple food, a go-to meal, it's daal. Each family has their own way of cooking it (and spelling it), each the best, each delicious. Lentils, much like potatoes, are so under-appreciated, but are the royals of the table: versatile, full of energy and goodness, a failsafe. It is pulses and beans, cooked with toasted spices, rice and aromatic oils, that make the bulk of our everyday meals at home.

Thanks to Mudrika Purohit, originally from Gujarat (via Uganda and Kenya), who moved next door to us in Cardiff, and who taught Mum to cook, we've been enjoying home-cooked Indian meals since the eighties. I'll always thank her for opening the door to the secrets of rolling chapatis, scorching aubergines on the gas ring, preparing the best vegetarian food this side of the sun. Further on down the line came more friendships and recipes from so many different regions. Mrs Boora and Apexa, I'm talking about you now. Whole leg of lamb marinated in yoghurt and roasted until golden, studded with cloves and whole black peppercorns and fluffy saffron rice, birianis, okra, spinach and paneer. With *Tosca* playing in the background, we were, right there in South Wales, feasting like the kings of Punjab.

I've been fascinated with the rich cultures of India and Pakistan for a very long time: the colours and intricacies of the silk saris, the gold, the *mehndi* (henna ink for tattoos), the ancient languages, medicines and holistic remedies, the yoga, the smoky red wines, the religions, social history, the migration of its peoples, not least the flight of musical tribes who left Rajasthan and Northern India between the sixth and eleventh centuries during the rise of Islam. They entered mid-west Asia and later dispersed across Europe, changing the musical landscape for ever with the 'gypsy' music they gifted to the world. Welcome in a myriad of forms, Macedonian, Serbian, Andalusian Flamenco, or in its dance with the Klezmer music of Eastern European Jews. Aye, we've arrived at music. The scales, rhythms, drones, the otherworldliness of Sufi performances and ghazal singers (ghazals are verses about love and praise) which still appeal across the religious divides. Then there's the glorious drama, choreography and escape of Bollywood. Imagine a world without it!

To spend time there was a hope realized: to visit the huge thirteenth-century Konark Sun Temple with its graphic freezes, an Indian music school, to ride through towns where front doors opened on to the road of honking, interweaving streams of traffic, bikes, mopeds, trucks, oxen, and cows roaming or napping in roundabouts. We rode through the countryside, passing rice fields where the women did the majority of the labour (ditto the towns, where young women in pink saris loaded bricks onto their heads in baskets, the mainstay of construction work), visited rural villages, wore necklaces of bright orange marigolds (the word 'orange' is thought to come from the Dravidian languages of South India), brushed our teeth in a lake where cows paddled, the laundry was washed and the dishes scrubbed in the shade of palmtrees. Smartphones everywhere, but sadly also skewed adverts. Coca-Cola, deliberately choosing pale-skinned models to sell tooth-decaying refined sugars to country folk, plastering posters on the rickety-shack stall walls, ironically dwarfed by palm trees whose coconut water we now favour in the West. The cooking on the floor, the fires, the endless industry. I came back thoughtful but inspired, with a huge bunch of curry leaves from a tree in Puri, which I froze in bags as soon as I got home. I'm still using them, and when they sizzle in oil, it's a little taste of Odisha.

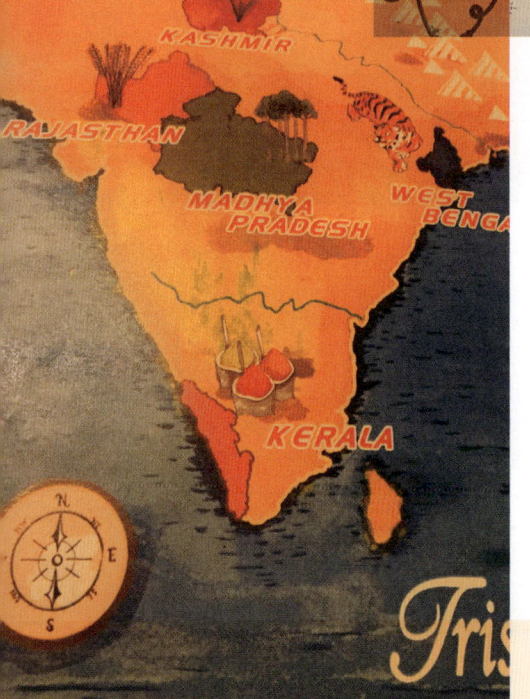

> 'Why shouldn't a moonlight night be
> a fit time for drinking wine?
> What if today there's no breeze
> nor black clouds in the sky?'
>
> **GHAZAL BY MIRZA GHALIB,**
> born in 1797 and considered one of the
> greatest poets in the Urdu language.
> (translated by Dr Sarvat Rahman)

Indian wine is smoky, try this above, Soul Tree or Sula.

INDIA

INDIA

ON THE MENU

SAAG PANEER

ROAST ALOO

FRESH PICKLED ONIONS

JEERA RICE

DAAL

CORIANDER CHUTNEY

VAGHAR

EGG CURRY

STORE-CUPBOARD CURRY

CHAPATI

RAITA

CARROT SALAD

VEGAN RICE PUDDING

DRINK

LASSI

chilli · curry leaves · mustard seeds · onions · coriander (fresh and seeds) · cardamom · garlic · cumin · turmeric · ginger · lentils

These are just some of the recipes I return to week-on-week, some vegan, all superb. The coriander and coconut chutney is a variant on a recipe I picked up thanks to the Madras Café, a vegetarian Indian food restaurant which is the best pop-up restaurant at the WOMAD world music festival, held each year in Wiltshire.

Asha Bhosle 'Karle Paar Karle'

Kishore Kumar 'Main Hoon Jhoom Jhumroo'

Saag Paneer

VG **GF**

Although we used to make paneer at home, you can get it ready-made from supermarkets. It freezes well, and if rushed, I have cooked it from frozen, though ideally defrost it first.

Ingredients

2 tbsp vegetable oil
1 onion, very finely chopped
salt and pepper
2 cloves of garlic, very finely chopped
1 tsp grated ginger
1 tsp whole cumin seeds, toasted and roughly ground
fresh whole green chillies, split lengthways
¼ tsp cayenne pepper
¼ tsp ground turmeric
100ml water
250g paneer, cubed
200g spinach (or 160g greens like callaloo, kale, cavolo nero)
juice of ½ lemon (2 tbsp)

Method

1. Heat the oil in a pan and fry the onion with a pinch of salt on a medium heat until soft and golden – about 5–7 minutes.
2. Add the garlic and ginger and stir for a few minutes until soft, then add the cumin and stir for a minute to release the flavours.
3. Add the chillies, cayenne, turmeric, water and paneer, stir, then add the greens and lemon juice.
4. Put a lid on the pan and cook for 5 minutes, or until the spinach is wilted.
5. Stir, taste, season, turn the heat down low, and it's ready to serve.

For a vegan version of this dish, replace paneer with firm tofu.

Option:
Add 1 tsp ground coriander seeds when you add the cumin.

Mohammed Rafi 'Kya Hua Tera Vada'

Roast Aloo

(V) (VG) (GF) (DF)

Ingredients

600g potatoes (4 medium), chopped as for small roast potatoes
2–3 tbsp vegetable oil
1 tsp mustard seeds
1 tsp cumin seeds
300g tomatoes (cherry tomatoes are nice in this dish, otherwise 2–3 tomatoes cut into small pieces)
¼ tsp ground turmeric
sea salt
juice of ½ lemon

Method

1. Preheat the oven to 220°C/gas 7.
2. Parboil the potatoes and drain, keeping the water.
3. Heat the oil in a shallow tray/dish on top of the grill. Fry both kinds of seeds until the mustard seeds pop (use vegetable oil, not olive oil, as the latter won't be hot enough to make the mustard seeds pop).
4. Add the potatoes and tomatoes, sprinkle on the turmeric and a pinch of salt, add 5 tablespoons of the potato water and stir.
5. Roast in the oven for 20–30 minutes, adding more potato water if it dries out completely.
6. When the potatoes are roasted and cooked through, squeeze over the lemon juice, taste, add more salt if needed, and serve.

Fresh Pickled Onions

(V) (VG) (GF) (DF)

Finely chop ½ a white or red onion, or 2–3 spring onions. Add the juice of 1 lemon and stir so that the onions are covered by the lemon juice (you can use vinegar if you don't have lemon). Leave the onions to sit and pickle if you have time.

Before serving, add a sprinkle of cayenne pepper and some chopped fresh coriander if you have some.

Jeera Rice

(V) (VG) (GF) (DF)

Jeera is cumin. Cook your rice in the usual way, but before serving, fry 1 teaspoon of whole cumin seeds with 8 curry leaves in 3 tablespoons of hot vegetable oil (not olive oil). Sizzle for a minute or so, then pour the *vaghar* (see p. 219) on to the rice.

Option:
Use ghee if you have some, instead of oil.

Ghazalaw with Tauseef Akhtar, Gwyneth Glyn, Georgia Ruth 'Seren Syw (Teri Aankhon Mein)'

Daal

VG GF

Ingredients

2 tbsp butter

2 tbsp vegetable oil

1 large onion, finely chopped

1 generous tsp grated ginger, or ½ tsp ground ginger

1 tsp cumin seeds, toasted

½ tsp cayenne pepper (or less, to taste)

200g red lentils

1.1 litres boiling water

¼ tsp ground turmeric

1 fresh green chilli (or to taste)

½ tsp salt (or to your taste)

fresh coriander, chopped, to serve

Method

1. In a casserole or a large pan, heat the butter and oil on a medium heat until the butter starts to brown.
2. Add the onion with a pinch of salt and cook until soft and golden – about 7–9 minutes.
3. Add the ginger and cumin, stir a few seconds, then add the cayenne and the lentils, stirring so that they absorb the flavours.
4. Pour on 900ml of the boiling water and add the turmeric. Turn down the heat, put a lid on the pan, cook for 15 minutes, then add a further 200ml of water.
5. Keep simmering, stirring every once in a while, checking that it isn't sticking.
6. After 40 minutes, the lentils should be soft and incorporated. Taste, adding more salt if needed.
7. If you'd rather a thicker daal, cook it for a little longer with the lid off.
8. Garnish with fresh coriander, and serve with chapatis or rice.

Option:
Browning the butter in oil like this is also a good base for making tomato sauces for pasta.

Coriander Chutney

V VG GF DF

Ingredients

large bunch of fresh coriander (approx. 100g)
40g desiccated coconut
100ml water
2 green chillies (or to taste)
½ tsp grated ginger
juice of ½ lemon
¼ tsp sea salt

Method

1. Blend together all the ingredients.
2. Now make a *vaghar*: into 1 tablespoon of hot oil, put ½ teaspoon of mustard seeds, ¼ teaspoon of cumin seeds, and 4 curry leaves if you have some.
3. Put the chutney into a serving dish and pour over the *vaghar*.

Option:
Add some yoghurt to this.

Vaghar

V VG GF DF

Spices and other ingredients may be flash-fried in hot vegetable oil to enhance their flavours. This flavoured/tempered oil is then poured over a main dish, and is known as a *vaghar*.

My favourite *vaghar* is made like this:

To a pan of 2–3 tablespoons of vegetable oil, add ¾ teaspoon of mustard seeds, 10 curry leaves and a pinch of asafoetida. Pour over your cooked daal, rice or raita.

Adding chopped tomatoes and cumin seeds is another variation.

Arun Ghosh 'Punjabi Girl'

Egg Curry

VG GF

A family favourite. The title might not appeal, but once tasted it becomes a staple.

Ingredients

2 tbsp vegetable oil
1 onion, finely chopped
¼ tsp salt, or to taste
1 heaped tsp grated ginger
1 tsp cumin seeds, toasted and ground
1 fresh green chilli, sliced lengthways (or 2 dried chillies)
200ml vegetable stock (or water with ½ stock cube, dissolved)
squeeze of tomato purée
juice of ½ lemon
¼ tsp garam masala (see below)
250ml cream
8 eggs, medium hard-boiled, shelled and halved
¼ tsp ground turmeric
¼ tsp cayenne pepper (or more, to taste)
fresh coriander, chopped, to serve

Method

1. Heat the oil in a large pan and fry the onion with a pinch of salt on a medium heat until soft, about 5–7 minutes.
2. Add the ginger, cumin and chilli, and cook for another 1–2 minutes.
3. Add the stock, tomato purée, lemon juice, turmeric, cayenne pepper and garam masala and turn down the heat. Stir in the cream, taste and season, then add the halved eggs.
4. Simmer on a low heat until the sauce reaches a lovely consistency, about 15–20 minutes.
5. Serve sprinkled with fresh coriander.

Garam masala:

Freshly made garam masala (literally, 'hot mix') makes all the difference, but it is pungent rather than hot; it is named for its warming properties and is very similar to the aromatic baharat spice mix (see p. 197). Garam masala is a mix of ground toasted whole spices: the ratio and choice of spices varies, but I include approximately equal proportions of the following: cardamom pods, bay leaves, peppercorns, cassia bark, then a half measurement of cloves and nutmeg. Toast the spices on a heavy pan for a minute or two, until fragrant, then grind in a pestle and mortar or a blender. Store in a jar for a week or two, then make a fresh batch.

Ananda Shankar 'Jumping Jack Flash'

Store-cupboard Curry

GF DF NV

Whatever you have in your fridge, you can make a spicy meal fit for kings.

500g of your choice of the following: chopped vegetables, cooked beans or other pulses, tofu, paneer, prawns or meat (e.g. browned chicken thighs, no skin)

Fresh coriander, chopped, to serve

Ingredients

3–4 tbsp oil
1 onion, chopped
salt and pepper
1 clove of garlic, chopped
1 tsp grated ginger (a thumb-sized piece)
1 tsp cumin seeds, toasted and ground
1 tsp coriander seeds, toasted and ground
1 fresh green or dried chilli, or to taste
1 x 400g tin of tomatoes
¼ tsp ground turmeric
¼ tsp cayenne pepper
¼ tsp garam masala
200ml stock (or water with a stock cube, dissolved)
fresh coriander, chopped, to serve

Method

1. Heat the oil in a pan and fry the onion with a pinch of salt on a medium heat until soft and golden – about 7–10 minutes.
2. Add the garlic and ginger and fry for 1–2 minutes, then add the cumin, coriander and chillies, and stir to release the flavours.
3. Add the tomatoes, stir then reduce down for 10 minutes – don't let it catch – you need it to turn a darker colour.
4. Now add your main ingredient of choice: vegetables/prawns/paneer/pulses/meat.
5. Add the turmeric, cayenne, garam masala and stock, stir, then put a lid on the pan and cook until heated through. Turn the heat right down and simmer for 30–45 minutes, adding more water if it gets too thick.
6. Taste, season with salt and black pepper, and serve with fresh coriander and rice.

Option:

If you like it rich, add 100ml of cream or yoghurt at the end. Stir in, and heat right through before serving.

Asha Bhosle and R. D. Burman 'Piya Tu Ab To Aaja'

Chapati

V VG DF

I use chapati flour, but if you don't have any you can use a ratio of 1:1 wholewheat flour with white flour (plain or even self-raising).

Ingredients

200g chapati flour

½ tsp salt

1–2 tbsp vegetable oil

100ml (or more) water – enough to make a soft dough

Method

1. In a large bowl mix the flour and salt, add the oil, then gradually add the water, gently working it until you get a soft dough.
2. Cover with a damp tea towel or clingfilm and leave for 10 minutes.
3. On a floured surface take the dough and knead for 5–10 minutes until elastic.
4. Divide mix into 10 balls and roll each to a 2mm thickness.
5. Heat a pan, griddle or bake stone until very hot and cook each chapati for about 45 seconds each side. (At this point you have an option to try to bloat them up by placing directly on a gas flame.) Keep hot in a tea towel until you ready to serve.

Mukesh 'Mera Joota Hai Japani'

Raita

VG GF

We used to stir a teaspoon of mint sauce into yoghurt, a British twist you still see in some restaurants, offered with poppadoms. I prefer this raita.

Ingredients

200ml yoghurt
¼ small onion or 1 spring onion, finely chopped (about 40g)
1 tomato, finely chopped
¼ cucumber (about 40g)
sea salt
2–3 tbsp vegetable oil (not olive oil)
½ tsp mustard seeds
5 curry leaves
pinch of cayenne pepper
¼ tsp ground cumin seeds, toasted
fresh coriander leaves, chopped

Method

1. Mix the first four ingredients in a serving bowl and add a pinch of salt.
2. Heat 2–3 tablespoons of vegetable oil (not olive), and add ½ teaspoon of mustard seeds (and 5 curry leaves if you have some) until they pop.
3. Pour the oil and spices on to the yoghurt mixture and serve immediately, garnished with a pinch of cayenne, the toasted ground cumin and some chopped coriander leaves.

Carrot Salad

V VG GF DF

The southern Indian taste of the popped mustard seeds rules in this. It's so simple to make and so, so good.

Ingredients

2 tbsp vegetable oil (not olive oil)
1 tsp mustard seeds
4 carrots, grated
juice of ½ lemon
pinch of sea salt

Method

1. Heat the oil in a pan, then add the mustard seeds and cook until they pop.
2. Pour this *vaghar* on to the grated carrots and stir in the lemon juice and salt.

Kishore Kumar 'Eena Meena Deeka'

Lata Mangeshkar 'Gore Gore O Banke Chhore'

Vegan Rice Pudding (aka the one-tin wonder)

(V) (VG) (GF) (DF)

I love this fuss-free dessert and use a tin to measure out the ingredients. You can throw everything into the pot and pretty much leave it for the next hour.

Ingredients

1 x 400ml tin of coconut milk
2 x 400ml tins of water (use the coconut milk tin to measure)
1 x ¾ full tin of brown basmati rice (240g – again, use the tin to measure)
4 cardamom pods, split
1 x 5cm long strip of cassia bark or cinnamon stick
pinch of saffron
4 cloves
soft brown sugar (or honey) to taste

Method

1. Put all the ingredients into a saucepan and bring to the boil.
2. Turn down the heat, put on the lid, and cook until the rice is soft and the liquid has been incorporated to make a creamy dessert – about 1 hour, checking during the last 10–15 minutes of cooking that it's not burning at the bottom.
3. Stir, taste, and leave off the lid for the last 10 minutes if you need to lose more liquid.
4. Serve with chopped toasted pistachios or other chopped nuts or seeds, e.g. almonds/pumpkin seeds/sunflower seeds.

Option:
Stir in ½–1 tsp rose water near the end of cooking.

Lassi

(VG) (GF)

I like the ratio of 1:1 yoghurt to water.

Ingredients

200ml yoghurt
200ml ice-cold water
pinch of sea salt
3 ice cubes (optional)
cumin seeds, toasted and ground

Method

1. Whisk together the yoghurt and water with a pinch of salt until frothy, or put into a blender (adding the ice cubes if you like).
2. Serve, sprinkled with toasted ground cumin.

Options:

Mint lassi: add a sprig of fresh mint to the blender.

Turmeric lassi: add ¼ teaspoon of ground turmeric.

Cardamom lassi: add the black seeds from inside 2 cardamom pods.

Mango lassi: omit the salt and spices, and add the pulp of a fresh mango to the blender. Serve with a sprig of mint.

A turmeric nightcap:
To a mug of hot milk, add ¼–½ teaspoon of ground turmeric. It is meant to relax and deepen sleep. (Don't add too much turmeric, though, as it can, apparently, make you itch.)

Debashish Bhattacharya 'Gypsi Anandi'

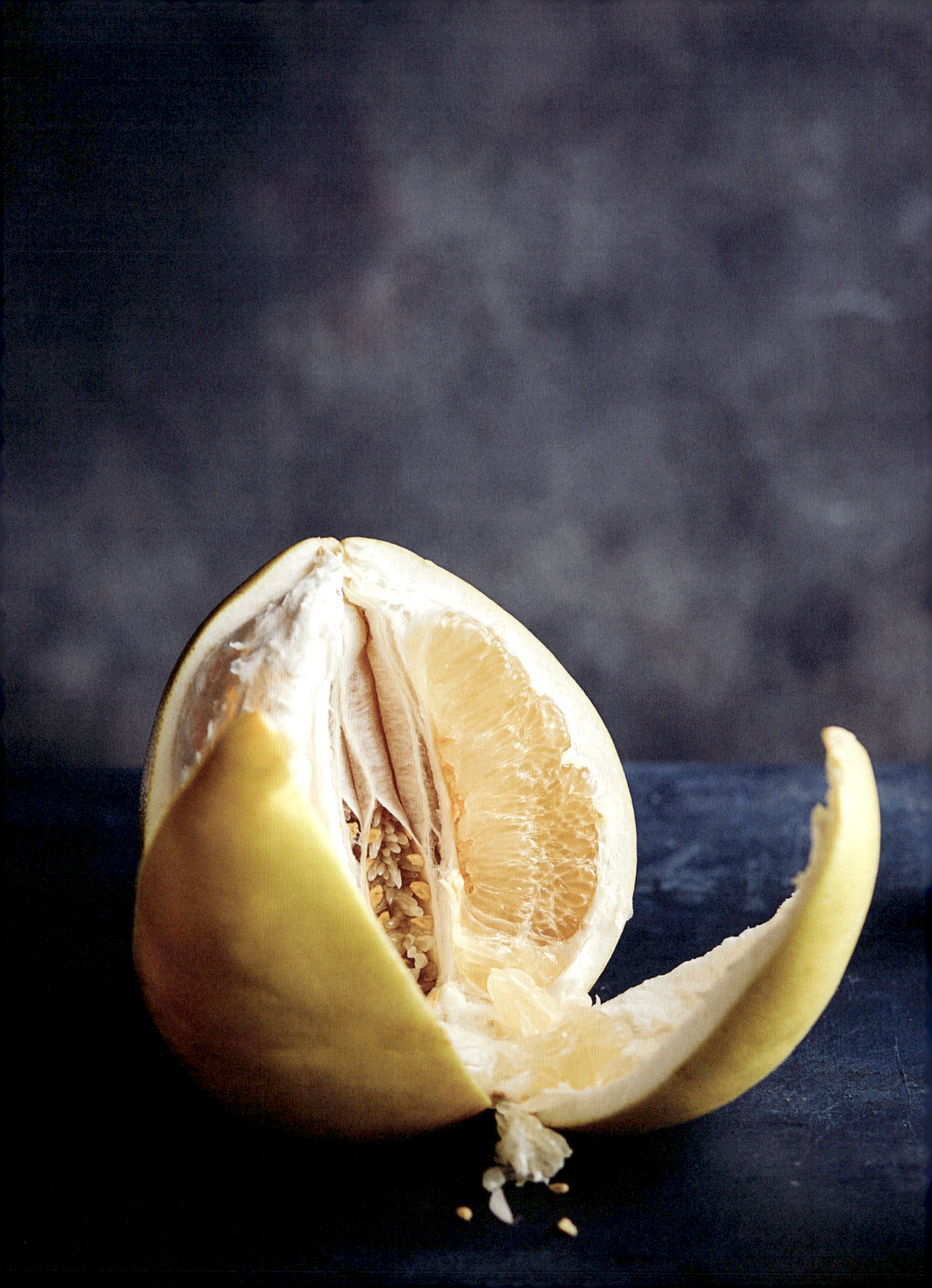

CHINA

'On the Road'

Sadness at the hairs in the mirror is no longer new,
　　The stains on my coat are harder to brush away.
　　　　I waste my hopes by river and lakes, a fishing-rod in the hand
　　　　　　Which screens me from the Western sunlight as I look toward Ch'ang-an

Translated by A. C. Graham

TU MU, FROM *POEMS OF THE LATE T'ANG*
In this poem, the scene is set by an ageing down-at-heel romantic, who escapes by fishing, much as I do with my cauldron and fire. Tu Mu (803–852) was a master of a kind of poetry called *chueh-chu:* four lines bursting with life. He seemed to love his time on Earth and is a joy to read, delighted as he was with the natural world, wine and women.

Entrevue de Confucius et de Lao-tse.

CONFUCIUS (551–479 BCE),

China's 'first teacher' was a sage, scholar and philosopher. He described himself as a 'Transmitter who invented nothing', and advocated enlightenment and education. One of the most important and influential thinkers in the history of the world, Confucius remains a towering figure in today's China. Though born to a poor family, and schooled humbly, he rose through the ranks of government, first as book-keeper and animal carer then as teacher and governor of a small town, at one point holding the title 'Minister of Justice'. Famously, Confucius was drawn to walk away from all this, to go on a **LONG SET OF JOURNEYS** through various regions of China, and not returning home until he reached the age of sixty-eight.

His philosophy, Confucianism, is followed almost like a religion, but its values are secular, like a set of moral codes or ethics. Its greatest emphasis is on the importance of study.

Confucius was also a **FOODIE** whose directives for a healthy lifestyle have proved valuable despite being established over 2,000 years ago. Here is some Confucian wisdom on eating and drinking:

Do Not Eat:
Food that smells bad, rotten fish and meat;

Food that has changed colour, smells bad, is not cooked right;

Food in the wrong season.

Even if there is an abundance of meat, one must not eat more meat than staple grains.

One can drink wine without limit, but one mustn't get drunk.

———

Confucius' family surname is **Kong.** Members of this family have the longest known family tree. There are over eighty father-to-son generations recorded, with 2 million known descendants.

Confucian wisdom:

'If you are planning for a year, sow rice; if you are planning for a decade, plant trees; if you are planning for a lifetime, educate people.'

'What you do not wish for yourself, do not do to others.'

'Treat your neighbours as you would be treated.'

———

I love this advice on drinking and his nod to the wisdom of not consuming too much meat, echoed here in a quote from a Song Dynasty poet, Su Shih:

'One can manage without eating flesh; but one cannot manage without the bamboo.'

———

The **kumquat** fruit is named from a similar sounding Cantonese phrase meaning golden tangerine/orange.

FACING HEAVEN CHILLI

Chillies, Sichuan peppercorns, aromatic spices and toasted sesame seeds make the most delicious **CHILLI OILS.** I often fry up dried bullet-head chillies to serve as a condiment.

Plum blossom and peony, flowers of riches and honour, are traditional floral symbols in Chinese culture.

CHOPSTICKS have been used for over 6,000 years, and were probably invented as far back as 9,000 years ago. The Chinese symbols for chopsticks are translated literally as 'quick bamboo'.

The Kiwi fruit is native to China and used to be called the **CHINESE GOOSEBERRY** until New Zealand producers renamed it the Kiwi fruit in 1962 to help exports.

The phrase 'Gung-ho' comes from the Chinese language, originally meaning 'to work together'.

I had a huge **BAMBOO** grove in my garden in Nashville; we ate the buds as they started poking through the soil. They are starchy, tasting like raw potato.

The English word 'chopstick' was first seen in the 1699 book *Voyages and Descriptions* by William Dampier.

The **GINKGO** tree, native to China, is the national tree and has been found in fossils dating back 270 million years.

Six ginkgo trees survived the atomic bombing of Hiroshima, Japan. It is known as the 'Giant panda of plant' and the 'No. 1 living fossil'.

'Beneath these green mountains where spring rules the year. The irbarbutus and loquat in season appear, and feasting on lychee – 300 a day, I shouldn't mind resting eternally here.'

SU SHIH

I once travelled to the far-off island of Nauru, en route to the Central Pacific islands known collectively as Kiribati. We landed and disembarked from the tiny plane; people, live chickens and televisions were to wait for some five hours in the airport before being marched back on the plane and flown onwards to Tarawa, our final destination. Nauru has a dramatic history of boom and bust but is notorious now as being home to some questionable offshore refugee encampments belonging to Australia. The boom came from selling guano, bird poo fertilizer. In the eighties it was the richest country per capita in the world, before the guano ran out. So did the cash, hence the refugee camps in exchange for money, and this enforced landing for tourists, to demand landing tax. I became bored and hungry during the stopover, went for a swim and almost drowned. Nauru is a continental shelf island, with lethal offshore currents. I was pulled out to the vast Pacific Ocean at extraordinary speed, but before I was completely out of my depth, I stuck my big toe into the sand and half swam, half waded to shore. I survived and went to find a restaurant.

The only one I could find anywhere on this parched atoll was a Chinese restaurant, a wooden shack, nudged between the few remaining palm trees, covered with white powder from the guano mines. I ordered hot steaming dumplings, and was served chicken feet and some pigskin. I returned to join the queue to board, thinking about the old quote, 'We the Chinese conquered the world through our food', and the gall and resilience of the restaurant's owners. I began to wonder about the challenges of opening businesses in remote places like this, navigating a foreign land, foreign law, bureaucracy, language, alphabet, unfamiliar crops and products – I felt admiration for the world's migrant entrepreneurs and chefs. China, master of the Silk Road, is renowned for its trading acumen, its explorers, far-travelling workforce and innovations: here paper, gunpowder, the compass and, quite probably, alcohol were first produced. It was therefore a total thrill to visit for the first time back in 2016.

Beijing, my first port of call, smelt of roast duck. What did I expect? It was formerly known to us as Peking and, of course, is home to Peking Duck. The bloated white carcasses of these birds are seen hanging on hooks; their distinctive bright red colour comes from braising and roasting in the log fire ovens of the duck restaurants. Red is everywhere; the red and gold hanging lanterns symbolize booming life and prosperous business. It was summer when we visited. Squeezed between the high-rise new developments remained older housing in streets and alleys called *hutongs*, which were covered in pumpkin plants. I love this kind of guerrilla market-gardening bang in the centre of cities. In heaving, polluted Beijing, these green shoots with their yellow flowers climbed all over old walls and chainlink fences. Food is everything in China, regarded as high art and central to every aspect of life. Tea, too, with every meal, and shops entirely dedicated to different teas; rows upon row of glass jars, shades of various greens, and dried flowers, each purporting to possess special medicinal properties.

We took in the views from the Great Wall of China, learning more about the harrowing lives of those who built and then protected it. Some parts of the wall were built as early as the seventh century – the main reason for the construction was to stop raiding from nomadic tribes from the west, but it was also used as a kind of border control both for people and the taxing of goods. We took an overnight train to Xi'an, famous for its terracotta warriors and bang bang noodles: 4 inches wide, 2 metres long and handmade – the best I've ever tasted. Bang bang noodles are named after the slapping sound made as you bang them on the table to stretch them. I tried making them at home: there's a lot of kneading and stand-by time that renders the dough elastic enough to stretch. They were delicious, though not as good as those tasted in Xi'an, dipped in divine chilli oils made with Szechuan peppercorns, chillies and sesame seeds. These oils, oozing with nutty, toasty warming spices – ginger, bay and star anise – were served wherever we went in China. Also popular was the smashed cucumber side dish with more chilli, so easy to make at home, and I've included a recipe in the coming pages.

CHINA

'Learning without thought means labour lost; thought without learning is perilous.'

CONFUCIUS

Xian'r Lao Man
Our dumplings Are The Fullest

'A peasant must stand a long time on a hillside with his mouth open before a roast duck flies in.'

CHINESE PROVERB

CHINA

'We have two lives,
and the second begins
when we realize we
only have one.'

CONFUCIUS

'It does not matter how slowly you
go as long as you do not stop.'

CONFUCIUS

Night-time dance meetings in Xi'an.

ON THE MENU

EASY AND QUICK CHINESE DINNER

CHARGRILLED GREENS

TOFU AND PEANUT STIR-FRY

EGG FRIED RICE

SMASHED CUCUMBERS

DESSERT

POMELO AND LYCHEE

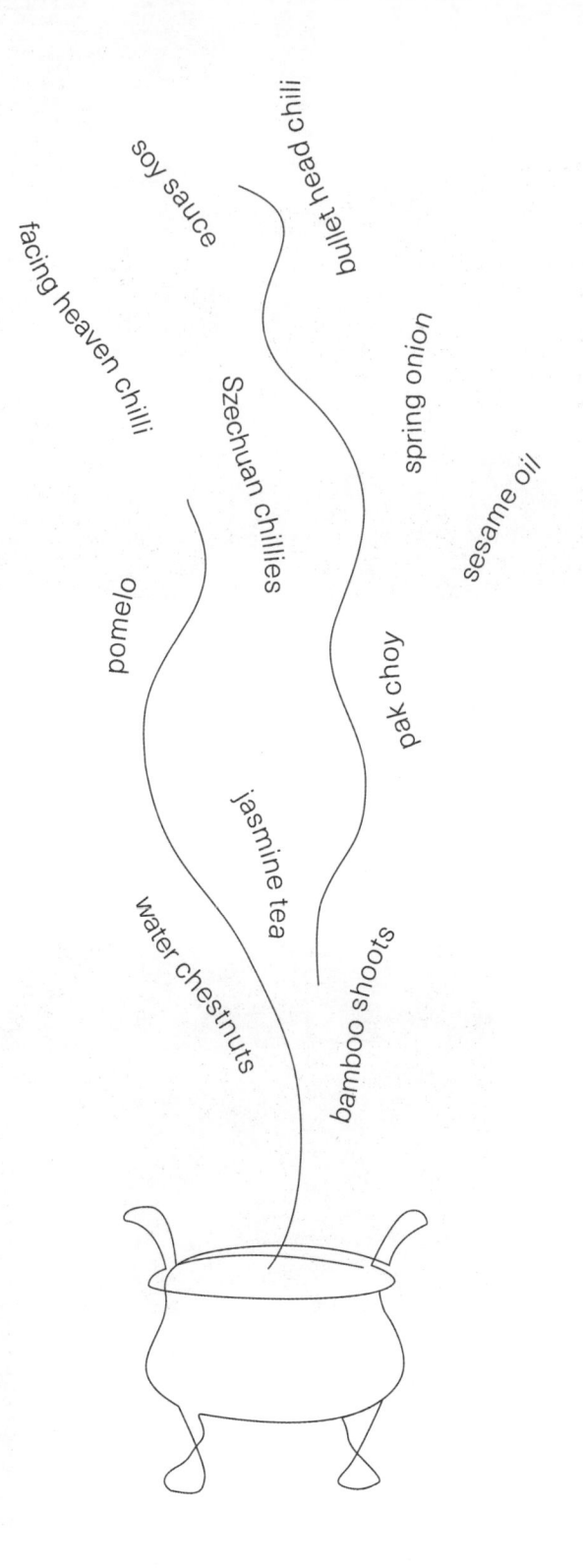

soy sauce · bullet head chilli · facing heaven chilli · Szechuan chillies · spring onion · sesame oil · pomelo · pak choy · jasmine tea · water chestnuts · bamboo shoots

The City of Prague Orchestra 'Once Upon A Time In China', from *Farewell My Concubine*

Easy and Quick Chinese Dinner

(V) (VG) (GF) (DF) (NV)

You are simply flash-frying food with ginger, garlic and onion, with a sauce made with stock and soy, thickened with cornflour.

Prepare the food first as this is a quick dish to cook. You can substitute any finely sliced/julienned vegetables like courgettes, carrots, mushrooms, peppers, baby corns, aubergine. Try also with 100g cooked black beans or chickpeas, and for a change try adding 1 tsp of Shaoxing or dried sherry to the dish, at the same time as the soy. The combination is up to you. Prepare everything before any cooking, cutting all the vegetables to a similar size. You'll need about 500g in total (not including the cornerstones: ginger, garlic and onion).

For example:
500g of 3 types of vegetables: pak choy, Chinese cabbage, green pepper, mange tout, broccoli, courgettes, green beans, mushrooms, carrots, water chestnuts, bamboo.

Or:
Vegetables and pulses/peas: 400g vegetables with 100g of cooked peas, chickpeas, black beans, broad beans.

Or:
Tofu, prawn or meat stir fry: 250g vegetables with 250g tofu or uncooked prawns or meat. (Make sure the meat is very thinly sliced and add at step 3, just after the garlic and chilli, and cook through before adding the vegetables.)

Add a handful of pre-toasted nuts, peanuts, cashews to any of these combinations.

Method

Follow the same steps as the recipe for Tofu and Peanut Stir-fry (p. 237), but using your choice of 500g of ingredients.

Chargrilled Greens

(V) (VG) (DF)

Ingredients

2 tbsp groundnut or vegetable oil

200g greens, such as chopped kale and cavolo nero, sprouted and broccoli

2 tsp soy sauce or tamari (to taste), or the juice of ½ lemon

sprinkling of toasted sesame seeds

sea salt

Method

1. Massage the oil on to the greens.
2. Heat a large heavy saucepan, add the greens and cook on a high heat for 7–9 minutes, turning them from time to time as they scorch/char.
3. Either: add soy sauce (or tamari) to taste, and serve with a sprinkling of toasted sesame seeds.
4. Or: squeeze over the lemon juice and sprinkle with sea salt.

Option:
If using kale and cavolo nero, continue to cook them on a low heat for another 10–20 minutes until they get crisp, to get a kind of cheater's crispy seaweed. Then choose either the soy or the lemon dressing (steps 3 and 4 above) and serve.

You can also try adding grated garlic with the greens.

The Gentle Good and members of the UK Chinese Ensemble 'Antiffoni', from *Y Bardd Anfarwol*, about Tang Dynasty poet Li Bai

Wild Children 'Incantation'

Drinking Song

Bai Guang 'Qiu Ye (Autumn Night)'

Tofu and Peanut Stir-fry

(V) (VG) (GF) (DF)

Cornerstone ingredients

2 tbsp groundnut or vegetable oil

1 clove of garlic, finely chopped

2 dried red chillies (e.g. bullet chillies, optional)

1 inch cube of ginger (same size as the garlic), finely chopped

½ onion or 2 spring onions, finely chopped

Sauce

200ml vegetable stock

2 tbsp soy sauce

1 tbsp cornflour

500g choice of ingredients

50g sliced water chestnuts (drained and sliced)

50g bamboo shoots (drained and sliced)

150g pak choy, chopped

250g firm tofu, drained

Also: a handful of peanuts (unsalted, skinned)

Method

1. Cook your accompanying rice or noodles first so that they are ready.

2. Mix the stock, soy sauce, cornflour (and the rice wine, if using) in a cup, to make the sauce.

3. Heat a large frying pan or wok until very hot, then add the oil. Flash-fry the garlic, chillies and ginger for thirty seconds, then add the onions, vegetables and tofu and fry, stirring, for 2–3 minutes.

   (If using meat, add at this step after the garlic, chillies and ginger, and cook through before adding the vegetables)

4. Add the sauce mix and the nuts, turn heat down low or remove pan from time to time to avoid burning, stirring as the sauce thickens.

5. Taste, adding more soy sauce if needed, add a drizzle of sesame oil if you fancy.

6. Serve with steaming bowls of rice or noodles (with added garnish options of fresh coriander and/or fine slices of spring onions and sesame seeds).

Wu Junde 'Ma Ni Gan Ge'

Wu Man 'White Snow In A Sunny Spring'

Chang Jing 'In The Past'

Red Chamber 'Sunny Spring And White Snow'

Egg Fried Rice

VG GF DF

If there's leftover cooked rice, this is especially swift; great when you're hungry and tired.

Ingredients

1–2 tbsp sesame oil, plus extra to taste

4 eggs, beaten

400g cooked rice

100g frozen peas (or cooked fresh peas, or cooked green beans, chopped)

50ml water or light vegetable stock

soy sauce, to taste

toasted sesame seeds and/or sliced spring onion, to garnish

Method

1. Heat the sesame oil in a large saucepan. Pour in the eggs and begin to cook.
2. Add the rice and peas, and stir.
3. Add the water or stock, stir, then put on the lid and heat through on a low-medium heat.
4. Once heated right through (3–4 minutes), add sesame oil and soy sauce to taste.
5. Serve sprinkled with sesame seeds and/or spring onion.

Hani Union 'Greek Text'

Herbert Stothart and the MGM Studio Orchestra 'Home From The Meeting', from *Dragon Seed*

Lei Qiang 'Boys And Flowers/Raise The Red Lantern'

The Gentle Good and members of the UK Chinese Ensemble 'Meddyliau Distaw'r Nos', from *Y Bardd Anfarwol*, about Tang Dynasty poet Li Bai

Smashed Cucumbers

(V) (VG) (DF)

A refreshing foil to any dish: the crunch, the garlic, the vinegar, the chilli. It's your choice whether you peel some of the green skin, or whether you remove the inner pulp – it depends on how much time you have and what your preference is. Being a gung-ho cook, I leave it on.

Ingredients

1 large cucumber
2 tsp fine salt
2 cloves of garlic, very finely chopped
1 tsp toasted sesame oil
1½ tsp Chinese black rice vinegar (also called Chinkiang vinegar), or rice vinegar
2 teaspoons light soy sauce
½ tsp mirin rice wine (optional, or use ½ tsp sugar or honey if you want)
½ tsp chilli flakes, or chopped fresh red chilli
½ tsp toasted Szechuan peppercorns (optional)

Method

1. Place the cucumber on a chopping board and roughly bash it with a rolling pin until flattened slightly but not broken open. You are aiming to break the cucumber up inside without splitting the skin too much.

2. Slice the cucumber in half lengthways, then cut into 2-cm chunks. Place in a bowl and sprinkle with the salt. Leave for 10 minutes, then discard the liquid, rinse the cucumber and blot dry with kitchen paper.

3. Mix together the remaining ingredients in a small bowl (making sure the sugar is dissolved if using). Taste and adjust the seasoning if necessary. Pour over the cucumber chunks and stir to coat. Serve immediately.

You can make this without salting and standing for 10 minutes, if you don't have time – just don't add the wet mix until just before serving.

To drink
Jasmine tea in a teapot with small porcelain cups.

Pomelo and Lychee

(V) (VG) (GF) (DF)

A beautiful dish of Asian fruit: kumquats, lychees and pomelo (peel like a grapefruit, discard the white pith). Pomelo is one of the four original citrus species from which the rest of the cultivated citrus hybridized, and is very good for you. Also add some 'fire dragon fruit', as the pitaya (native of the Americas) is called by the Chinese (eat the white and black speckled insides, not the pink), and some kiwi fruit and lychee.

Shigeru Umebayashi 'Battle In The Forest', from *House of Flying Daggers*

Roc Chen 'Deep Love Of Yu Zhanao', from *Red Sorghum*

Wang Li and Wu Wei 'Sun and Snow'

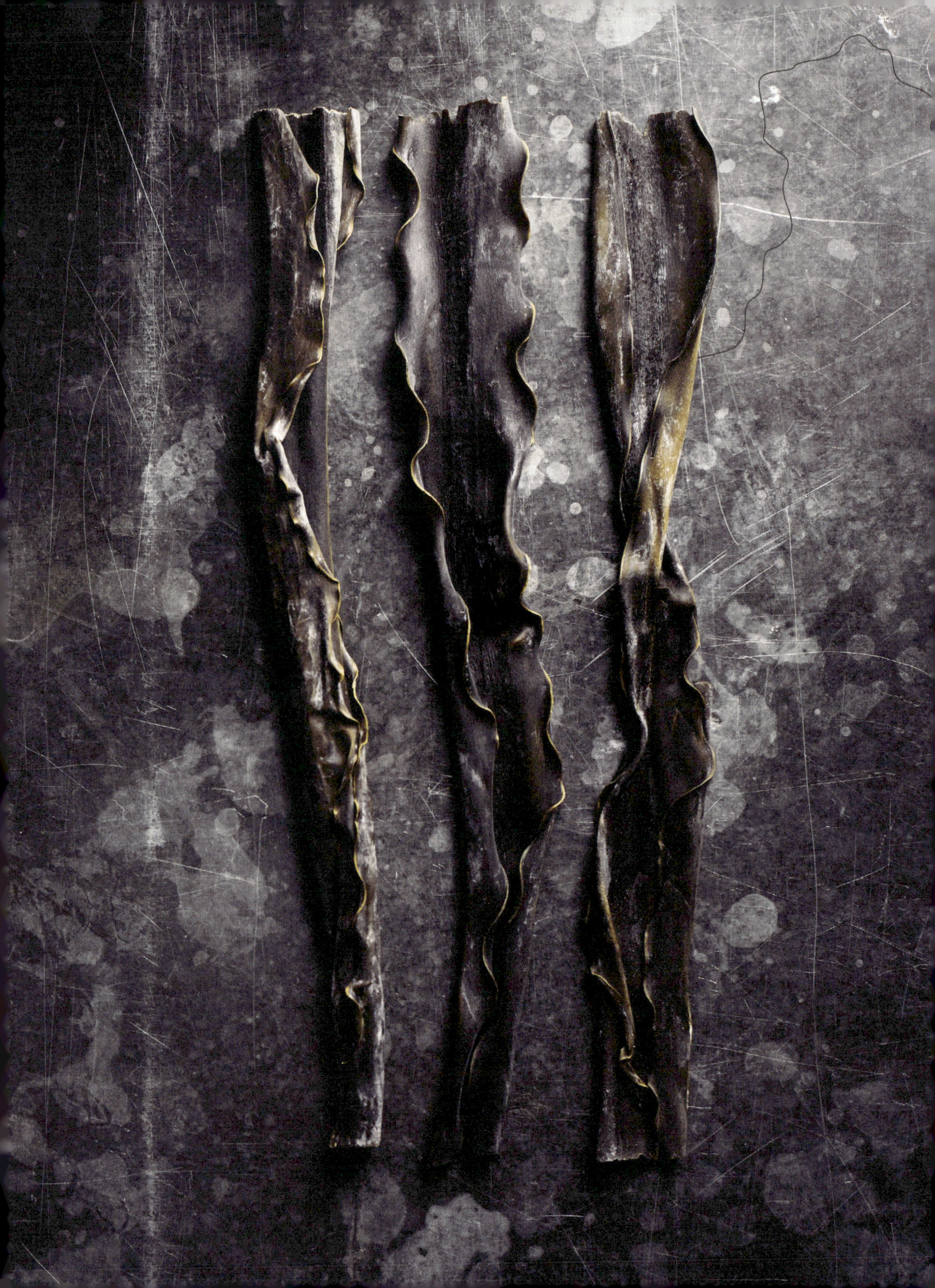

JAPAN

Nozarashio
Weather Beaten

Kokoro in kaze no
Wind pierces my body

Shinu mi kana
To my heart

There's a wonderful economy to Japanese poetry, but these few words leave you with such vibrant images. One master of the haiku was **MATSUO BASHŌ** (1644–1694), a famous poet of the Edo period in Japan, born in Ueno, Mie.

The goddess **AMATERASU**-omikami (her name means 'the great august god who shines in the heaven') is revered as the guardian of Japan. She is both a mythical figure and a major deity of the Shinto religion, the indigenous (Buddhist) religion of Japan that focuses on ritual practices 'to be carried out diligently, with the aim to keep or establish a connection between present-day Japan and its past'.

Amaterasu first appeared in tales written in the oldest records of Japanese history around 712 CE, and the Emperors of Japan are considered to be directly descended from her. She is the sister of the god of storms and sea (Susanoo) and the god of the moon (Tsukuyomi). According to myth, these siblings painted the landscape to create ancient Japan and separate night from day.

Japan has overtaken France in number of **Michelin-starred** restaurants.

Sake, made by fermenting rice, is drunk hot or cold and also used to flavour cooking.

Dashi is made with kombu seaweed (see photo p. 242) and dried bonito fish flakes, and is used as a stock base for dishes.

SUMO is a centuries-old wrestling sport heavy with ritual elements that come from Shinto. There is a height requirement of 5ft 8ins but famously Mainoumi Shūhei had silicon injected in to his scalp to meet this as he was 2cm too short. He became a popular wrestler in Japan in the nineties.

改善

KAIZEN: the idea that positive change can reap improvement.

SHINTO

stems from a collection of Japanese mythologies and beliefs that were labelled as Shindo (now Shinto) in the sixth century.

There are shrines all over Japan, where people go to worship a number of gods who cover various purposes: war, harvest, peace and prosperity.

The ancient Japanese realized that **BOILING WATER** freed it from contaminants, thus avoiding sickness (predating John Snow's tracing of the cholera outbreaks in Soho, London, in 1854 by some time).

The world's best-selling bourbon, **JIM BEAM,** is owned by a Japanese company, Suntory, which also owns Maker's Mark, Knob Creek, Laphroaig and Teacher's blended Scotch.

Nori sheets were invented in the Edo period, around 1750.

EKIBEN are bento boxed meals sold for train journeys.

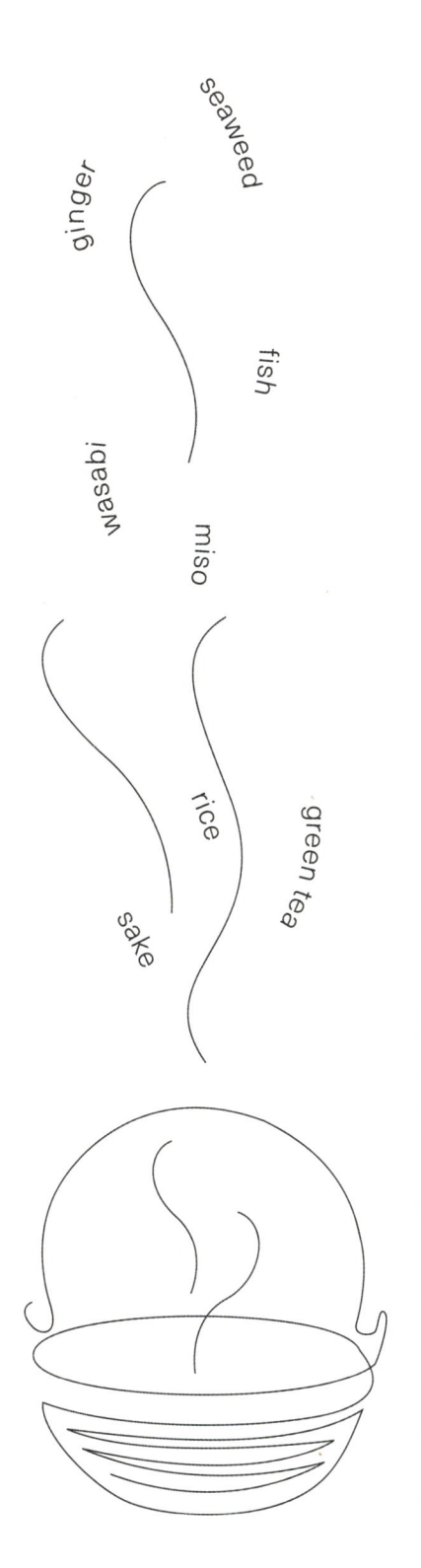

The national tree is the cherry tree, and at the end of March into April, when the trees burst into flower, families and friends picnic under the blossoms of pink and white. The ethos of these cherry blossom festivals is: **LIFE IS FLEETING, ENJOY IT.**

The **NATIONAL ANTHEM** is one of the oldest and shortest in the world. Its lyrics take the form of a 'waka' poem, originating from the Heian period (794–1185 CE) and first popularized by the Samurai:

*'May your reign
Continue for a thousand,
eight thousand
generations,
Until the pebbles
Grow into boulders
Lush with moss …'*

Sa Shi Su Se So: the flavours of Japanese food:

Sato: sugar (**mirin** is often used to add sweetness, it's a kind of sweet sake)

Shio: salt

Su: vinegar
(rice vinegar)

Seuyu: **soy sauce**
(Shōyu in modern Japanese)

Mi**so**: **miso paste**
(fermented soy beans)

Irasshaimase:
Welcome!
(Heard when you enter a restaurant or business in Japan)

Oishii:
It's good, delicious

Kanpai:
Cheers

Hai:
Yes

ginger
seaweed
fish
wasabi
miso
rice
green tea
sake

'It's good when food tastes good, it's kind of like proof you're alive.'

HARUKI MURAKAMI, *NORWEGIAN WOOD*

Some meals can leave you feeling like the bloated, snoring uncles in Dylan Thomas's *A Child's Christmas in Wales*; eating Japanese food (if you skimp on the deep-fried stuff, the *agemono*) feels like you're doing your body a service. If you're like me and prefer unadulterated food, i.e. not messed with too much, no cheesy sauces, or balsamic reduction drizzled on everything, then raw fish sashimi, edamame and seaweed salads (as served in the old Japanese way) are ideal. Apart from the tempura (which is very light usually), and other fried offerings (like *tonkatsu* and *korokke*), very little oil is used in Japanese cooking. We're so used to thinking that a stew, sauce or curry begins with frying onion and garlic, that Japanese cooking requires a mental reset. The warm heart of a Japanese broth dish is *dashi*, a stock made of fish flakes and kelp. Despite the different approach, you can easily start cooking with a Japanese bent at home. One meal I prepare regularly when I have no time at all is this: sushi rice, a bowl of drained cooked red kidney beans sprinkled with rock salt (protein alternative to edamame which aren't so good frozen, and not easily available fresh), cut-up omelette, tofu with sesame oil and seeds, avocado, spring onion and cucumber slices, all plonked on the table with some nori sheets and reduced-salt soy sauce. You roll your own 'sushi' and eat what you fancy. I buy tiny tins of wasabi powder (like the mustard powder of yore), and add water to make paste.

I remember trying sushi for the first time: mackerel nigiri in the studio, recording in London, circa 1998. I think that was the date; it's hard to believe now that back then the idea of raw fish was new-fangled, at least to most people in the UK. Forward wind the clock, and sushi has even reached Marks & Spencer's and wasabi peas can be found in even the remotest pubs. As for the mackerel, as with olives, beer, crab and sea urchin, I wasn't convinced at first, but kept trying it. It was the mix of wasabi and soy that did it, by which time I became rather obsessed, carrying chopsticks around with me for the next fifteen years, and the first port of call in any new city on tour would be to a Japanese restaurant.

When eventually we headed on tour to Japan, it didn't disappoint: nattō (the stickiest, gooiest, fermented beans, now known to be – so good for you), miso soup, sashimi and agedashi tofu, mountains of beer, edamame and karaoke sessions. There were the shabu-shabu nights, where they served big pots of steaming *dashi* and plates of kobe beef, mushrooms and cabbage, served with sesame sauce. We'd spill on to the streets of Tokyo, milling with youngsters carrying ultra-modern gadgets (phones with toys attached is how I remember it), and glass skyscrapers juxtaposed with ancient wooden temples, intense industry right next to the zen calm of moss and monks with wind prayer sticks. There were singing cicadas, and carp swimming under our feet in the hotel – where apparently the Beatles had stayed some decades before. The Japanese breakfast of salmon, pickled veg, rice and green tea... And the audiences – quite memorably silent during the songs – but as soon as we stopped, they started clapping frantically. There was the Fuji Rock Festival: thousands of bobbing heads covered in white handkerchiefs, watching Blur, then an escape to the crystal clear spring water streams, multi-coloured pebbles at the bottom, with the Stone Roses and Happy Mondays, who seemed always present at breakfast no matter what had happened the night before. Summer months were great like this, you'd keep bumping into other touring bands in festivals across the world, the Loreley festival on the Rhine, Benicassim, Spain, Roskilde in Denmark, you'd say 'Hey', lark about, play your set, and then leave for the next.

I love the seasonality of Japanese cuisine. They call it 'shun', where you eat food only when it is in season and at its peak. So for example, with 'fruit of the mountains' (fruit and veg), you look for bamboo in spring and chestnuts in autumn. When I was living in South Carolina, in the middle of nowhere, but surrounded by Piggly Wiggly stores, Popeyes, Chick-fil-A, Wendy's and other fast-food outlets, there was this oasis to be found, a beacon of culinary common sense: one tiny little Japanese restaurant, Sushi Masa, which served shishito peppers and the prized matsutake mushrooms. When a basket appeared on the sushi counter during September/October, you knew you were in for something special. Served as a clear broth in an earthenware teapot, every sip was a distillation of autumn. You feel every mouthful is a thank you to the ground that made it, to the chef that prepared it. That's how it feels, and I wasn't aware at the time that saying thanks like this is part of Japanese custom: Before a meal say 'Itadakimasu!', to show appreciation to Mother Nature for her bounty, and to those who have gathered, hunted or prepared the food on the table, and, after the meal, 'Gochisousama;' a second thank you for the feast and the effort involved, including that of your host.

I love the rituals: pouring each other's drinks but not for yourself, the hot towels before eating, the individual dishes, the *shiso* leaf garnish, pickled ginger and lump of wasabi and tiny bowls for soy. This meticulous attention to detail and presentation was the polar opposite of the grab-it-while-you-can eating experience of touring.

Huge thanks to my friend B. from Tokyo for welcoming me into her kitchen, talking deities, feasts and sharing with us her family recipes, included in this chapter.

'It is useless to talk with those who do not understand one and troublesome to talk with those who criticize from a feeling of superiority. Especially one-sided persons are troublesome. Few are accomplished in many arts and most cling narrowly to their own opinion.'

MURASAKI SHIKIBU,
DIARIES OF COURT LADIES OF OLD JAPAN

Okinawan rice wine with snake 'awamori'.

Sea grapes

> 'It is the man who drinks the first bottle of sake; then the second bottle drinks the first, and finally, it is the sake that drinks the man.'
>
> **JAPANESE PROVERB**

> 'There are as many types of women as there are women.'
>
> **MURASAKI SHIKIBU, *THE TALE OF GENJI***

ON THE MENU

HORENSO GOMA-AE

TOFU AND SESAME

CHIRASHI

EASY PICKLED CARROTS

TERIYAKI SAUCE

DASHI

JAPANESE HOTPOT

SUNOMONO

DESSERT

GREEN TEA ICE CREAM

Horenso Goma-ae (Spinach with Sesame Sauce)

(VG) (DF)

Ingredients

400g baby spinach (or chard), washed

4 tbsp sesame seeds, toasted in a heavy pan until golden

3–4 tbsp *dashi* (or water)

2 tsp soy sauce

2 tsp honey

2 tsp sake (optional)

Method

1. Blanch the spinach for 2 minutes in 150ml of salted boiling water, then drain in a colander, squeeze out the excess water, and set aside.

2. Using a pestle and mortar, grind 1 tablespoon of the sesame seeds. Take out and set aside, then grind another 1 tablespoon of seeds and repeat until all the seeds are ground. Put them all back into the pestle and mortar.

3. Add 3 tablespoons of the *dashi*, the soy, honey and sake (if using) and mix well. Some people prefer a thick sauce, but I like a light creamy consistency – add more dashi or water as you prefer.

Tofu and Sesame

(V) (VG) (DF)

Ingredients

1½ tbsp sesame oil

300g silken or firm tofu, drained and cut into cubes

2 tsp soy sauce

1 tsp toasted sesame seeds

sichimi – to taste (if you don't have any, use chilli powder or paprika)

Method

1. Heat 1 tablespoon of sesame oil in a frying pan on a medium/low heat.

2. Add the tofu and heat through.

3. Add the soy, the remains sesame oil, sesame seeds and shake on some sichimi or chilli powder.

Note:
Sichimi Togarashi is a 7 spice seasoning, which includes some orange peel, that you can buy in supermarkets to season soups and noodle dishes, meat, fish or vegetables.

Buck Owens 'Made In Japan'

Django Reinhardt 'Japanese Sandman'

Nanae Yoshimura, Kifu Mitsuhashi and Noriko Tamura 'Wind Dream Dances op. 98 number 1: Kaze No Mai I', by Takashi Yoshimatsu

Hideo Osaka Ensemble 'Samurai Song'

Masayo Ishigure 'Sunae'

Nanae Yoshimura, Kifu Mitsuhasho and Satomi Fukami 'Seoto'

Chirashi

GF DF NV

Chirashi means 'scattered sushi', and is a dish of sushi ingredients served on top of a bowl of rice.

Ingredients

For the rice

400g sushi rice
1 tbsp sake

For the rice vinegar

2½ tbsp rice vinegar
1 tbsp honey
½–1 tsp sea salt (to taste)

For the chirashi vegetables

3–4 dried shiitake mushrooms (optional), soaked in hot water – once rehydrated, cut off stems and slice thinly, keeping the water
1 carrot, cut into matchsticks
1 x 125g tin (120g drained) bamboo shoots, cut into matchsticks
1 tbsp sake
1 tbsp mirin
1⅓ tsp soy sauce

For the shredded egg (kinshi tamago)

1 egg
⅔ tsp honey (or sugar)
1 tsp sake
a pinch of salt
vegetable oil

To finish

250g smoked salmon (optional), cut into small strips
1 sheet of nori, cut into strips 40mm x 3mm

Method

1. Cover the sushi rice with water (about 600ml), leaving 2cm or a knuckle above level of rice. Add the sake, bring to the boil, then turn down the heat and put a lid on the pan. After 20 minutes, taste the rice – it should be pretty much done. Turn off the heat and leave for another 10 minutes, keeping the lid on.

2. Put the rice vinegar, honey and salt into a bowl and set aside – you'll use this to dress the cooked, cooled rice.

3. Pour the reserved shiitake water into a saucepan and add the mushrooms, carrots, bamboo, sake, mirin and soy sauce. Add water to just cover the vegetables. Bring to boil, then turn down the heat and simmer for 5 minutes, skimming off the scum, until the vegetables are tender. Drain and set aside.

4. Once the rice is cooked, tip it on to a large shallow surface and let it cool for 10 minutes. Pour on the rice vinegar mix from step 2 and fold it evenly into the rice. When cooled (about body temperature), cover the rice with a damp tea towel.

5. Beat the egg with the honey, sake and salt.

6. Heat a well-oiled 18cm frying pan over a medium heat. Pour in half the egg mixture and spread it evenly in the pan. When one side is cooked, turn it over. Remove from the pan when both sides are done. Cook the remaining egg mixture in the same way. Leave to cool, then cut into fine shreds.

7. Mix the vegetables into the rice and serve in a big bowl, garnishing with the smoked salmon, egg and nori.

Nobuko Miyazaki 'Camera'

Hideo Osaka Ensemble 'A Ri Rang'

Easy Pickled Carrots

(V) (VG) (GF) (DF)

Ingredients

3 medium/large carrots, cut into matchsticks
6 tbsp rice vinegar
3 tbsp mirin
3 tbsp sesame oil
1 tsp cup black sesame seeds (toasted – use white seeds if you don't have black)
pinch of sea salt

Method

1. Blanch the carrots in boiling water for 20 seconds, then drain and cool.
2. Put the vinegar, mirin and sesame oil into a bowl and add the carrots and sesame seeds.
3. Serve. You can keep these in a pickling jar in the fridge for days.

Teriyaki Sauce

(V) (VG) (DF)

This marinade is so easy and so good.

Ingredients

6 tbsp soy sauce
2 tbsp mirin (or 1 tbsp each of sake and honey)
2 tbsp rice vinegar
2 tbsp sesame oil
1 tsp grated ginger
1 clove of garlic, finely chopped

Method

1. Mix all the ingredients together.
2. Use as a marinade for firm tofu or chicken, for example; marinate for 30 minutes to overnight, then grill/roast or sauté.

Dashi (Japanese Stock)

(V) (VG) (GF) (DF) (NV)

You can buy sachets of dried *dashi* in Japanese supermarkets or make your own vegan *dashi*: soak roughly 25g konbu (dried kelp) in water for 3 hours, then bring to the boil, discarding konbu just before boiling point, and then leave to cool. To make non-veg *dashi*: add 2 generous handfuls of bonito flakes (dried shaved tuna) to the *dashi*, bring to the boil, simmer for a few minutes, then turn off heat and allow to cool. Filter off the solids and the stock is ready.

Japanese Hotpot

(V) (VG) (GF) (DF) (NV)

Vegan *dashi* is a great base for Japanese hotpot. Cook Chinese cabbage, pak choi or spinach, shitake, enoki or chestnut mushrooms, carrots, leeks, or spring onions, tofu and noodles in steaming hot *dashi*, adding more boiling water if needed, so vegetables are covered in broth. Serve with soy sauce, ponzu, sesame or/and chili oil. (You can make a 'quick' ponzu sauce by mixing soy sauce, rice vinegar and citrus juice (lemon, lime or yuzu).

Sunomono (Cucumber and Seaweed Salad)

(V) (VG) (DF)

Ingredients

½ large cucumber (or 3 small), sliced as thinly as possible

¼ tsp sea salt

3 tbsp rice vinegar

1 tbsp mirin (or ½ tbsp honey and ½ tbsp sake)

¼ tsp soy sauce

1 tbsp dried wakame (a handful), rehydrated for 10 minutes, then water squeezed out

1 tsp toasted sesame seeds

Method

1. Put the cucumbers into a bowl, add the salt, and leave for 5 minutes.
2. Squeeze out the water (I use a sieve to do this), then rinse and dry.
3. Mix together the vinegar, mirin and soy sauce.
4. Add the vinegar mixture to the cucumbers, along with the wakame, and sprinkle over the sesame seeds.

Green Tea Ice Cream

(VG) (GF)

Make homemade ice cream.

Ingredients

75g sugar or honey

200ml milk (semi-skimmed or whole)

200ml double cream

2 tbsp matcha/green tea powder

Method

1. Put a Pyrex glass dish into the freezer.
2. In a saucepan, dissolve the sugar (or honey) in the milk and cream, then mix in the green tea powder and leave to cool.
3. Once cooled, pour the liquid into the ice-cold Pyrex dish and return it to the freezer.
4. Every 20 minutes, take out the dish and churn the mix with a hand-held mixer.
5. Repeat four or five times. That's it. Eat when it gets to the consistency you like.
6. If time poor, buy ready-made vanilla ice cream and allow it to soften, stir in the green tea powder, then return it to the freezer.

Nanae Yoshima, Kifu Mitsuhashi and Noriko Tamura 'Wind Dream Dances op. 98 number 7: Kaze No Mai II' by Takashi Yoshimatsu

INDEX

A
ackee: salt fish ackee 50
amlou 67
    thousand-hole pancakes with amlou 68
apples: baked apples 156
artichokes 78
    roast artichokes 78–9
avocados: guacamole 32
Ayrshire shortbread 139

B
baghrir 68
baharat 197
beans and pulses x
    bean burgers 15
    cawl 114
    chickpea and vegetable tagine 63
    daal 218
    falafel 199
    ful medames 202
    green beans 168
    green lentil shepherd's pie 154
    green lentils with preserved lemon 66
    green lentils with whole head of garlic 80
    haggis (vegan) 135
    pilaf 204
    rice and peas 47
    stewed black beans 29
    store-cupboard soup with dumplings 155
beetroot salad 65
berries: cranachan 138
    see also raspberries
black beans: stewed black beans 29
bread: bread with tomato 86
    brown soda bread 99
    chapati 222
    cornbread with jalapeño 16
    homemade bread 119
    homemade tortillas 31
breakfasts 148
broad beans: pilaf 204
burgers 14
    bean burgers 15
    classic burger 14
butter beans: cawl 114

C
cabbage: colcannon 97
    coleslaw 9
cacik 201
callaloo 47
Campari spritz 189
cardamom lassi 225
carrots: cawl 114
    chickpea and vegetable tagine 63
    easy pickled carrots 254
    Indian carrot salad 223
    Moroccan carrot salad 64
cawl 114
celeriac mash 171
ceviche 34
champ 97
chapati 222
cheese: *labneh* 197
    lemon spaghetti 185
    queso fresca 33
    rocket and parmesan 186
    saag paneer 215
chestnuts: nut roast 150
chicken: cock-a-leekie soup 137
    roast chicken 153
chickpeas x
    bean burgers 15
    chickpea and potato curry 46
    chickpea and vegetable tagine 63
    falafel 199
    hummus 205
    pilaf 204
chillies: *chiles toreados* 33
    cornbread with jalapeño 16
    homemade hot chilli sauce 32
    pineapple with chilli 34
    spaghetti *aglio e olio* 185
chips: roast chips 101
chirasi 253
chocolate: chocolate and Guinness fondants 102
    hot chocolate 171
chorizo in red wine 84
cinnamon baked peaches 16
clams: seafood paella 82
    spaghetti vongole 188
cock-a-leekie soup 137
cockles: laverbread and cockles 117
colcannon 97
coleslaw 9
coriander chutney 219
corn on the cob 33
corn tortillas 31
cornbread with jalapeño 16
courgettes: pilaf 204
    roasted in cumin 66
    roasted zucchini and garlic 188
couscous 63
cranachan 138
cucumbers: cucumber and seaweed salad 255
    smashed cucumbers 240
cumin: courgettes roasted in cumin 66
    jeera rice 216
Cumnock Loaf 137
custard 123

D
daal 218
dandelion: hedgerow salad 121
dark and stormy 51
dashi 254
    Japanese hotpot 254
Death by Chocolate (cocktail) 102
dumplings 155

E
eggs: *chirasi* 253
    easy poached eggs 9
    egg curry 220
    egg fried rice 238
    eggs en cocotte 168
    homemade custard 123
    homemade mayonnaise 79
    kuku sabzi 198
    shakshuka 203
    Spanish tortilla 84
    Yorkshire pudding and pancakes 153
espinacas a la catalana 81

F
faggots 113
fajita mix 21
falafel 199
fava beans: falafel 199
    ful medames 202
fish and seafood: ceviche 34
    chirasi 253
    curried prawns 49
    easy and quick Chinese dinner 235
    fried fish pieces for tacos 29
    laverbread and cockles 117
    mussels in wine 101
    paella with brown rice 83
    prawns a la *plancha* 81
    salt fish ackee 50

sautéed scallops with lemon 167
seafood paella 82
shrimp and grits 12
spaghetti vongole 188
tequila prawns 28
frittata: *kuku sabzi* 198
ful medames 202

G

garam masala 220
garlic: green lentils with
  whole head of garlic 80
    roasted zucchini and garlic 188
gin: sloe gin 157
granola 138
gravy: vegan mushroom gravy 152
green beans 168
green soup 155
green tea ice cream 255
greens: chargrilled 235
  kuku sabzi 198
  see also callaloo; kale; spinach
grits 12
  shrimp and grits 12
guacamole 32
Guinness: chocolate and Guinness
  fondants 102
    Death by Chocolate 102
gunga peas: rice and peas 47

H

haggis: haggis (vegan) 135
  home haggis (non veg) 136
harissa 67
hazelnuts: hedgerow salad 121
  nut roast 150
hedgerow salad 121
horenso goma-ae 250
hotpot: Japanese hotpot 254
hummus 205

I

ice cream: green tea ice cream 255
ital soup 48

J

jambalaya 11
Japanese hotpot 254
jeera rice 216
jerk marinade 49
jerk seasoning 49

K

kale: colcannon 97
kidney beans x

bean burgers 15
kuku sabzi 198

L

labneh 197
lamb: cawl 114
  home haggis 136
lassi 225
laverbread and cockles 117
leeks: cock-a-leekie soup 137
  colcannon 97
  leek and potato soup 118
lemons ix
  lemon spaghetti 185
lentils: bean burgers 15
  daal 218
  green lentil shepherd's pie 154
  green lentils with preserved
    lemon 66
  green lentils with whole head
    of garlic 80
  haggis (vegan) 135
  store-cupboard soup with
    dumplings 155
lime leaves: hedgerow
  salad 121
limes ix
  ceviche 34
liver: faggots 113
  home haggis 136
lychee 240

M

mangoes: mango lassi 225
  mango and mint sorbet 51
matcha: green tea ice cream 255
mayonnaise 79
melon: half a melon with
  sherry 87
Mexican mushrooms 28
mint: mango and mint sorbet 51
  mint lassi 225
  mint tea 67
mole sauce 27
Moroccan rice 61
mushrooms: haggis (vegan) 135
  Mexican mushrooms 28
  vegan mushroom gravy 152
mussels: mussels in wine 101
  seafood paella 82

N

nasturtium: hedgerow
  salad 121
neeps 133

nettle soup 149
nuts ix
  nut roast 150

O

oats: cranachan 138
  porridge 148
  smoothies 148
  super bowls 148
onions: fresh pickled onions 216
  Moroccan tomato and onion
    salad 65
  Spanish tomato and onion salad 86
  see also spring onions

P

Padrón peppers 85
paella: paella with brown rice 83
  seafood paella 82
pan y tomate 86
pancakes 153
  thousand-hole pancakes with
    amlou 68
parsnips: cawl 114
  chickpea and vegetable tagine 63
pasta: cooking 183
  homemade 183
  lemon spaghetti 185
  spaghetti *aglio e olio* 185
  spaghetti vongole 188
peaches: cinnamon baked
  peaches 16
peanuts: tofu and peanut
  stir-fry 237
pears: poached pears 172
peas: pilaf 204
  rice and peas 47
peppers: *pimientos de Padrón* 85
pesto: wild garlic pesto 186
pico de gallo 31
pilaf 204
pimientos de Padrón 85
pine nuts: spinach with pine nuts 81
pineapple with chilli 34
plantain 41
pomelo 240
pork: faggots 113
porridge 148
potatoes x
  cawl 114
  champ 97
  chickpea and potato curry 46
  colcannon 97
  green lentil shepherd's pie 154
  leek and potato soup 118

potato scones 133
potatoes boulangère 170
potatoes dauphinoise 170
roast *aloo* 216
roast chips 101
Spanish tortilla 84
prawns: curried prawns 49
    easy and quick Chinese dinner 235
    paella with brown rice 83
    prawns a la *plancha* 81
    seafood paella 82
    shrimp and grits 12
    tequila prawns 28

Q
queso fresca 33
quinoa x

R
raita 223
ras el hanout 67
raspberry 'gelato' 189
red soup 155
rhubarb: roast rhubarb with yoghurt 205
rice ix
    chirasi 253
    egg fried rice 238
    jambalaya 11
    jeera rice 216
    Moroccan rice 61
    paella with brown rice 83
    pilaf 204
    rice and peas 47
    seafood paella 82
    vegan rice pudding 225
rocket and parmesan 186
rum: dark and stormy 51
    rum punch 51
    sorrel 51
    Ting-a-ling 51

S
saag paneer 215
salmon: *chirasi* 253
salt fish ackee 50
sausages: jambalaya 11
scallops: sautéed scallops with lemon 167
scones: potato scones 133
seafood *see* fish and seafood
seaweed: cucumber and seaweed salad 255
    laverbread and cockles 117
sesame seeds: spinach with sesame sauce 250
    tofu and sesame 250
shakshuka 203
shepherd's pie 154
sherry: Gramma's sherry trifle 122
    half a melon with sherry 87
shortbread 139
shrimp and grits 12
sloe gin 157
smoothies 148
soda bread 99
sorbet: mango and mint sorbet 51
sorrel (drink) 51
sorrel (plant): hedgerow salad 121
spaghetti: lemon spaghetti 185
    spaghetti *aglio e olio* 185
    spaghetti vongole 188
Spanish tortilla 84
spice mixes viii
    baharat 197
    garam masala 220
    jerk seasoning and marinade 49
    ras el hanout 67
    za'atar 197
spinach: *saag paneer* 215
    with sesame sauce 250
    spinach with pine nuts 81
spring onions: champ 97
    tabouleh 202
squid: seafood paella 82
stir-fry: easy and quick Chinese dinner 235
    tofu and peanut stir-fry 237
stock viii
store-cupboard curry 221
store-cupboard soup with dumplings 155
sunomono 255
super bowls 148
sushi: *chirasi* 253
swede: cawl 114
    neeps 133
sweet potato salad 65

T
tabouleh 202
tacos: fried fish pieces 29
tagine: chickpea and vegetable tagine 63
tahini sauce 201
tattie scones 133
tequila prawns 28
teriyaki 254
thousand-hole pancakes with amlou 68
Ting-a-ling 51
tofu x
    curried tofu 49
    easy and quick Chinese dinner 235
    tofu and peanut stir-fry 237
    tofu and sesame 250
tomatoes x
    bread with tomato 86
    fresh tomato sauce 61, 187
    fried green tomatoes 8
    Moroccan tomato and onion salad 65
    pico de gallo 31
    shakshuka 203
    Spanish tomato and onion salad 86
    tabouleh 202
    tinned tomato sauce 186
tortilla: Spanish tortilla 84
tortillas: homemade tortillas 31
trifle: Gramma's sherry trifle 122
turmeric: turmeric lassi 225
    turmeric nightcap 225

V
vaghar 219
vegetables: ital soup 48
    store-cupboard soup with dumplings 155
    see also individual vegetables

W
watercress: hedgerow salad 121
Welsh cakes 123
whisky: cranachan 138
wild garlic pesto 186

Y
yoghurt: *cacik* 201
    labneh 197
    lassi 225
    raita 223
    raspberry 'gelato' 189
    roast rhubarb with yoghurt 205
Yorkshire pudding 153

Z
za'atar 197

ACKNOWLEDGEMENTS

The author is grateful to the following publishers for granting permission to quote from: Kei Miller, 'Place Name', *The Cartographer Tries to Map His Way to Zion* (Carcanet 2014); Una Marson, 'Home Thoughts', *Selected Poems*, (Peepal Tree Press 2011); Al-Fassi trans. Fatima Sadiqi, 'Hold the Grinder'; Arthur Rimbaud trans. Wallace Fowlie, 'Novel', *Complete Works, Selected Letters* (University of Chicago Press 2005); Hafiz, trans. Daniel Ladinsky, 'Every City Is a Dulcimer', *The Gift* (Penguin 1999); Tu Mu, trans. A.C. Graham, 'On the Road', *Poems of the Late T'ang* (The New York Review of Books Classics 2008); Haruki Murakami, *Norwegian Wood*, (Vintage 1987). Every effort has been made to trace copyright holders and obtain permissions for the use of copyright material. The publisher apologises for any errors or omissions in the above list and would be grateful if notified of any corrections that should be incorporated in future reprints or editions of this book.

PICTURE CREDITS

19 Jean-Pierre Courau / Bridgeman Images; **21** Granger/REX/Shutterstock; **38** De Agostini Picture Library / A. Dagli Orti / Bridgeman Images; **38** De Agostini Picture Library / A. Dagli Orti / Bridgeman Images; **39** John Greim/REX/Shutterstock; **39** Design Pics Inc / REX / Shutterstock; **42** De Agostini Picture Library / G. Dagli Orti / Bridgeman Images; **42** British Library Board / Bridgeman Images; **54** British Museum, London, UK / Bridgeman Images; **55** Matthew Taylor / REX / Shutterstock; **71** Prismatic Pictures / Bridgeman Images; **72** British Library Board / Bridgeman Images; **73** Roger-Viollet/Shutterstock; **90** Granger / Bridgeman Images; **91** Look and Learn / Bridgeman Images; **106** Look and Learn / Bridgeman Images; **107** Brian Seed / Bridgeman Images; **107** British Library Board / Bridgeman Images; **126** Museum of Fine Arts, Houston, Texas, USA / Gift of Marjorie G. & Evan C. Horning / Bridgeman Images; **126** Keith Corrigan / Alamy Stock Photo; **127** Bridgeman Images; **127** Look and Learn / Illustrated Papers Collection / Bridgeman Images; **142** Shutterstock; **143** Amoret Tanner Collection / REX / Shutterstock; **143** Universal History Archive / Universal Images Group / REX / Shutterstock; **160** Jaime Abecasis / REX / Shutterstock; **160** Shutterstock; **161** Chronicle / Alamy Stock Photo; **161** Shutterstock; **175** Look and Learn / Elgar Collection / Bridgeman Images; **176** Bridgeman Images; **176** Metropolitan Museum of Art, New York, USA / Bridgeman Images; **177** Alinari / Bridgeman Images; **192** Bettmann / Getty Images; **193** Shutterstock; **207** Granger / REX / Shutterstock; **208** Bridgeman; **208** Universal History Archive/ UIG / Bridgeman Images; **209** Tim Gainey / Alamy Stock Photo; **228** Archives Charmet / Bridgeman Images; **243** The Picture Art Collection / Alamy Stock Photo; **244** Pictures from History / Bridgeman Images; **244** Brooklyn Museum of Art, New York, USA / Bridgeman Images.

SCOTLAND
Neeps
Tattie Scones
Haggis (Vegan)
Home Haggis (Non-Veg)
Cock-a-Leekie Soup
Cumnock Loaf
Cranachan
Ayrshire Shortbread
Whisky
Scottish Spring Water

IRELAND
Champ and Colcannon
Brown Soda Bread
Mussels in Wine with Chips
Roast Chips
Chocolate and Guinness Fondants
Cocktail: Death by Chocolate

AMERICAN SOUTH
Fried Green Tomatoes
Coleslaw
Easy Poached Eggs
Jambalaya
Grits
Shrimp and Grits
Classic Burgers
Cornbread with Jalapeño
Cinnamon Baked Peaches

JAMAICA
Chickpea and Potato Curry
Rice and Peas
Callaloo
Ital Soup
Curried Tofu or Prawns
Homemade Jerk Seasoning
Salt Fish Ackee
Mango and Mint Sorbet
Cocktails

WALES
Faggots
Cawl
Laverbread and Cockles
Leek and Potato Soup
Homemade Bread
Hedgerow Salad
Gramma's Sherry Trifle
Welsh Cakes
Homemade Custard

SPAIN
Roast Artichokes
Homemade Mayonnaise
Green Lentils with Whole Head of Garlic
Prawns a la Plancha
Spinach with Pine Nuts
Seafood Paella
Paella with Brown Rice
Spanish Tortilla
Chorizo in Red Wine
Pimientos de Padrón
Tomato and Onion Salad
Pan y Tomate
Half a Melon with Sherry

MOROCCO
Fresh Tomato Sauce
Moroccan Rice
Chickpea and Vegetable Tagine
Moroccan Salads
Amlou
Thousand-hole Pancakes
Fresh Mint Tea

MEXICO
Mole
Mexican Mushrooms
Tequila Prawns
Fried Fish Tacos
Stewed Black Beans
Homemade Tortillas
Pico de Gallo
Guacamole
Homemade Hot Chilli Sauce
Queso Fresca
Chillies Toreados
Corn on the Cob
Ceviche
Pineapple with Chilli